About the Author

Dr Stephan Rechtschaffen has more than twenty years' experience as a physician and leader of workshops on personal growth. He is a pioneer of the wellness movement and a founder of the Omega Institute for Holistic Studies in New York state, a world-renowned centre for the holistic study of health, culture, spirit and the arts.

'Stephan Rechtschaffen's book clearly explains that time is manufactured in consciousness, processed in the mind and metabolized in the body and the material world. Highly recommended.'

Deepak Chopra

'. . . a masterful job of articulating the effect of time perception on our health and sense of well-being. This book is an excellent guide . . .'

Christiane Northrup, author of *Women's Bodies, Women's Wisdom*

'. . . this fascinating book shows us how to . . . experience moment to moment fulfilment.'

Ram Dass, author of *Be Here Now* and *How Can I Help?*

'Unusually insightful.'

Jon Kabat-Zinn, author of *Wherever You Go, There You Are*

TIME
SHIFTING

A Revolutionary New Approach
to Creating More Time
for Your Life

STEPHAN RECHTSCHAFFEN

RIDER

London · Sydney · Auckland · Johannesburg

First published by Doubleday,
a division of Bantam Doubleday Dell Publishing Group, Inc.
Published in 1996 by Rider,
an imprint of Ebury Press, Random House,
20 Vauxhall Bridge Road, London SW1V 2SA
New edition 1998

Random House Australia (Pty) Limited
20 Alfred Street, Milsons Point, Sydney,
New South Wales 2061, Australia

Random House New Zealand Limited
18 Poland Road, Glenfield
Auckland 10, New Zealand

Random House South Africa (Pty) Limited
Endulini, 5A Jubilee Road, Parktown 2193, South Africa

Random House UK Limited Reg. No. 954009

Book design by Julie Duquet

Cover photograph by Ellen Schuster/Image Bank

Papers used by Rider Books are natural, recyclable products made from wood grown in sustainable forests. In addition, the paper in this book is recycled

Printed and bound in Great Britain by
Cox & Wyman Ltd, Reading, Berkshire

A CIP catalogue record for this book
is available from the British Library

ISBN 0–7126–7126–9

CONTENTS

To my three boys—Rahm, Daniel, and Eli—who have helped me understand the preciousness of time.

FOREWORD

My daughter was born when I was fifty-one, and many an afternoon I have wistfully counted the days of our possible future. "When she's graduating from high school," I'll muse, "I'll be sixty-nine, God willing." Sometimes my wife and I, who met during my mid-forties, wonder what it would have been like to have known each other from our teens. These thoughts are motivated by love and the wish that our time together will be long and full and that we can gather as much of our lives as possible in the bundle of our common experience.

These melancholic reflections also teach me that time is a fantasy, part of the imagination of experience, and not something that can be fully measured and explained with reference to a clock or calendar. It's this imaginal aspect of time that stands out for me in Stephan Rechtschaffen's remarkable book. He doesn't theorize, as I tend to do, but rather offers inspiring rhapsodies and occasional recipes. For me, a musician and lover of food, these are good words and excellent forms for thoughtful writing, as they help us consider many issues that usually go by unnoticed.

Stephan's book is a workshop on time. It has led me into precious reverie about the time of my life: how I imagine it, how I shape it or "shift" it according to my imaginings, conscious and unconscious, and how I'm influenced by habit and by the society around me. These are helpful considerations, because time, as Stephan's book demonstrates so vividly, is a primary window on experience, a telling prism through which the emotions, meanings, and values of a life can be perceived.

As I've read Stephan's words, I've noticed how often my own life follows the lines set by a fast-paced society. I find my days full of business that I haven't initiated, deadlines that aren't nearly as important as the messages I get about them, and projects that may or may not be "worth my time." I realize how difficult it is to keep promises to myself, such as setting two hours aside each day for exercise and play, and turning down invitations to travel so I can stay home with my family.

Busyness is a fantasy, a story we tell ourselves that is not as factual or literal as we might think. In all my reading of literature written before this century, I've never come across the cliché one often reads or hears today: "Sorry I haven't written—I'm just too busy." The "busy" fantasy seems to be part of modern life, even though people in the past accomplished much without timesaving technologies. Without a computer, Freud and Jung wrote many volumes of essays and letters, and without airplanes, they made significant journeys.

It's fascinating to me how close Stephan's discussion of time runs to my interest in the soul, but I've long known that the soul has its own sense of time and its own odd forms of clock and calendar. The sundial and hourglass seem more appropriate to the soul than the quartz watch, because they picture the passage of time in elemental, natural, and imagistic ways. Like anything else, time can be imagined in a wide variety of ways, and not all of them serve the humane life.

Maybe the most dangerous quality of modern notions of time is its distance from nature. We eat lunch quickly because the second hand is running, rather than slowly in time with the ascendant sun. We structure our workdays according to a nine-to-five custom, instead of according to the rhythms of the moon or our own circadian pulse. As Stephan says, we rise in the morning to the violence of an alarm rather than to the tuneful crowing of a bird or the gentle, warming wake-up call of sunlight.

For many years I've been drawn to ancient forms of astrology, a variant reading of time that stays close to the natural order of the sky, elaborated by mythology, tradition, and intuition. When the telescope brought the planets and stars closer to our eyes, and we saw that they were not made of pure light or moved by pure magic, our sense of time lost its enchantment, becoming a mental measuring out of quantities rather than a soulful elaboration of qualities. We strayed far from the rhythmic dance of seasons, solstices, retrogrades, and conjunctions, turning instead to evenly measured, image-free months, hours, minutes, seconds, and even nanoseconds.

When such a fundamental aspect of daily life as time loses its rich imagination, our lives become disenchanted, and we have to struggle to find meaning and value. Now we battle time, rather than find our lives colored by it. When I lived in a monastery in my early years, each day of my life was dedicated to a saint or a liturgical season, and even the hours of the day took on the rhythm of the hours of Divine Office—the hymns, readings, and psalms of matins, vespers, and compline. I felt a relaxation of ego in these traditional "hours," allowing ritual to determine the pace of my life rather than moment-by-moment decision.

Everyone knows that time refuses to fit neatly into the even boxes of the clock and calendar. Some days are long, some short; some minutes go by like an hour, some hours like a minute. You meet an old friend and wonder where the years have gone since your last meeting, and sometimes it seems you've never parted and time hasn't interfered with your feelings of friendship.

We cannot only shift time to invite more spirit and soul into our lives, we can also be shifted by the colorings of natural time—the melancholic mood of old memories, the sweet gift of moments of bliss, the bitter taste of times of anger and conflict. As a writer I have had one ambition: to be able to make my living by writing so that I can get up in the morning and have before me a stretch of time that will vary from morning to evening and from day to day. I don't want to be free to do things, as much as I want the variety of life's possibilities to wrap time around me in the many different colorings and tonalities that are possible.

By trying to live efficient and productive lives, we struggle against time's entropy, but time will have its way, as we age and change, and as the world around us shifts and never stays the same. I've come across a lovely English folk song collected by Cecil Sharp that expresses the melancholy brought on by natural time. The song uses a gentle play on words to demonstrate that time "grows" on its own schedule and for its own purposes:

O once I had thyme of my own, and in my own garden it
    grew;
I used to know the place where my thyme it did grow,
but now it is cover'd with rue, with rue, but now it is
    cover'd with rue.

. . . so beware of a young man's flattering tongue,
he will steal your thyme away . . . And that's how my time
   has gone, has gone,
and that's how my time has gone.

In our inescapable sentimentality, we may think that time is space for growth, but we all discover rue growing in our gardens, and many developments that steal our time away, making us wonder if we have enough left to give it all meaning. The secret of time, like thyme, seems to be that its loss and theft are part of the human condition, and the melancholy that so often lies like a dark mist around thoughts of time is not actual loss, but merely the ache of having lived our time, having chanced happiness and growth while winning only regret and longing.

We talk about "having a good time" and about "the best time of our lives," and so it's clear that time is not a pale measure of unqualified particles, but is a coloring of life. We can grow time in a garden and tend it and treat it with care, and can enjoy its fruit and its blossoming. Time is a quality of life, not a measurement of its units. When we remember a time in our past, we are not rewinding a tape, but looking back at a facet of the dark gem that is the gift of our time on earth.

In recent years time has played a trick on me, done something I didn't know it could or would do: It has circled around my present awareness, bringing back to me thoughts and feelings of a time abandoned long ago. My days as a Catholic friar have returned twenty-five years later at the interval of an octave—as a renewed participation in the monk's life and in my general Catholic upbringing, but not at the same level of density. Without losing any of the developments of the intervening years, I find myself loving a period of time once rejected, seeing it with fresh eyes and in a way I could not have appreciated those many years ago. Something of time has come back as a *renaissance,* one of those glorious words of ours that acknowledges time's potential beauty and the power of its retrograde movement.

I'm grateful to Stephan for gently reminding us of both the dangers and the gifts of time, of the possibility of reimagining it, and of its malleability. The Greek philosopher Heraclitus said: "Time is a child moving counters in a game." Time need not be imagined in modern terms only as an abstract structure into which life is poured. This is a serious old man's saturnine version of time. We might also think of time as a child at play—full of unknowing chance and serendipity. The game is over when "time's up," but until that point we are in play, and it is time that gives us the pleasure of the game.

Time is simply one facet of life itself, and life is the gift of time. To wish for time is to wish for life, for the opportunity to live with fullness and vitality. Therefore, time calls for artful attention on our part. We can craft the time that is given to us as we follow the many recommendations Stephan has taken the time to give us. We may discover that time is indeed like thyme, full of flavor, natural, savory, a condiment as well as a staple, a growing thing that needs planting, weeding, and harvesting.

THOMAS MOORE

TIME AWARENESS

————

> *Eternity has nothing to do with the*
> *hereafter. . . . This is it. . . . If you*
> *don't get it here, you won't get it anywhere.*
> *The experience of eternity right here and*
> *now is the function of life. Heaven is not*
> *the place to have the experience; here's the*
> *place to have the experience.*
>
> —JOSEPH CAMPBELL

ONE NIGHT MANY years ago, I was working as the attending physician in a hospital emergency room when Barry, a local politician, was rushed in, suffering from an apparent heart attack. I immediately sent him up to the coronary care unit. Two days later, when I next returned to the hospital, I went to the CCU to see how he was doing, only to discover that he had checked himself out of the hospital against medical advice.

Ten days after that, he was rushed into the emergency room once again, back with a second heart attack. I admitted him again, and asked him why he had skipped out before, when it was clearly against all doctor's orders, not to mention common sense. He told me, "I don't have time to be laid up in a hospital. I have so many more important things to do."

Clearly, unless Barry changed his orientation toward using and prioritizing time, he was not going to have much more time to worry about. Unfortunately, his attitude is all too common. I'd go so far as to say that *most* of us prioritize our use of time this way:

First comes work;

Second, our primary relationship and family life;

Third, the mundane chores of everyday life;

Fourth, our social responsibilities; and

Finally (if there is any time left over), ourselves.

It's sort of a "trickle-down" approach to time, similar to the "Reaganomics" trickle-down theory—neither works. Just as our national economy is deeply in debt, so we always feel in debt when it comes to time. The reality is that there is simply never enough time "left over" to be used for our own health, well-being, or inner growth processes. Yet we know that if we want to be healthy, we need to create time for ourselves.

Do you have enough time in your life?

When I ask this question in my seminars on wellness and time, only one or two people generally say yes—out of a class of fifty. When I ask these one or two how they feel, they tend to give a knowing smile: "I feel great about my life!" is the common answer. Invariably, these few people say that they *consciously changed* their relationship with time into one that brings them far more happiness.

The other 95 percent—like most of us—are experiencing what I call "time poverty." When asked what it feels like never to have enough time in the day, they say things like:

"Frustrating. Stressful."

"Like I can't breathe."

"I feel like I'm under constant pressure."

"Whatever I'm doing, I feel like I should be doing something else."

"I feel trapped."

"I hear the clock ticking. I keep thinking, 'Oh my God, my life is slipping away.'"

"Like life is zooming by, and I'm missing it."

Sound familiar? Statements like these are the refrain of contemporary life. Since almost all of us have these feelings, we consider them normal. It's difficult to imagine another way to live. No wonder W. H. Auden dubbed ours the age of anxiety.

This has become so deeply ingrained that a woman recently told me she has been having recurring nightmares about always running late. Our anxiety about time has become a core issue, even operating subconsciously in our life.

Thomas Moore starts his magnificent *Care of the Soul* with the following statement:

> The great malady of the twentieth century, implicated in all of our troubles and affecting us individually and socially, is "loss of soul."

Substitute "time" for "soul"—*equate* time and soul—and you will begin to have an idea of the relationship to time I'm talking about.

To most of us, time means clock-time, sixty seconds a minute, sixty minutes an hour, twenty-four hours in the day: unchangeable, inexorable clock-time.

But if we can think of time in a different way, if we become aware that it contains myriad rhythms and that any individual moment can be expanded or contracted *under our control,* then I believe we can make time our servant—and in doing so, fill our lives with happiness and health to a degree most of us don't experience and cannot even imagine.

Many people come to my seminars expecting advice on time management. The time management taught at business seminars is essentially designed to make you more materially productive. Time is broken into manageable segments, and in each time frame you complete a project (or several; the horrid word for this is "multitasking"). Once one project is finished—if you've allocated your time wisely—you'll have time for the next.

But this simply turns up the speed on the treadmill of our lives— and, to the applause of those around us, we run faster. The reward for those who "manage" time well is usually just more to do. After all, as the saying goes, "If you want something done, just ask a busy person."

The time awareness I teach is *not* time management. Practicing time awareness is not about producing efficiently. (Although it *will* in fact make you more productive; indeed, there are vast practical benefits to timeshifting.)

Time awareness is about living fully. When we truly need to meet a deadline, when speed is essential, we can always call on time management skills. But when we can exist fully in the present moment, we've achieved time awareness, which lifts us *away* from clock-time, into time freedom.

To be aware of time, we must develop new attitudes and new skills. This involves focusing on one thing at a time, learning to slow down and notice—really experience—our physical and emotional states. It involves reacquainting ourselves with our senses, our friends, our spouses, our children, and just what it is to be in this moment. It involves learning when to speed up (increasing the speed of our rhythm can be as valuable as decreasing it) and when and how to downshift. It involves facing ourselves directly, and truly showing up in each moment of our lives. In fact, the "time management" I teach is an individual process, governed by only one rule: Live life in the now.

"Now" is a puzzling concept. Read or say the word and you are already beyond it: "Now" is a thing of the past.

Einstein showed, and contemporary physicists agree, that time does not exist on its own; it is only a gauge of how long an object takes to move through space. When we drop a ball, for example, we can measure precisely how long it takes to hit the ground—but we can't tell where the "now" is in the process.

Still, to me—and, I trust, to you—the now *does* exist. We *feel* present.

In fact, we can only know the present subjectively. Time stands still when we're at a boring meeting, and flies all too quickly when we're making love. The time we call the "present" is always, and only personally, felt.

There is a well-known story of a Zen monk who, pursued by a ravenous tiger, climbed halfway down a cliff—and hung by a branch above a ledge he found inhabited by an equally ferocious tiger. Growing next to the branch was a bush with a single strawberry, which the monk picked. The monk smelled the strawberry, felt the strawberry, bit the strawberry . . . and thought to himself, "How delicious!"

If we are aware of the now, if we experience it, we are in the flow of time. The rush of the past and the pressure of the future—those twin tigers—are cast aside. There is only the present; there is only what is at hand.

When we realize that there is only what is at hand, we also realize that time does not march at our back or lead us on, although it often seems to. Time simply *is*. It is this moment, *right now:* a medium for our own rhythms and the rhythms of the universe—nothing more.

Most of us aren't conscious of this aspect of time—its essential emptiness, apart from our experience of it—because we live by clocks and the "sureness" of past, present, and future. In fact, we cling desperately—much more desperately than that monk to his branch—to our clocks, our watches, our guarantors of surety.

Students in my seminars love it when I suggest that they tape the word "now" over the face of their watches—yet I've rarely seen anyone actually do it. At est training sessions, the participants are asked to take off their watches—yet a significant number refuse, secretly hiding their watches when the trainer insists. At the end of World War II, American soldiers stripped the Germans of their watches, a sure metaphor for mastery: They knew what time it was—real time and victory time—and the Germans did not.

People constantly look at their watches, yet when asked immediately afterward, do not know what time it is.

Patently, the watch is a kind of security talisman. We don't even need to know the time—as long as we have it on our person.

Knowing "what time it is," we think, grounds us in the world, lets us know where we are. But it is linear time we're relying on, and by so doing, we neglect the soul.

* * *

The good news is that the way we deal with time is neither inevitable nor unchangeable. We don't *have* to live with a chronic time shortage. We don't *have* to wear our watches like shackles.

A day holds both twenty-four hours and an infinity of time. But our society doesn't recognize time as infinite; quite the opposite. We have been taught to value time only by how productive we can be in it. We are caught by the disrhythms and dysfunction of modern life—so much so that we rush through life without experiencing it.

This sort of time pressure is a peculiarity of recent history. Keeping precise time is a social invention, and only about a hundred years old. For all the aeons of human existence before that, time was generous with us, and we lived in time freedom.

We can learn to live that way again, to shift into a more natural, biological rhythm. We must strive for "soul time," a different time for each of us; one that corresponds to our individual soul's rhythm, our inner beat, but that is in tune with the soul—the pulse—of the universe.

My purpose is to create more time for you in your life. Yet surely I'm not increasing the day from twenty-four to thirty hours. So what does it mean to create time?

It means becoming present, here in this moment, more of the time. We create time each moment we step into awareness of the present.

If you feel your life rushing by, as though you can't keep up with all your obligations and the demands upon you—just stop! Begin with just a moment. Allow yourself to be aware and to feel in this moment. Creating time is about becoming alive and authentic.

We have the capacity to *look* at time—and by doing so step into a new awareness of it and experience its next dimension, time freedom. But we cannot just look with our eyes and understand with our mind; we must experience it with all facets of our being: with all our senses, with our perceptions, with our feelings, with our hearts. Timeshifting is the method for doing this, and how *you* can learn timeshifting is what this book is about.

This is not a theoretical or philosophical book (although there is much theory and some philosophy in it), but rather, at its core, a practical one. My own experiences, and those of the thousands of people who have attended my seminars, have shown me that when we learn to shift time, our relationships become more rewarding, our time spent alone is richer, our aging is more satisfying, our work is more fruitful, and our stress and anxiety are less paralyzing—or even nonexistent.

We've all experienced it: that feeling when everything seems to be flowing; when we truly have enough time; when we are relaxed, calm, at peace with ourselves, and in harmony with the people and the world around us.

We've all experienced it, but far too rarely. This book is about learning to experience it more.

Timeshifting can make us richer by giving us more of that most precious commodity: life itself.

PART ONE

Time is the substance I am made of. Time is a river that sweeps me along, but I am the river; it is a tiger that rips me apart, but I am the tiger; it is a fire that consumes me, but I am the fire.

—JORGE LUIS BORGES

CHAPTER ONE

TOWARD TIME FREEDOM

———

I am not this steeply sloping hour in which you see me hurrying.
—RAINER MARIA RILKE

W E F L E W O U T of a raging blizzard in New York and landed in the magical, warm blue of the Caribbean. I was leading a group of people to the island of St. John to take a series of workshops on wellness and personal growth from the Omega Institute for Holistic Studies, which I direct. To get from St. Thomas, where we'd landed, to the other island, we boarded an open-air ferry.

The scene from the boat was the very definition of idyllic. We were rocking gently in the turquoise sea, with islands of forested hills in the background. It was a warm day with a flower-scented breeze, even a rainbow in the distance. Because of inevitable schedule changes, the ferry waited for several minutes in the harbor.

I noticed Vicki, a woman from our group, sitting on the ferry, repeatedly beating her fists on her knees, her face showing impatience and tension. I watched her for a while. She stared straight ahead, seemingly unaware of the beautiful scenery, just thumping her arms up and down. Finally I walked over to her and asked, "Is anything the matter?" She looked up at me. "When are we going to get there?" she asked plaintively.

Immediately I thought, "Where else could we possibly be that would be better than right here, right now?" "No place," I answered myself. There's no "there" that could be any more beautiful, more fragrant, more peaceful than where we were right then. Right at that moment.

Of course, Vicki didn't see it that way. Like most of us, she was so accustomed to extreme time pressure that just sitting still for a few minutes felt like she was "wasting" precious time—felt, in fact, "like a sin," she told me later. She was so used to running at top speed, often doing several things at once, that slowing down became stressful, and she literally couldn't see the stunning scenery all around her, couldn't feel peaceful in the midst of an atmosphere of peacefulness. She was so habituated to time urgency that even on a trip to "get away from it all" she had taken it all with her—the feeling that she had to hurry and be productive every moment. She also felt the guilt associated with taking time "off," and had the nagging worry that she should be doing something else. Like most of us, Vicki had spent her daily life stuck in high gear, and couldn't figure out how to downshift into relaxation, even though that's what she desperately wanted and needed to do.

Vicki's problem is all too common; our turbulent relationship with time is the curse of modern life. If you've picked up this book, you probably feel that you never have enough time—and that you are always moving at a relentless pace. This constant rushing robs us of the peace of mind and basic pleasures that are our birthright—and denies us the time for meaningful communication with others, leisurely meals, play and laughter, relaxed and comfortable time with ourselves, and the ability to experience the beauty of life all around us.

Imagine a world without clocks.

We would be, at best, disoriented. At worst, the organization of our lives would collapse.

Most of us set the alarm each night so we can be sure to wake up at the precise moment we think we should—so that we can prepare breakfast, get to work on time, and make sure the kids don't miss the school bus. Those of us who have the luxury of waking without

an alarm still look at our watches first thing, if only to place ourselves in relation to the day. If it's late, we think, "I've overslept"—
as though letting any part of the day pass without being conscious
of its passing is a sin.

Without clocks, we would not know when the movie started,
the train left, the restaurant opened, the meeting convened, or the
date was to be picked up. Workers punch time clocks; if they're
late, their salaries are docked and the work doesn't flow as
smoothly. We work from nine to five (and get paid for overtime),
pick up the children at three, have dinner at seven, and watch the
eleven o'clock news. High schoolers have three hours to finish their
SATs, quiz contestants must answer within thirty seconds, professional basketball players have twenty-four seconds to shoot, runners
set world records in hundredths of seconds, NASA officials calibrate
liftoffs to the thousandth of a second, and physicists work in nanoseconds.

Everything is lived according to a clock, by now so accurate that
we can measure the speed of subatomic particles. We wear time like
a manacle on our wrists, and move to its inexorable beat.

Time is what we use to measure our lives: a second, a minute, an
hour, a year, a decade, a lifetime. All of us depend on clocks because we have become slaves to time.

But there were no such things as clocks in the Middle Ages. Even
the hourglass, hardly a precise instrument of measurement, wasn't in
use until the late thirteenth century. We tend never to question
whether time was experienced differently by our ancestors. We
relate to time as a phenomenon outside ourselves, a universal
"clock" that keeps ticking as it quickly passes by. Yet those who
came before us experienced time as a flow very different from the
speed of modern life.

Even today, in areas of Africa, for example, and in Papua, New
Guinea, the concept of time as *we* understand it does not exist. In
many languages there are no equivalent words for "hour," "minute," or "second." It is day when the sun comes up, night when it
sets; the seasons are measured by the way crops grow or wither, and
no one knows how old his parents were when they died—only that
they *were* old, and dying was an inevitable and blessed event.

What backward people, we're apt to think. What backward

times. Yet I doubt that the Papuans would agree with us, and I'm not at all convinced that someone living in the Middle Ages would see our society as having advanced very much. Indeed, they might regard us with pity. What frantic people, they might think. What frantic times.

Both attitudes, of course, are right.

It is simply a fact that, as Westerners living in an industrial-atomic-space-age world, clock-time is part of us—and it is something to be valued, something to be used. But we must learn to keep a different kind of time as well, if we are to savor life most fully.

Unless we consciously learn to control time in our lives, the stress we suffer will only get worse. We are at the mercy of all the messages in our society that tell us to go faster, do more, produce more, buy more—and above all, never sit still and just experience being alive. Until we learn to control time consciously, our lives will continue to speed away from us, and we won't even notice the beauty or the events around us. We'll simply be left with the feeling that something's missing, something's disappeared. Like Vicki on the ferry, we could be in Paradise itself—and not even realize it.

My own fascination with time goes back as far as I can remember. It took me years to realize that when I was an infant, before conscious memory, I ate and slept and learned on my own schedule, without a clock. Back then, when I was most contented, I was time's master.

I was about six years old when my grandfather, an inventor who delighted in the workings of the mechanical world, gave me a clock and explained how it worked. He spent hours with me, exploring the world of numbers, explaining their relationship to time and time's relationship to us. At first, I was less interested in the face of the clock than in its inner mechanism. But I soon realized that the information it imparted—the time of day—was particularly important in our household.

My father, a physician, was acutely aware of time, since his work demanded a rigorous schedule. My mother, too, was time-conscious, and taught us to use our time efficiently. "Time's valuable," she told us. "Don't fritter it away."

On schedule, I attended college and then medical school. My parents were pleased. *I* was pleased. I was using my time to my best advantage.

Yet there was a restlessness or rebelliousness in me, also imparted by my parents. I began looking for something other than the prescribed life I was leading—and in 1973, just before I got my degree in medicine, I took a trip to India, which changed my perspective and approach.

It was around this same time that I reread a book written in the early seventies that suddenly took on new meaning for me: *Be Here Now,* by Ram Dass, who has since become a cherished friend and mentor. The book focuses on "being" rather than "doing," on existing in the present moment rather than in the past or future. Although many people considered such ideas heresy, thinking that following them meant simply "dropping out," I was inspired. I was determined to incorporate these ideas into my life and my medical practice.

After I became a doctor, I concentrated on holistic medicine, a new concept in the West at that time. The focus in my practice became wellness, prevention, longevity, and the mind-body connection in disease and stress. I taught exercise and nutrition, stress reduction, and relaxation—and I began to notice, even though I could not yet codify it into a theory, the role that time played in all aspects of health.

The effects of "time poverty" were clearly beginning to reveal themselves to me in my work with patients. Patient after patient complained that "there wasn't enough time." Their sense of anxiety and pressure was enormous; there were simply "not enough hours in the day" to accomplish everything they *had* to do. I listened sympathetically, prescribed exercise and a healthy diet, and—with a kind of smugness I shudder at now—thought proudly to myself that I was working twice as hard as any of them, yet shared few if any of the symptoms of stress they exhibited.

But I noticed something else, too. Like so many successful people, I had come to adopt the strategy that, since life is a mortal event—there was only so much time for me, after all—the way to make the most of my years was to cram in as much activity as possible. I thought that living life to the fullest meant doing as much as possible.

By the time I reached my thirties, however, I began to feel an emptiness, a sense of dissatisfaction. Although I was doing more in order to experience more, I actually felt as if I were experiencing *less*. I had a nagging feeling that, somehow, I was missing the point.

In fact, I was, because I wasn't really *present* for any of it. My life was speeding by so fast, I was missing it.

"I'd better do even more, then," I told myself. "I'll just have to speed up."

But, as we'll discover, the reverse is true. We need to learn how to make the time to slow down. We need to drop *in*, to notice things, to really settle in to our lives and pay attention moment to moment, instead of simply rushing ahead.

In 1977, I founded the Omega Institute for Holistic Studies in Rhinebeck, New York, as a center where people can develop skills to help them become more fully alive in daily life. From the beginning, a critical objective of Omega has been to create a truly nurturing and safe environment, where people can feel a sense of community and spirit. In order to do this, we found a setting in the Hudson River Valley, where the woods, the gardens, and the sounds of nature combine with the curriculum to allow participants to slow down and feel comfortable. The Omega experience becomes a vacation combined with learning, and allows the participants to leave the rush of their daily lives behind for a while.

The response to Omega's offerings was dramatic from the start. Now, some twenty thousand people come to our programs over the course of a year, and that number continues to grow. Omega has become an oasis for people seeking to feel connected with others, with nature, and, ultimately, with their own inner selves.

Key to this response, I believe, is the role of time and rhythm. At Omega, people come to a country setting. There is no emphasis on clocks, but rather the attendees are encouraged to attune to the rhythms of nature, rhythms they tend to overlook in their work lives, but which are very much part of them. For them, time shifts in ways that are healing and healthful.

I'm still at Omega—but I'm not the same person I was in 1977.

Time has changed me. I don't mean only the *passage* of time—yes, I'm eighteen years older and have that much more accumulated wisdom and folly. I mean that my understanding of time, and my *use* of time, have changed as well.

In America, time is the enemy. We speak of "wasting time," "passing time," "killing time," "doing time"—to the point where idleness makes us anxious and we fill silence with the sound of boom boxes and television. I had bought into the American way, believing I could do two or even three things at once: writing lectures while I watched my children play, preparing dinner as I kept up with the current news. But a series of events occurred that altered my way of thinking, remodeled my lifestyle, made time my special subject—and led to this book.

The first event was seemingly mundane: I saw a man walk.

He is, of course, a special man, and the walk was unlike any I had ever witnessed. The man was Thich Nhat Hanh, a Vietnamese Buddhist monk and peace activist, who had honored Omega by coming as one of its visiting teachers.

One day, while he was leading a meditation retreat, I was talking about business with someone in my office, the windows of which overlooked a garden on the Omega grounds. Thich Nhat Hanh was walking through that garden, followed by a group of about a hundred people. I stared outside, transfixed, my visitor and our business together forgotten.

The way Thich Nhat Hanh was walking made it seem that, with each step, he was kissing the earth. He was totally present, obviously immersed only in the act of walking. I could almost *feel* him savoring each moment, feel the sensation of grass on sole, feel the way his body seemed at one with each movement.

He was *present* in that walk. At that moment, nothing else mattered; he was living only in the now. Even as I remember it today, I can feel completely present in that moment when I experienced him walking.

That night, as I was walking to dinner, I suddenly stopped short. My mind, I realized, was on the business discussion of that afternoon, and a phone call I had forgotten to make and would have to put through after eating. In other words, I was existing in the past and future, but not in the present. That evening—just as on so many previous evenings—I was not conscious of my walk, of my breathing, or of the glow of the lights from the Omega dining hall.

So I thought of Thich Nhat Hanh—and as I allowed myself to enter into the present moment, to become aware of my present activity and simultaneously drop the preoccupying thoughts of past and future, I began to notice a very deep peacefulness coming over me. It was as though my whole being was shifting into relaxation. I could have such an experience at any time, I realized. All I had to do was bring myself into the present moment and be *here*. And I could stay as long as I wanted! I learned that I could control—and thus create—time!

Walking slowly and consciously can look, from our typically frenetic, "time-poor" point of view, like a "waste" of time. But I along with countless students have found that the impact of just a few moments of becoming present like this is so calming and refreshing that it goes a long way toward creating more peace and relaxation in the rest of the day.

As we'll see later, when you set up a peaceful rhythm in your life, like the walking meditation—or even walking your dog, taking the time to play with children, or having a deep conversation with a friend—it can help to balance the pace of your life. What's wonderful and surprising is that a brief period of conscious downshifting does not have the effect of sucking time away from your day. Instead, it creates time for you, paying you back in what I call "time freedom" all day long. That's timeshifting.

In 1986, my wife and I were divorced. We're friends now—indeed, coworkers at Omega—but at the time the separation was bitter and painful. As an antidote, I threw myself into my work with redoubled energy. Omega expanded rapidly. I took on more private patients. I filled my days and nights with activity—anything to escape from the hurt that was at my core.

I was working hard—but I wanted to work still harder. Although I was running Omega and continued to carry a full medical practice, I took on the development of a major health-wellness spa in Lenox, Massachusetts—a multimillion-dollar project—and thereby underwent a crisis that became another pivotal experience in my personal relationship with time.

I knew I was already doing too much, yet I let myself be seduced into this project because it had been a dream of mine. I also knew that, if it worked, it would make me wealthy. In addition, the gamesman in me responded to the challenge: Friends told me that if anyone could pull this off, I could.

One day, though, I found myself driving to a meeting . . . and pounding my fist on the dashboard, something I had never done before. My inner voice was telling me to stop this insane overloading of my life with activity—but who listens to inner voices when logic dictates? I went ahead, full speed.

But the timing was all wrong for the spa. The American economy had entered a recession, we encountered lots of problems, and it didn't take long before the whole enterprise came tumbling down. Certainly, I can look back now and say that I would prefer to have been successful—after all, who really prefers failure?—and I would love to have made a few million dollars. But when I look deeper, I realize that, although it was an expensive lesson, it was one I needed to absorb. In truth, the subsequent bankruptcy was a blessing in disguise.

Rather than slowing down to feel the pain of the loss of my marriage, and resolving those difficult feelings, I had plunged forward with a new project just to keep myself fully occupied. I was forcing myself to race past the pain—and thus allowing myself to race through precious moments with my children and my friends, moments I appreciated only in retrospect. My life was plainly way out of rhythm. Only a major event was going to wake me up to the fact that I needed to make some changes. The bankruptcy did just that.

In the wake of the crisis, I took a hard look at my life and how I had been relating to the world. It became clear that proceeding along the same path—always putting work first, and doing as much as possible—was only going to lead to an increasing sense that the important things in life were eluding me, no matter how "successful" I became.

Since that time I have learned, step-by-step, to dramatically change my awareness of time and my relationship with it. I have learned to experience a deep peacefulness and profound satisfaction in the ordinary moments of living—largely by slowing down enough to savor them. I still work hard when I work, and move fast when I need to. But I am learning to let go of my work when I'm not working, and to slow down when I wish. I can relax and enjoy just being alive in a way I never dreamed possible when I was stuck in high gear all the time.

Sound appealing?

This book offers a set of concepts and teaches skills that will enable you to understand time better—and, by doing so, shift it. I'll show you how time affects your sense of self, your relationships, your experience of work, play, health, aging, dying, society, and the future.

But understanding time with your brain isn't enough, although it's essential. When you learn to *embody* time, when you can shift it at will, *then* you will experience a wholeness, a freedom—time freedom—you never dreamed possible.

CHAPTER TWO

ENTRAINMENT AND THE RHYTHM OF LIFE

---

*Artur Rubinstein was once asked by an ardent
admirer: How do you handle the notes as well
as you do?
The pianist answered, "I handle the notes no
better than many others, but the pauses—ah!
that is where the art resides."*

EVERYTHING MOVES IN rhythm. Atomic particles, waves of electrons, molecules in wood and rocks, grass and trees, amoebas, mammals and birds, fishes and reptiles, the earth, the moon, the sun and stars . . . and we ourselves. All are dominated by rhythm.

In us, as in all animals, the heart is most noticeably rhythmic; but the blood pumped by our heart, along with the organs, muscles, and sinews nourished by our blood, also move in rhythm, whether we're conscious of it or not. Our breath, the most obvious manifestation of our inner condition, quickens or slows according to our state of mind or level of physical excitement.

The world is thus alive with a myriad of rhythms. "Entrainment" is the process by which these rhythms fall into synchronization with each other.

Rhythmic entrainment is one of the great organizing principles of the world, as inescapable as gravity. It explains how one rhythm works with another, and how separate entities, from molecules to stars, will fall into rhythm as automatically as a pulse beats or a butterfly flaps its wings.

If you set two out-of-sync pendulum clocks side by side, by the next day they'll be keeping time together. In fact, it looks as if they *want* to be locked into sync with each other. When you adjust the knobs on your radio, you're adjusting the set's oscillators: When they come reasonably close to matching the frequency of a station's signal, they suddenly lock and pulse together, and your program jumps into focus.

That moving bodies tend to entrain was discovered by the Dutch scientist Christian Huygens in 1665. Since then, entrainment has become a well-accepted concept in the physical and natural sciences, where our increasing understanding of it has led to fantastic technological achievements.

But we are still only beginning to understand, or even recognize, entrainment as it applies to people. In fact, most of us take it so much for granted that we don't consciously realize it exists. Even if we're aware of it, we don't take the time to understand it.

Our entrainment—our coming into sync with another person, object, sound, mood, rhythm—can be short term or long. It can take the form of a shared smile; a dance either solo or with another; the act of love; an intense discussion; teamwork in sports, business, during a crisis; a feeling of community with a whole town or city against a common enemy or for a common cause, good or bad (think of the way the nation wept when Christa McAuliffe died, or rejoiced when Neil Armstrong set foot on the moon); a sense of kinship with nature in the woods or on a silent lake; or even a oneness with the great mysteries—the rhythm of the spheres, the pulse of the universe, the flow of time.

Women who live together in college dormitories often find that their monthly menstrual cycles begin to coincide. Mothers and babies entrain when the baby is in utero. See a baby smile, and I dare you not to smile with it. And think of sex with and without entrainment: The first leads to bliss, the other produces frustration and anger.

Frederick Erickson of the Interaction Laboratory at the University of Pennsylvania has shown that entrainment takes place even at the dinner table. When family members talk, the syllables they stress carry the same rhythm. When the conversation lapses, the shared rhythm continues: Someone reaches for the salt on a beat; a knife hits a plate on a beat; and, when the meal is over, the family members' departing footsteps continue to tap out the beat.

Great orators are well aware of the power of the rhythm of their speech to pull people into their orbit. Members of his congregation said that just listening to the young Martin Luther King, Jr., made you feel like part of a human wave, rising to what he was saying. John F. Kennedy had that kind of power as well—so did Adolf Hitler. Entrainment in itself is neither right nor wrong; it simply exists as a force in nature. (As the author René Daumal once wrote, in his *Mount Analogue:* "A knife is neither right nor wrong, but he who holds it by the blade is surely in error.")

The African drummer, the great violinist playing Brahms, the orator, the politician . . . all use entrainment. They have caught the rhythm of the music or of the words, and they experience the same rhythm coming back at them from their audience. In my seminars, I know I've captured the right rhythm when I am actually so present that I'm not consciously monitoring what I'm saying—I am just "being" in the flow of speaking. At such times, I get the palpable feeling from my listeners that they're "with" me just as I am "with" them.

Entrainment need have nothing to do with words or sound, though. The great basketball player Bill Russell writes in his autobiography, *Second Wind,* of those moments in a game when teammates and opponents are playing to the maximum of their ability, when they're entrained not only with each other, but with the game itself. At those moments, says Russell, winning or losing doesn't matter. What is sublime is the *act* of basketball, players united in sport on the highest level.

Earlier religious leaders and shamans knew the power of rhythm to transform mundane or profane time into sacred time, where contemplation supersedes pace, where timelessness overcomes social time. Ceremonies and religious rituals have always relied on a drumbeat or choral chant to induce a state that brings the community into a slower rhythmic frequency, enabling a more profound and spiritual experience of existence.

In some cultures, the trance state is induced through the ritual of drumming. Anthropologist Michael Harner has researched many different cultures and found that a specific and particular kind of drumming brings an entire group into a shared rhythm that is considered sacred, and thus an opening to the "other world." Shamans speak of the drum as the "canoe" that carries them to the other shore.

In Africa, the drum was and still is used not only in religious ceremonies, but also in dances and other ceremonies to create a rhythm that reflects a story or an aspect of the environment. When there was no written history, the drum and its accompanying dance carried the story. If there was a drought, or a harvest, or a birth, or a war, the drum conveyed the appropriate rhythm. It was not a measured beat as we have known it in the West, but a rhythm that reflected the changing natural environment. It created an entrainment field for those involved. Even today, each village often will have its own dances and rhythms, reflecting the differences between communities, indicating that each community is entrained to its own particular beat. Even cities have their own particular rhythms. The pace of life in Seattle, say, is far different from the pace of Los Angeles.

A drum beats at an African festival. Slowly at first, then faster and faster goes the beat; then it slows, then speeds up again. The dancers, moving in a circle around a fire, match their pace to the drum's. Some of the onlookers, caught in the rhythm of the dance, tap their feet in time with the drum; others clap their hands. Soon, each of the participants, onlookers as well as drummers and dancers, has lost consciousness of his immediate surroundings; indeed, there is no *thinking* at all, but rather entrainment with the rhythm, which in fact contains every beat, every rhythm in the world.

The drummer, if inspired, is tuning in to the rhythm of the moment, of the universe, becoming an instrument himself, relaying the rhythm to the crowd. Babatunde Olatunji, who introduced the African drum to the West, once told me that the rhythm moves through him, but he feels no sense of domination or power. It is merely given to him to be the messenger.

In the West, too, since early times, societies have used the rhythm of song to reflect and determine the tempo of life. Farmers sang in the fields, guests danced at a wedding, bells tolled the hours, rowers chanted as they pulled their boats through the water. People gathered for songfests, both religious and secular. In ancient Greece, Homer sang his stories rather than recited them. In the Middle Ages, each German guild had its own song to depict its own rhythm.

Everywhere, music—not solid sound, but sound *and pause,* with the rhythm of silence as well as sound—has always been, and still is, the most effective entrainer. And its power is enormous. My father told me of a performance of Beethoven's *Fidelio* in Salzburg, with Toscanini conducting, where the audience—an elite and sedate crowd if there ever was one—was so moved that they danced in the aisles, much to the surprise of the singers onstage.

The trumpet player Miles Evans told me, "Miles Davis created great music by opening the space between the notes and stepping inside." And percussionist Tony Vacca says, "If you can't find your rhythm, you can't find your soul."

But today we have little time for any music that doesn't draw on a narrow range of accelerated rhythms. Today our music, like our society, has grown more raucous; rock and rap dominate our airwaves. And according to anthropologist Edward T. Hall, our popular music doesn't determine, but rather reflects, the pace of our lives:

> Music can been seen as a sort of rhythmic consensus. One reason you get hit tunes is that someone composes something that is so close to what people are doing, feeling, and the rhythms they use that they recognize it immediately. The music releases feelings and rhythms that people are familiar with.

Since music is the great entrainer, our music *had* to speed up. Our society was telling it to.

Entrainment is something that's so much a part of our lives that we don't usually notice it—but sometimes we catch a glimpse of it. For instance, when my son Eli was two and a half, he wanted to listen to the tape of *Aladdin* again and again, as small children do. Unfortunately for me, even when the tape was off, it was still going round and round in my head. It would be playing inside my skull and I wouldn't even realize it; things would quiet down and all of a sudden the *Aladdin* theme would pop back up, full blast. It was actually there all the time, as sort of an undercurrent rhythm—and I was unwittingly moving to that resident rhythm.

Most of us haven't internalized *Aladdin,* but we are intimately in touch with the ambient clip of society. We're living a rhythm that goes snap-snap-snap all the time—and it's there *all* the time, even when we don't notice it. Unconsciously, like a poison ingested by our bodies in a deceptively sweet syrup, we have entrained with a faster rhythm. It controls the way we walk, the way we speak, the way we respond to intimates and strangers, the way we *don't* relax. Just notice your annoyance when someone sitting in a meeting with you is tapping his pen on the desk, or his foot on the floor.

This habituation to simply skim the surface of experience, then move on, permeates our life. For instance, we may go to the zoo to watch the animals. But a recent study of zoo-goers at the National Zoo in Washington, D.C., found that the average time people spend looking at any one exhibit of animals is barely a blink of an eye: five to ten seconds. You might as well be flipping through a picture book for all the experience that amount of time can give you on how an animal acts, reacts, moves, eats, or communicates. In the same study, a tour guide at the National Zoo in Washington, D.C., noted that many people assume hippos stay underwater for long periods of time. "Actually," he explained, "the average is ninety seconds and the maximum is five minutes. Tourists just don't stay around long enough to watch them emerge." Our press to move on virtually guarantees that we miss what we came for.

This absurdly fast internalized rhythm, this rhythm we scarcely notice because it is so pervasive, is urged on us by our society. And modern society's rhythm provides perhaps the most powerful—and potentially the most pernicious—entrainment of all.

For the last hundred years or so, Western society has set an overly fast rhythm, a rhythm that varies only in that it is continually getting faster, urging us to do more, produce more, learn more. All our machines are geared to the acceleration of an already too-frantic speed. Computers, faxes, voice mail, E-mail, the Internet, portable phones, automatic redial: These are handy for business and sometimes convenient, but they each add to the speed of the rhythm around us, constantly increasing the pressure—allowing us little time for reflection, and none for feelings.

This rhythm of fast and still faster is a relatively new phenomenon, and no one seems to know how to vary it. Most of us don't even think of varying it, because society judges it "productive," and because we as individuals are so entrained with it that we don't consciously realize we want to change it.

Even if we recognize something is wrong, we don't know *how* to change the rhythm, how to entrain with something slower, more "human." Most of us don't know how to shift time. We don't know how to entrain with slower rhythms when society hammers at us relentlessly. We don't know how to pause for contemplation, to take time for ourselves, to go from the frenetic to the peaceful, to truly relax, to take note, to feel.

Let's look at the life of a Colonial family, circa 1750.

Those were tough times. The land had to be tilled, the crops planted and harvested, the clothes washed by hand, the bread baked without benefit of electricity, the children reared, the clothes washed, the (rudimentary) machinery kept in working order. There were no timesaving devices, no home appliances, no boxes of one-minute rice or TV dinners.

Yet how do we explain that wedding ceremonies often lasted five days, celebrations of holidays or the harvest, a week? Where did those oppressed, overworked Colonials find the time to enjoy themselves—which all their literature suggests they did? Why did they have so much more time than we have for religion and meditation? Why was there more joy, more friendliness, more consideration than in our *angst*-ridden, angry, no-time-for-civility society?

The Colonials were working within the rhythm of *their* society's time, one completely different from ours. Of course the Colonials struggled, but usually not against time. The stress disorders that plague so many of us today were essentially unknown then; relaxation was built into their lives. They were in a peaceful rhythm with the daily course of events. Their rhythms were defined not so much by days, hours, and minutes as by seasons.

For them (as for all people until the beginning of the Industrial Revolution, and for most people in non-Western societies today), time was circular. It was marked by changes, certainly. Wet seasons and dry. Heat and cold. Birth and death. Planting, cultivating, and harvesting (each part of the cycle marked by celebration). But existence went on without fundamentally changing. The cycle of the years started over again as surely as day followed night, and babies were born as surely as people died.

We can see a sudden, dramatic shift from this sort of circular time to modern, linear time in a place called Ladakh, a district of North India high in the Himalayas.

Ladakh was totally isolated until the mid-seventies, and work was hard. Its citizens used the simplest tools, grew their own food, raised their own animals, and made their own clothing. But, as Swedish linguist Helena Norberg-Hodge noted in *Ancient Futures: Learning from Ladakh,* work was done collaboratively, usually accompanied by singing, and there was a tremendous amount of time, particularly during the winter, which was spent in virtual nonstop partying and celebration.

In 1974, the Indian government built a road to Ladakh, encouraging tourists and "development experts" to visit. The Ladakhis quickly got caught up in a money economy. And now, although they had never needed money before, many cannot imagine how they had gotten along without it. They now buy timesaving devices, goods from other countries—the ways of the Western world.

This sudden entry into modernity has changed every aspect of life in Ladakh—right down to the basic level of human relationships. As a Ladakhi friend told Norberg-Hodge:

I can't understand it. My sister in the capital, she now has all these things that do the work faster. She just buys her clothes in a shop, she has a jeep, a telephone, a gas cooker. All of these things save her so much time, and yet when I go to visit her, she doesn't have time to talk to me.

The Ladakhis had, unconsciously, shifted from circular to linear time. I wonder how many of them would be happier if they could shift back.

I encountered the concept of circular time myself when reading about the Hopi people of the Southwest United States. Like most Native American societies, the Hopis dwell in circular time, a concept peculiar to our modern linear sense of the flow of time. In circular time, just as day comes after night, the seasons continually repeat themselves, the crops are yearly planted, grown, and harvested—so the future is seen as a return of what has already occurred in the past. The present moment is the center of a continually repetitive flow of past events that will recur in the future once again. Change takes place against a backdrop of constancy.

Thus, for the Hopis, if the days, the seasons, even lifetimes come around again, then time never runs out. What is not completed in the circle of today may be accomplished tomorrow. If not this year, then the next; if not in this lifetime, then in another. Things don't progress as you look to the future, nor do they get worse.

The *present* is where life happens.

By contrast, our modern rhythm is distinctly *unnatural,* mirroring society's pull, not the magnetism of the earth. We're taught to think quickly, act quickly, accomplish quickly. *Buy* quickly, our television sets implore us: only ten more shopping days till Christmas! We have superimposed on nature the rhythms of greed, of materialism, of "having it all."

We do this even in childhood. A friend described with chagrin how his daughter tends to react to Christmas:

> Sarah goes through this absolute frenzy of anticipation. Instead of looking at each gift, handling it and thinking about it and really getting into it, she goes through this little cyclone of opening things. She'll tear the wrapping paper off one present—and then immediately she puts it down and frantically digs into the next one. It's like a feeding frenzy.

Sarah is, of course, acting out her own entrainment to the weird speed at which we live. She is picking up her cues from us, for we, too, anticipate what's to come, then ignore what's actually here.

* * *

I'm not suggesting that we become Colonials, or shape our lives like the Hopis. We couldn't, even if we tried. I'm advocating only that we *learn* from them. For they lived—and many still live—their lives in the flow of time, rather than racing to be on time, racing *against* time.

We have forgotten what the vast majority of people who ever lived—who are living now, in fact—knew and still know. We have forgotten that life itself—time itself—is the unfolding of a myriad of rhythms. Like music, the pulse of the universe is filled with sound and silence, activity and rest.

We have forgotten how to rest.

To remember, we must entrain with rhythms other than society's. And we are best off, I think, starting with our own.

Take your pulse. Run for ten minutes. Take it again. Rest for a minute. Take it again. Your pulse will of course beat to different rhythms, faster when you're active, slower when you're calm. We are born through a series of contractions and rests, not just one continuous cramp. Our muscle cells must relax to work again.

As it is with the human pulse, so it is with human emotion. Anger, fear, love, peace: All produce a different pulse rate, a different rhythm.

And as it is with us, so it is with the universe. Quantum physics and chaos theory verify what an ancient sage once said: A butterfly beating its wings can affect the weather half a world away. The sun and stars burn, not with a steady heat, but cooler and hotter as their inner gasses explode.

If our pulse beats in different rhythms—if life does, if the universe does—why is it, then, that we feel we must spend our lives at one speed? Why do we wish only to go faster, since we don't have enough time to accomplish everything we're "supposed" to do?

The answer is that society dictates it. We are creatures of habit who have become habituated to society's pulse. But society is our master only if we allow it to be. Even the most ingrained habit can be broken.

As we shift our rhythm, serenity is the reward.

Rhythm is powerful; sometimes you must fight against it, sometimes let yourself flow with it. Knowing whether to fight it or flow with it depends, first, on recognizing it for what it is. Later on, I will suggest various ways of finding serenity by shifting rhythms and forming different entrainment patterns. For the moment, I ask that you begin by simply becoming aware of different rhythms as you go through your days. Do that, and you can learn to change them, and by so doing, set your own pace.

I'm asking you to be *proactive* rather than *reactive*. I'm asking you to take *conscious responsibility* for the rhythms you entrain with.

Taking this responsibility begins with slowing down. It begins with experiencing the now, entraining with the people and environment we are with and in at *this moment*. We can only entrain effectively with different rhythms by being consciously in the present.

In every fulfilling relationship, the parties are entrained in the same rhythm, have fallen into its flow, and are in the same present. Then and only then is true communication possible.

Being consciously aware of rhythms, your own and those of the people around you, will allow you to shift the rhythms, and therefore, shift time. But you must *slow down* in order to listen and feel. Understanding is impossible without serenity; serenity only exists when time moves slowly.

Feeling rushed? Take a deep breath before you continue. In a fierce argument? Prescribe silence so you can both reflect on what you've been saying. Worried about the future? Come into the present moment.

These are simple—even simplistic—suggestions, but they are the first steps toward becoming aware of ourselves *in the rhythmic flow of the present moment*. With this awareness, through the conscious focus on the present, we can regain the mastery of the speed and rhythm of our lives.

We can choose to create a slower rhythm that will allow us the time to feel and sense and enjoy the ordinary. Or we can choose to be in sync with the faster rhythms of the world around us, but we can do this *consciously*, with a sense of being present, and with the knowledge that if we want to, we can always get off the runaway train.

Indeed, I'm not suggesting that slowing down is the *sole* aim of mastering rhythm. Timeshifting, in fact, means constantly changing our rhythm, slowing *or* accelerating in order to feel present and in the flow of time. A rock band is meant to produce a frenzied ecstasy—and frenzy can be fun if it's joined with awareness—just as a band at a football game is used to make the spectators cheer and the athletes "fight." Throughout history, countless troops have been "psyched up" by the driving rhythms of a trumpet or military band.

In a world where faster is automatically better, timeshifting is essential if we are to thrive in the business of everyday life. Still, given the rhythm of modern life, I believe that slowing down— through awareness of time, consciousness of the present, and knowledge of the subtle, poisonous entrainment society imposes— is more often than not what we must strive for.

I believe that just being conscious of our ability to shift our rhythms within the fabric of a frenetic society will make our hours less anxious, our days less stressful, and our lives more complete. It will, simply enough, make us happier.

Happiness has a rhythm, too. Happy people seem to live less frenetically. They have more time in their lives. They are more in the moment. This happiness is available to all of us.

CHAPTER THREE

MENTAL AND EMOTIONAL TIME

———

*Many of us spend our whole lives running
from feeling with the mistaken belief that you
cannot bear the pain. But you have already
borne the pain. What you have not done is
feel all you are beyond the pain.*

—BARTHOLOMEW

R ECENTLY, A WOMAN came to see me with a health
problem: She had a history of weight fluctuations due to binge
eating, and wanted my help in shifting her behavioral patterns. Everything she had tried until then had been focused on strengthening
her willpower.

"I've told myself, dammit don't eat—and then there I am with a
pint of ice cream or a box of Oreos, eating it all. I don't understand
it. What can I do instead of eating?"

"When do you feel this urge to binge?" I asked.

"When I get upset or anxious."

"Or depressed? Or angry? Or when you feel worthless?"

She became more dejected. "Yes. All those times."

Her eating was a knee-jerk reaction to uncomfortable feelings, a
way of fending off pain. Of course, as she well knew, by avoiding
the distressing feelings with food, she was only exchanging one
source of unhappiness for another.

Willpower alone is never enough. Although having it can be
helpful, it doesn't address the root cause of binging, which is the

desire to avoid troubling feelings. I suggested she try a completely different tack.

"I'd like you to try something that won't be easy. In fact, it's going to get you in touch with your emotional pain even more."

"I'll try anything."

"Then I'd like you to notice, right when it happens, what you're feeling when you feel the urge to eat—and just stay with it. Let the feeling rise, and just keep noticing it. But don't *do* anything."

She grew uncomfortable. "But I feel I *have* to eat then. I hate the feelings that come up."

"Exactly. And sometimes you may have to run from them and eat. But if you can begin to stay with your feelings, just be in the moment and slow down, you'll begin to get control of them. Stay with the sadness or the loneliness or the feeling of unworthiness. *Feel it.* And when it begins to hurt, don't move into action. Let the feelings rise. Feel them fully in that moment, and I assure you the bad feelings will gradually subside. If you don't run away by eating, if you learn to stay with your feelings when they rise, they'll become less threatening, and they'll soon pass without your needing to act."

She returned in two weeks.

"Did it work?" I asked.

"Not a hundred percent, but most of the time," she said, grinning. "And most importantly, the urge to eat doesn't seem to have the same grip on me anymore."

All of us sometimes behave like a binge eater. When I was going through a painful separation from my wife, I was struck by how much the strategy of avoiding suffering by nonstop work was ingrained in me. I worked so hard, I literally did not allow myself to feel. My mother said, "I hope you're keeping busy; it'll keep your mind off you troubles," and I was able to answer, "You bet, Mom." It kept me from feeling the pain.

Painful feelings are difficult to face, and we'd rather not feel them if at all possible. So we get busy. We speed up. We substitute action for contemplation. We turn on the television, prepare a meal, do the chores, surf the Internet, work out, think about anything rather than allow ourselves to be with the feeling we're trying to avoid.

When we do this, we're living in our heads, in what I call "mental time." All because we're trying to avoid feeling what's in our hearts, to avoid falling into "emotional time."

Our thoughts and feelings operate at drastically different rates and carry very different rhythms. The brain communicates electrically, its synapses registering thoughts and ideas in tiny fractions of a second. Notice how quickly you can follow the many fleeting thoughts that go racing through your mind at any moment. Think about a red balloon, now a pink elephant, now what time it is. See how easy it is to move from thought to thought? It's so easy that you hardly ever think about how quickly you're doing it.

Now: Feel sad. Feel angry. Feel rapturously in love.

Seem like a silly request? It is—because these feelings can't be conjured up just like that. We can *think about* them quickly, without feeling them. In fact, to induce a feeling in ourselves, we literally *have* to think about something concrete first, something that makes us feel sad, or angry, or loving.

Feelings are experienced by way of chemical communication within the body. They are a hormonal surge, a wave that washes over us—sometimes with such force that we feel drowned. Feelings that are authentically experienced in the present moment take time to emerge. Which is why we either run from them—or take the time to process them.

Of course, since emotional and mental processing varies in speed—by a magnitude of difference similar to that between a carrier pigeon and a modern telecommunications system—it seems more "efficient" to depend solely on our brains for making decisions. The brain has been called the world's most efficient computer: communicating impressions, giving commands, making calculations so rapidly that most of the time we aren't even aware of the activity.

Thoughts occur constantly, whether we're awake or asleep. Just try to turn off your thoughts, to sit quietly without thinking. The mind is ever active, continually processing thoughts, darting from one idea to another. Try not thinking of a bright red juicy strawberry. Once suggested, the mind jumps toward it immediately. Our thoughts take us instantly into the past and future, and just as quickly back to the present. The very essence of thought is speed.

Some emotional reactions can emerge more quickly than thoughts. How many times have you yourself "blown up" unexpectedly when a more rational reaction would have been appropriate? How many times have you read of the murderer who "didn't know what he was doing"? How many times have you felt so scared you wanted to run, so angry you wanted to kill, so elated you wanted to "dance on air"?

In *Emotional Intelligence,* Dan Goleman calls these reactions "emotional hijackings":

> At those moments, evidence suggests, a center in the limbic brain proclaims an emergency, recruiting the rest of the brain to its urgent agenda. The hijacking occurs in an instant, triggering the reaction crucial moments before the neocortex, the thinking brain, has had a chance to glimpse fully what is happening, let alone decide if it is a good idea. The hallmark of such a hijack is that once the moment passes, those so possessed have the sense of not knowing what came over them.

Most of the time the emotional reactions triggered in us are not so consuming that they'll cause an emotional hijacking. Yet reactions based on the emotions triggered by past experiences demand attention, even though, caught as we are in the daily speed of work and life in mental time, we try to deny them or hold them off.

An outburst (display of anger, flare-up of passion, crying fit, etc.) takes only a moment, but the associated feelings persist. To adequately deal with any real feelings takes time—first just to be with those feelings, to consciously experience them, and then to integrate them into our lives.

Still, the speed of the reaction can become very intense as events occur. If we are continually focused in mental time without any outlet for processing the emotional content of what's happening to us, the feelings are pent up within, undigested and unexperienced. In this condition there is a buildup of emotional pressure and turmoil, until something happens that pushes us over the edge. It is like a volcano erupting. The energy has been building until it can no longer be contained.

Goleman shows that this reaction often sets the neural alarm in action at inappropriate times:

> Its method of comparison is associative: when one key element of a present situation is similar to the past, it can call it a "match," which is why this circuit is sloppy: it acts before there is full confirmation. It frantically commands that we react to the present in ways that were imprinted long ago, with thoughts, emotions, reactions learned in response to events perhaps only dimly similar, but close enough to alarm the amygdala.

As the pace of society quickens, we will find ourselves more and more in mental time, and there will be less and less time to process the feelings. It may become more likely that we will have inappropriate emotional reactions flooding society. We will see an increase in violence and irritability. Unless we can slow down enough to consciously experience our feelings, balance between emotional and mental time will be further lost.

So, when we are rushed, we habitually go to our mind and repress our feelings. The mind gets the job done; feelings just get in the way.

And when we pause, and unpleasant feelings have time to intrude and rise up within us, we just as quickly find something to distract ourselves. These feelings are unpleasant because they are the ones we've pushed away in our busyness; indeed, we often *get* busy so we don't have to deal with them.

In my seminars, I often ask participants, "Let's say you have a free moment. You sit on your couch, prepared to do nothing. How do you feel?"

These are some of the common answers:

"I think about everything I should be doing and get incredibly anxious."

"I get up and turn on the TV."

"I feel sad. I feel like crying."

"I feel guilty and get up to wash the dishes or clean the house."

"I fall asleep."

One of the Omega participants last summer was an environmental scientist who led a typical workaholic's life: up at five, children fed and off to school, work and research all day, the results written up in the evening. She had come to Omega simply to get away from all the stress, and to try to put what she called her "out-of-kilter" life back in order. She happened to be having trouble in her relationship with her husband; they both seemed distant from each other, going through the motions, with professed but not profound love.

I asked her what it was like when she was still.

"Terrifying!" she immediately replied. "Well, not really. I'm having a wonderful time, taking all those courses and talking to the most fascinating people."

There was nothing overtly frightening going on in her life, yet it was obvious to me that stillness truly did scare her. She'd belatedly signed up for courses, and entered into one conversation after another, so she would not have to be quietly alone—even though that's what she had supposedly come to Omega to do.

I decided to give her an assignment. I asked her to sit—just sit—for an hour under a tree.

"It was amazing," she reported later. "At first, all I wanted to do was run. I don't think I've ever been so frightened in my life. I didn't want to sit there another second. An hour seemed an eternity. But then a miracle happened. I was transported back to a wonderful experience of my childhood. I felt myself back in nature for the first time in years. It was a remarkable experience. Full of wonder."

Try it yourself. See what happens when you slow yourself down, all the way to a stop. Right now, try entraining to a slower rhythm, letting your mind as well as your body relax.

Before you read any further, take a long pause. Don't do anything special, just wait: Breathe.

Stay with your feelings.

★   ★   ★

Most of us bemoan the fact that we don't have enough time to relax. There's too much pressure, from work, family, or community. Meanwhile, as we saw in the last chapter, we have subconsciously entrained to the ever-accelerating tempo of modern life.

But I believe there's another reason we avoid setting a slower pace. It's not just outside pressure, or social entrainment, that makes us feel guilty and nervous if we're not being "productive."

Why is it so hard for most of us to simply sit still, and do nothing but be in the present moment? Because there's something in the present moment that we're trying to escape.

That something is "feeling" itself.

The sitting-on-the-couch experiment shows this clearly. When we first try to "relax," we don't feel relaxed at all. Instead of joy or serenity, we feel anxiety and guilt. And we jump from the couch and get busy—because we sense, consciously or not, that this vague discomfort is merely the leading edge of a wave of negative emotions that have been waiting there all along. People often tell me they get busy fast because as soon as anxiety intrudes, they fear the "slippery slope." They're afraid to allow their emotions free reign; they worry that there will be no end to them; and that the floodgates will open and they will be consumed.

It's a simple fact that these seemingly overwhelming feelings build up over the course of our lives—arising from early childhood right up until today—and that we suppress them in order to get along. At work, we have no time to deal with the difficult feelings engendered when the boss criticizes us, a colleague betrays us, a coworker comes on to us, or a new job is offered. In a family setting, there are so many practical concerns—budgets to meet, school for the kids, different agendas for husband and wife, investments for the future, sickness, aging parents, unexpected crises—that there's often no time to address, let alone feel, the underlying emotional factors.

Besides, people are counting on us, counting on us to cope with all the deadlines, the problems, the pressures. So we do. We cope by keeping a lid on our own feelings like anger, sadness, and, at bottom, fear.

These can be strong emotions, and even frightening when we sense how *much* they've built up, how impatiently they're waiting to come surging forth at the slightest opportunity. When we let them leak out, we feel discomfort, and often outright pain; if they rush out, the pain is enormous. No wonder we turn on the TV or get off the couch entirely.

But emotions don't evaporate. You can ignore them, repress them, or deny them, but they're still there, accumulating. No matter how hard we try to tamp them down, they're inside us waiting to surface; the harder we suppress them, the more urgently they seek release.

Of course we want to feel the pleasant emotions, particularly joy and love, but they are only part of what we feel. Life contains grief as well as joy, pain as well as pleasure. No one gets through without both being part of the curriculum.

We often prefer to think about these things abstractly, rather than feel them. As A. H. Almaas notes in *Diamond Heart,* too often we're trapped either in our rational minds or in an overwhelming emotional drama.

But being present is ultimately beyond mind and emotions. It is just being aware of existence itself. We must experience the feelings as they come, when they come: whatever is so in this moment.

Usually, we avoid the feelings of the present. If we feel pain, we want to avoid it and don't want the present as it is. If we feel good, we want more of the same; the present is okay, but we immediately imagine another scenario that could be even better in the future.

Learning to accept the present simply as it is, without demanding it be different, is what opens us to the fuller dimensions of life.

Very few of us feel we have the wherewithal to *sit through* all these feelings, and get to the peacefulness at the other side. But we do. It just takes practice.

America is a society that treats emotion contemptuously. Men who cry are thought of as sissies; women who cry are considered hysterical. And so we keep busy.

This attitude, of course, fits a society that values working hard—and the material things that are hard work's reward—over anything else. In a similar society, Japan's, some ten thousand people a year are dropping dead from overwork—a phenomenon called *kashori*. Corporations have admitted that the problem exists, but when the Japanese government tried to shorten the work week from six days to five a few years ago, Japanese workers resisted it. What were they going to do with the "extra" day?

When I visited Japan not long ago, I was amazed to see large arcades where people play a game called Pachinko, a kind of vertical pinball, for literally hours on end. There is little skill involved, and no particular point in winning. But the game has a kind of hypnotic fascination, and even a kind of usefulness—if you're dead set against feeling.

Americans have their own version of Pachinko; it's called television. Time-use researcher John Robinson has discovered that 40 percent of an average American's "free" time goes directly down the tube. As Bruce Springsteen puts it, there are "fifty-seven channels and nothing on"—but we continue to watch.

Playing Pachinko, or compulsively channel-hopping, our minds are indeed in the present. Unfortunately, *we* aren't. We're numbed—which is exactly the point.

In order to live, we *must* feel. Only if we experience pain can we experience joy, along with the smaller pleasures and sorrows that lie in between. And most of life, even most of life lived in the present, is concerned not with "big" events or emotions, but with ordinary ones. That's why it's so important to feel. For if we don't continually repress our emotions, if we don't run from feelings to a television set or Pachinko parlor, then the ordinary moments take on a richness and flavor that bring us closer to the wonders that life provides.

Being in emotional time means not just being physically present when you're with your child, but emotionally present as well. It means being able to understand, appreciate, and share what he has to say and to offer, receiving as much from him as you are able to give him. It means being able to listen not only to someone's words, but also to the meaning and feeling tone behind them. It means being able to interact with another person, being *with* that person, without separate agendas. It means being able to feel not only anger at your boss, resentment at your spouse, annoyance at your child—but also enjoyment of your boss's praise, love of your spouse's love, pleasure and pride in your child's openness and honesty.

It means being open yourself. It means being alive.

The progression of a deep emotion to the point where you can truly feel it in the present often takes time—but you must consider carefully whether it is actually a present emotion you are feeling.

Think of grief, for example. A loved one dies. At first we are in shock, numb, barely registering the loss. Then the realization sets in, and we are *forced* into feeling, perhaps before we can deal with it. The pain is unbearable. We are overwhelmed by grief and cannot imagine how we will be able to go on. At this moment, it's perfectly natural—human—to try to escape.

In time, though, the acuteness of the grief recedes, and we are able to function again. But eventually, even years later, something—a song, a sunset, a stranger whose face or walk recalls the beloved's—brings back the person with such force that we are as overcome by sorrow as we were when we were most conscious of the loss. We are experiencing past emotions in the present. Again, this is human, and perfectly natural.

But here we enter a complicated and tricky area. For often, when a past event governs how we feel in the present, the feeling can be a way for us to escape from the present into the past, enabling us to circumvent the authentic emotion of the present. Psychotherapy has shown us that our reaction to a fight with our spouse, say, may have more to do with how our mother or father treated us than with the present fight itself. This is why most psychologists tell us that, unless we understand past emotions, we are destined to relive them, thus cutting ourselves off from living in the present.

In my view, understanding the past is important, but it's not the full answer to living in the moment. Too often, what we're doing in "understanding the past" is simply relating what's happening now to a past story line—and not authentically staying with what's happening *now*. Creating a "story line" can be an extremely effective way of resisting the reality of present emotion. By continually immersing ourselves in *its* drama, we become married to our past pain and suffering—and avoid going through the pain of the moment.

Therapist Bert Shaw suggests that there is a significant difference between our emotional reactions and the authentic feelings of the moment. For example, often we find ourselves in an argument with a spouse, child, or coworker that quickly escalates and worsens because of the emotional reactions each person is having.

These are not the feelings in the present moment that I'm suggesting we experience and stay with. Instead, they are emotional reactions triggered by past events, which serve to pull us out of the present. As Dan Goleman has suggested in *Emotional Intelligence,* our emotional radar in the lymbic system has picked up a potential attack, which in turn creates fear within us on some level, and so we seek escape. As Shaw indicates, those emotional reactions always result from a perceived fear or threat we experienced in the past—so we respond as we did in the past, often inappropriately to the current situation, thus avoiding the true feelings of the present.

If we can slow down, and allow ourselves a few breaths, we will be able to disengage from our emotional reactions. As Shaw goes on to say, "this enables us to stop just reacting to each other with our old baggage, instead to be present in a way that expresses what is really happening for us now."

Typical to all couples, as we will discuss in the chapter of relationships, my wife and I have become experts at "pushing each other's buttons." She tends to be more emotional, while I'm more rational in our process. Recently we got into an argument about going to a party given by a friend of hers. She wanted to go; I didn't. From what started as a simple conversation about it, we found ourselves deadlocked in a discussion of the core issue of whether or not she felt I was the right person for her and whether I felt, in fact, loved by her. The emotional reactions that we threw at each other had nothing to do with the upcoming party, but instead concerned issues that triggered my fear about social gatherings (I am rarely comfortable in groups) and her feelings of rejection when her mate doesn't want to share part of her life.

When we slowed down together, listened more deeply to each other, and became authentic with our feelings, I could express my discomforts and she her isolation. Then we met in real time, in sync in the present. We could feel our bond together, and the party disappeared as an issue, whether or not we went. (We did.)

It's not what's happened to us "then," but what we're feeling in the present that's most important. Instead of living our stories over and over again, instead of analyzing and reanalyzing them from every vantage point, we have an opportunity to truly bear witness—to just be with the depth of our feelings, to feel the pain until it is gone.

By choosing to be present for pain, we free ourselves to be present for the beauty and joy that are also there, all around us, all the time. Stuck in the drama, we can't believe beauty and joy even exist—but once we come into the moment, we begin to choose life.

This does not necessarily mean just sitting quietly with our feelings. It doesn't mean becoming "blissed out," or observing our pain dispassionately. Sometimes we may feel such rage that we can't help screaming, or such sadness that we can only sob—and we do need to be authentic with our feelings, as they are, not as we think they should be.

Too often in my life, in the name of letting my feelings pass, I have sat with them, or meditated until they passed. At those times, I was merely tricking myself into a kind of resistance to my feelings, avoiding them in the name of "Buddha nature"—when, in fact, beating my fists into a pillow would have been more real in the moment.

The important thing is to recognize the authentic present feeling, and *stay with it.* When we are able to be present with our feelings—quietly, sobbing, screaming, whatever comes—they begin to lose the charge that keeps us tied into replaying old issues in our minds.

Here is a client, Mary-Joe, talking about the aftermath of her divorce:

I found as time went on that there is indeed an underlying structure to the emotional process. Early on I was overwhelmed by the grief. I'd feel this irredeemable darkness; I feared I'd be dysfunctional forever, I'd have to be on medication. I noticed that if I kept busy, I didn't feel it so much. But when I slowed down, there it was again.

Finally, while I was in the midst of this wave of grief, something would shift—and suddenly I'd have a new thought or something positive would happen. After a while I began to trust the process. Seeing it like a wave helped me complete the trauma and deal with those feelings I've carried around and not allowed to crash over me. It's still painful, will always be painful, but when the ache comes up, I just watch it as it gets higher and higher, and then I'm through it and it dissipates.

Seeing the crest of the wave, we know we can get to the other side. And then we become free to see what else life has to offer us, to see its beauty and its joy.

Arnie, a close friend of mine, has gone through one of the most intense tragedies anyone can face—the loss of a child:

Initially, I couldn't find any peace of mind; I felt the pain of Jerry's death continually, no matter what I did or thought—it was completely overwhelming. As time went by, I found that the distraction principle worked—if I kept myself busy, it became somewhat easier to bear. But whenever I slowed down, even at a bus stop, or in between clients at work, I'd feel it well up—here it would come, back again with a vengeance.

Now, as time has passed, I still find it painful whenever I think about Jerry, but it's different now. I don't try to get busy and avoid it. Instead, this pain rises and rises, and then it peaks, and then I know I'm on the other side of it. It does actually pass. I feel a deep sadness—and I know it will go.

An interesting thing happened after I got to the point that I could sit out a wave of grief without resisting it. I can actually experience joy in my life again. The experience is no longer part of the vital present—it's part of the past, and I know I can go on.

All of our emotions are within us all the time, and all are operating simultaneously. A woman, at her father's funeral, found herself smiling at the feeling of pleasure, comfort, and oneness they had experienced together.

"How *dare* you smile?" a relative asked her.

The relative was a representative of conventional society, one where there's no tolerance and little understanding of the complicated emotions traumatic events engender. Only grief was allowed. The authentic mix of feeling, the authentic joy that welled up in the midst of this woman's sorrow, was condemned.

But this joy is a gift; the kind of gift that can only come when we allow ourselves to feel everything—whether it surprises us suddenly, or comes to us gradually, even in the midst of pain.

Giving ourselves permission to feel is like plunging into the ocean. Cold and uncomfortable at first, we soon adjust to the water to the point of exhilaration. We need time to adjust; if we thrash about, it will take longer. But once we master the waves, we will be carried to their crest and deposited gently when they recede.

This emotional work is very powerful and very difficult—but it is essential. It allows us to navigate through life in a more peaceful, more self-aware, more understanding way. It's the groundwork that lets us stay focused in the present and keeps us from running from our hearts to our minds, from relying on our busy hands to keep us distracted. And the present, after all, is where we live.

As Thich Nhat Hanh puts it:

> Our feelings play a very important part in directing all our thoughts and actions. In us, there is a river of feelings, in which every drop of water is a different feeling, and each feeling relies on all the others for its existence. To observe it, we just sit on the bank of the river and identify each feeling as it surfaces, flows by, and disappears.

We must learn to be comfortable watching the river, the ocean—and learn to swim.

CHAPTER FOUR

STRESS AND ANXIETY

*When you are immersed in doing without
being centered, it feels like being away from
home. And when you re-connect with being,
even for a few minutes, you know it
immediately. You feel you are at home
no matter where you are and what problems
you face.*

—JON KABAT-ZINN

I made a fire in the fireplace with some wood we'd collected in the country. One of the logs was still damp, but I put it on anyway. As the log heated up, a bunch of ants scurried out—apparently it had been their home—and began running up and down the log. Some of them jumped off and escaped the flames, but others just kept running, faster and faster, back and forth.

I found myself staring at those little guys who were about to cook, wanting to yell, "Jump! Jump!" And then I realized they reminded me of my own life. I wanted to yell for myself.

So relates my friend Josh, but his particular experience could stand as a metaphor for many of us in the twentieth century. When we are stressed, we become like those ants, desperate to avoid the fire, not knowing which way to jump.

The majority of us feel stress at work, stress at home, stress in a traffic jam, stress in a crowd, stress on a banking line or a checkout counter. Without stress, there would be no Valium or Librium—

the most commonly prescribed drugs of the 1970s and still among the top-ranking prescription drugs today.

Only on vacation do we supposedly avoid stress, yet when I take people on a retreat to a small island in the Caribbean, all I hear for the first few days are complaints: It's too hot, too humid; the chairs aren't comfortable; the food is too spicy, the showers don't work. Eventually, everybody relaxes and there are generally a few stress-free days. But then, as it nears time to go home, anxiety sets in: Will there be much work when we get home? Will the kids have wrecked the house in our absence? Will the car that I left at the airport start?

One of my students, Susan, announced that she had figured out how to relax:

> I often have to drive from my consulting business to the university where I teach. I look forward to the drive because I see it as much-needed time to slow down and relax.
>
> Before I leave I remember to bring a tape on management that I've been meaning to listen to. And, since I won't have time for lunch otherwise, I bring along something I can eat with one hand while the other's on the steering wheel. I also have a cellular phone in the car so I can catch up on some phone calls while I'm at it. So I figure, "Great! I can eat, listen to a tape, travel, talk to clients, and relax all at once!"

It may be her idea of relaxation. It's not mine. To me, it sounds like a way of staving off anxiety over not being able to get everything done.

This is a common enough "solution" to a common situation. I would say that 95 percent of the stress in our lives relates to our feeling of time poverty; it's the feeling that we cannot possibly accomplish all that we have to do.

Fear of what may come in the future provokes anxiety, the off-spring of stress, which comes from resistance to being with what is in the present.

Yet—and this is key to the entire concept of timeshifting—*in the present moment there is no stress.*

* * *

If stress comes from resisting what's actually happening in the present moment, then, as we saw in the last chapter, what's usually "happening" is emotion, or feeling. Thus, I could also define stress as the state of being in pain and trying to resist the pain at the same time.

If, for example, you're going through a divorce and you don't allow yourself to feel the pain of the divorce—but rather, as I did, you "get busy"—then the suppressed pain becomes a lens through which you see all of life. And life seen like that holds little *but* stress.

It's important to realize that stress, the tension that literally eats us up, is not the same as pain. We can be in pain, or disappointment, or confusion—but if that's what the present moment holds for us, and we allow ourselves to experience those feelings, then we needn't give ourselves the added burden of feeling stressed.

The notion that when we feel the emotion in the present, we can proceed more freely, is nicely illustrated on a metaphorical level by a Zen story:

Two monks, on a journey through a forest, come to a racing river. A frail young woman sits by its bank, unable to get to the other side. One of the monks picks her up in his arms and carries her across, and the monks continue on their way.

Hours pass in silence. Finally, the other monk bursts out, "How could you have done such a thing? You know we've sworn never to touch a woman!"

The first monk smiles. "I carried that woman for a moment and set her down hours ago," he says gently. "But you've been carrying her around all day."

Our painful emotions are our own burdens. If we can carry them across the river, and then set them down, we will be free to enjoy the softness of the forest and the glow of sunlight through the trees.

It bears repeating: *In the present moment there is no stress.* When we accept what is so right now, even if we're tired or frightened or hurt, we don't need to also feel stressed. We may not be happy, but we're open to the reality of what life is at this moment in time—and we're not allowing stress to do further damage to us.

★ ★ ★

Stress has distinct physiological as well as psychological effects, and the progression of physical maladies that are caused by prolonged stress has become widely and well understood. (It was Dr. Hans Selye who, fifty years ago, first formulated the correlation in his General Adaptation Syndrome.) In the early stages, stress weakens our adrenal glands, stomach lining, and immune system. Unrelieved, it eventually leads to the breakdown of vital body systems, causing heart attacks, strokes, degenerative diseases, and even cancer.

But if stress may be lethal, why don't we take significant measures to avoid it, just as we take precautions to avoid food poisoning or falling off a cliff? A simple biological experiment may help to explain.

If you take a frog and drop it into a pan of scalding water, he'll jump out immediately. If, however, you place him in a pan of cold water and heat it slowly, all the way to the boiling point, the frog never jumps. Because the heat is turned up gradually, the frog adjusts little by little and doesn't react even when the water turns deadly.

Day by day, year by year, we accept the turning up of the heat. Because of time poverty, we accept too little sleep; we take on a second job even though we fear we don't have enough time to do one; we ingest more and more information without the time to digest it. We're asked to do more, produce more, act and react more quickly—and we accede to the demand. As our stress level ratchets up, we get habituated to it, at enormous cost to our health.

Still, I don't think physical destructiveness is the worst aspect of stress. Rather, I agree with Jean-Louis Servan-Schreiber, who writes in *The Art of Time*, "What I fear most about stress is not that it kills, but that it prevents one from savoring life."

An acquaintance of mine commutes with a group of businessmen from New Jersey to Wall Street and back by catamaran. He loves the trip; the wind, the waves, and the slow rhythm of the boat are a welcome antidote to his workaday world.

On one particularly beautiful day, he found himself watching with fascination a scene he'd witnessed at the end of every workday, but which he'd hardly given a thought to before. A group of stockbrokers were sitting down to their nightly game of poker:

> They paid no attention to the weather, no attention to the rhythm of the boat. It was obvious they were completely engrossed by the game; it was all they wanted to do. The pots were huge. And I became aware, as the boat neared the Jersey shore, that the tempo of their game grew faster—the bets became higher, the hands dealt more quickly. Everybody stayed in every hand, their voices grew shrill, they didn't seem to care whether they won or lost—it was wild.

Those men were still in the New York tempo long after they had to be. Indeed, they speeded up the game, almost as if to ward off the threatened "slowness" of the night. And I'd bet they carried their fast rhythm home: Their day had been composed of "highs," and they literally could not slow down, even for a boat trip on a beautiful day.

But my friend, having slowed down, was feeling the beauty around him and experiencing a high. Although there was an enormous difference between the two highs, the poker players and my friend did have one thing in common: They were all very much in the present moment, though clearly in very different rhythms.

Since we need to feel in our lives, we search constantly for experiences that produce feelings. And our innate drive to seek pleasure includes a natural desire for what psychologists call "peak experiences."

Whether we call it a peak or a high, we know when we're having one. We're right here, fully absorbed, feeling totally alive and fulfilled. Our feelings, emotions, and mind are all engaged. It might be from white-water rafting or from tasting great chocolate; from playing some fast hands of high-stakes poker or savoring a boat ride across the Hudson River; from skateboarding or sitting in a garden.

But the pace of modern life makes it increasingly unlikely for us to experience peaks in the course of an ordinary day. Since the duration of a "moment" is shorter than ever before, we're usually moving much too rapidly to achieve an intense consciousness of anything much. Therefore, the only way for many of us to achieve a profound peak experience is to have an experience *so* dramatic that it makes a major impression, even in a very short dose.

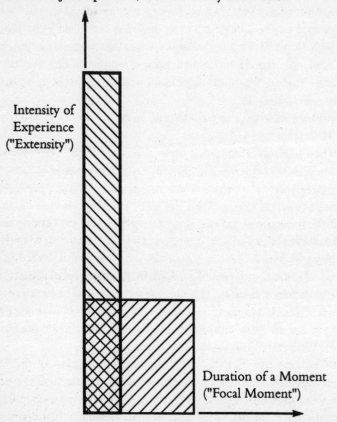

Intensity of
Experience
("Extensity")

Duration of a Moment
("Focal Moment")

The shaded area of the graph represents how deeply we feel an experience—the depth of consciousness or intensity of sensation we experience from a given event—called here "intensity." The external potency of the stimulation—how dazzling the sensation or how hard the hit—I call "extensity." The length of time we're able to focus our consciousness on the event is the "focal moment," the duration of our attention. With a long attention span, the focal moment is expanded; in our current habitual rhythm, it's short indeed.

So, if our focal moment is brief, then we need an event with great extensity to get us high. Only something as striking as skydiving, an orgasm, a high-stakes poker game, a sudden accident, or a major intellectual epiphany will do it.

If, however, we manage to maintain our focus over a longer period of time, then a much milder event—an event with a far lower extensity—can give us the same depth of internal experience, the same high. Then the quality of the high comes not from risk, but from the amount of time we can stay focused in the moment— feeling, hearing, smelling, touching, seeing, *aware* of all that is around us and in us.

In many instances, at least at first, many of the short highs are positive. After I took up windsurfing, as I got better at the sport I needed to take greater risks to attain the same peak. I didn't really put my life in danger, though. Sky divers, bungee jumpers, race-car drivers, and motorcycle racers do, but generally their expertise precludes calamity.

Drug users, however, do put their lives in danger. Taking into account the length of the moment gives us a whole new understanding of why we're such an addictive society. An addiction is simply an attempt to get that high from a particular activity or substance. Since our moments are too short to reach a peak during mundane events, we turn to drugs (or to sex, to work, to money, to power). But as the duration of focus shortens, we need more. And more. And more. Until we are addicted.

To become literally addicted is only one illustration of the fact that when positive highs become insufficient or unavailable, negative ones take their place. If we can't create a peak experience from ordinary life, if we can't *feel* it, many of us create external drama to achieve our highs. This is, I believe, why many of us constantly revisit the story line I discussed in the previous chapter; why some of us are "accident prone," why an adulterer finished with one affair will quickly start another. It's even why some of us enjoy watching stunt drivers, cliff divers or bungee jumpers: We're getting our (lesser) highs vicariously, but in our fantasies we're right there with the risk takers.

I'm not saying that the business deal, the mountain climb, the gamble, or the love affair aren't important parts of life; the high that accompanies them can be intensely pleasurable. But when the activities get addictive, they become dangerous. A glass or two of wine with dinner complements the meal, but steady, compulsive drinking destroys life.

There is such a significant difference in our lives when we are able to slow down, expand the moment, and become fully present for life around us. Then a walk in the woods, a game with our children, or a symphony by Beethoven can bring us to the same peak as parachuting. Smelling a flower, spending time in meditation, even doing household chores or eating a meal can be intensely pleasurable. Since most of our lives are not lived with the extensity of an Indy 500, think how much more rewarding it is to get most of our highs from everyday events.

We have provided ourselves with the greatest smorgasbord of diversions and pleasures that ever existed. Television, movies, books, CDs, Walkmans, spectator and participatory sports, spas, health clubs, etc.—all are supposedly aids to "getting away" from stress. But these diversions mean avoiding stress, not overcoming it. How many times have you been watching television when the thought of a work project left unfinished shoots adrenaline through you . . . and you switch channels to see if a different program might be a more effective means of escape?

Sometimes the sheer number of possible escapes *adds* to stress. If you go to a movie at a ten-screen multiplex cinema, you might think, "This one's okay, but maybe another would be better," and afterward, "Maybe I should have gone to that one instead." At a video store, notice how long many customers take to make their choices. Restaurants offer dozens of main courses, libraries thousands of books, and travel agencies offer hundreds of destinations.

Of course, there's *always* something else going on. We don't just feel we're missing something; we actually *are* missing something—the other movie, the other meal, the other destination. And this knowledge continually pulls our minds this way and that, each pull nourishing a little seed of stress.

Each choice may be the "right" one, and indeed there's nothing wrong with watching television, going to the movies, working out, or dining at a restaurant. But it's vital to realize that although you can escape emotion with diversion, which can be pleasurable and beneficial, continued escape can become addictive, like a narcotic. Stress can return with a vengeance, or manifest itself in other ways—in nightmares, in stomach disorders, or in the atrophy of the emotions and life in general.

One hallmark of stress is always being ready to launch into the next diversion. But if we keep jumping from moment to fleeting moment, we will never be content. Eventually, we'll not only lose the capacity to be diverted, we'll also lose the capacity to feel much joy at all in *anything* that's actually present. We'll doom ourselves to feeling as though, as performance artist Laurie Anderson puts it with deadpan irony, "Paradise is exactly like where you are right now. Only much, much better."

In truth, paradise *is* where you are right now. Period.

If we are going to learn to say yes to what is present—whether it's pain, paradise, or something in between—then we must also learn how to say no. And saying no is a tricky business.

Most of us want to be open to people, to help whenever we can, to "be there" for family, colleagues, friends. But we can only do one thing at a time, and sometimes an emotion or event has so filled the moment that we can only pretend to "be there" for anyone else. But we only add to our stress if we pretend to be available when we're not.

I used to face this regularly at my medical office. At the end of the day, I'd be finishing up charts, knowing I'd promised to be home a half hour earlier. Then the phone would ring: a patient with a problem. I wouldn't want to answer, but I'd pick it up anyway. I'd wind up talking on the phone while reading the charts, my attention split, and I couldn't wait to hang up. I wasn't present for that person on the phone, and I was stressed by wishing to be somewhere else.

"I need your advice," a friend says. "Got a moment?"

"I'm sorry," we answer. "Not right now. Can I call you when I'm free?"

This is much better than giving her only half our attention, or unreflective advice. Of course, if it's an emergency—if someone is sick; or there's been an accident; or the friend is at a true point of crisis—then we must come to her aid, dropping our focus for hers.

Saying no to others requires strength. But saying no—even at the cost of momentarily upsetting a friend or temporarily alienating a client—is also essential to living in the present. Just as facing an emotion—in effect, saying yes to it—is equally essential.

The ancient Greek philosopher Heraclitus said, "Nothing endures but change." Nowadays, we can be certain that our world will continue to change in the direction of more complexity, more choices, and more potential for stress.

So we conclude that there's nothing we can do, and we accept the stress we're under, knowing it will only get worse. But what strikes me as I speak to people is how much *is* in our control. For instance, we can learn to choose our reactions to events.

It was a client's turn to prepare a church supper, a weekly event involving considerable competition among the parishioners. Unfortunately, on the scheduled day, her husband was detained by an office crisis and couldn't get back to help, and her baby-sitter got sick, so she had to look after her child herself.

As time got "shorter," her anxiety increased, and so did a sense of being smothered. All she could do was move faster, do more. So, four-year-old in tow, she did the shopping, set the table, cleaned the house, cooked a turkey, made a pecan pie and a cherry pie . . . and, her anxiety at its zenith while she prepared a huge salad, dropped the glass bowl on her foot, cutting it so severely that her blood stained the dining room carpet.

What she did then might serve as an example to us all. She began to laugh. There, in the midst of chaos, she had the choice of becoming even more frantic, or breaking the rhythm—her laughter was that break.

She took a deep breath, then another, and decided to forget about what had happened. She couldn't change it, after all, and in that relaxed present, she knew she could let the dinner *be.* Her anxiety vanished. The dinner would get done.

My friend Sid used to be afraid of roller-coasters. He had never gone on one as a child, and had remained fearful of it as an adult.

But he was curious about them, so one day he put a telephoto lens on his camera, stood at the bottom of the roller-coaster track, and snapped pictures of people coming over the top—just as they were heading into a huge drop.

When the pictures were developed, he found the passengers had basically reacted in one of two ways: Either they were grimacing in fear and hanging on white-knuckled, or they had raised their arms in joy and wore ecstatic grins on their faces.

Sid studied the pictures and made a conscious choice about his response. He took his first roller-coaster ride—and his wife took a picture of him as he went over the top, arms raised, grinning with delight.

In short, society may throw us into stress-producing situations, but we can decide to be unstressed. We may be natural-born cowards, but we can learn to be brave.

Of course, much of the stress we experience is self-inflicted. We need to recognize that, to see that stress doesn't always come from outside pressures.

My friend Carole told me this:

I come from a family where a 3 P.M. flight meant showing up at the airport at 3 P.M. and hoping the plane would be there—amid loud debate over whether we should just give up and go home. After quite a bit of traveling by myself, I finally figured out that getting somewhere an hour early was not a "waste" of time. It simply meant I didn't have to cause myself an ordeal. Sure, I'll bring a magazine or some work in case I feel I have to "do something." And sure, sometimes I have only twenty minutes instead of an hour. But I think learning to plan my own arrivals and departures more realistically is the single largest stress-reducer I've found.

Carole learned to take her time, something I'm in the process of learning as well. For most of my own life, I've managed to run late. Before I started investigating timeshifting, in fact, I used to pride myself on getting to the movie theater just before the feature started; jumping onto a train seconds before it began to roll; being the last to board an airplane. I'd usually start out with enough time, but then I'd drop off a note, talk to the recipient, get caught in traffic—and barely make it to my destination in time.

Looking back, I think my behavior came partly from the fact that, when you cut things close, it appears you're making the best possible use of your time. It shows the world that your time is far too valuable for you to "sit around" while others watch the coming attractions or wrestle with overhead bins on the plane.

But as I began to study time, I became aware of the stress associated with such a closely and rigidly scheduled regimen. I realized that I was always wondering if I would be able to catch the first minutes of the movie, and I was putting myself through harmful bursts of adrenaline as I frantically ran down airport corridors.

In recent years, although I sometimes return to old habits, I've learned to give myself ample time. I don't try to get "just one more thing done" by stopping to drop off that note on the way, either. I leave early so I can take my time and, if I'm early, it isn't "wasted" time that lies ahead.

National Public Radio reported a test in which researchers studying commuter stress asked two people to drive the same stretch of road at rush hour. One was told to go as fast as possible—change lanes, pass slow drivers, run yellow lights, etc. The other was instructed merely to keep pace with the traffic. Then they clocked the two. The "lane changer" did manage to arrive five minutes before the "slow" driver. But the slow driver rolled in relaxed and composed, whereas the weaver was frenzied and depleted. He had "saved" five minutes—but endured enough stress, to take those five minutes, or more, off his life.

This literal rushing from place to place is only the most obvious instance of self-inflicted time pressure. If we don't put this sort of time pressure on ourselves, it's obviously going to be easier to stay in the moment, to have *time* for the moment. And again, in the moment, *there is no stress*.

You might say, "But my boss needs the report by this afternoon, and I'm not finished with it! What do you mean there's no stress?" My answer is, "If you allow yourself to be *in this moment*—this *now*—and just be with what *is,* then the stress will disappear. It's only when you move outside the moment, either backward or forward, that stress or anxiety exist. Eliminate them, and you'll write a better report anyway.

Yes, we are the only ones who can control our stress, even if we are by no means the only ones who cause it. We can run, we can hide, we can divert ourselves—or we can allow ourselves to be wholly in the moment.

Imagine yourself waiting at a doctor's office. What do you do when you're stuck there? You can resist the waiting, *hate* the waiting, harangue the nurses, wish adamantly you were someplace else. Or you can choose a more peaceful response.

What if, instead of considering this "wasted" time, you shifted your response and considered the wait "found" time—a surprise gift, like finding a ten-dollar bill in the pocket of a coat you haven't worn since last year? Your stress, I guarantee you, would dissipate.

Traffic jams, bank lines, check-out counters—all are places where you, like Sid on the roller-coaster, can consciously shift your inner response to one of peace and health. Judy, a student of mine, told me that when she's frustrated or stressed out, she tries to "see beauty":

I'll look around and let something catch my eye. It can be anything. I notice how the light, say, is shining through the leaves of a plant on the windowsill, splitting the green into a zillion hues. Some leaves are backlit and translucent, almost glassy, some are in shadow, and some are directly under a light beam. And there's the contrast of the greens with the earth colors of the soil and the pot. And all the little cracks in the pot that form patterns . . . I can just sit there and realize how beautiful, how wonderful is this ordinary object. I totally lose track of time.

It really doesn't matter where we "see beauty." Meredith, another student, pointed out the design and angle of the Exit sign in the conference room at Omega. The contrast of the red with the yellow wall makes it look like modern art. And it *is* art, it *is* beautiful—if you choose to see it that way.

Notice that when Judy talks about being in the moment—for that is what she's doing—she "loses track of time." That's because when you're in the present moment, time surrounds you and does not rush past you. You join with it, as a part of the flow.

CHAPTER FIVE

EXPANDING THE MOMENT

———

*An eternity is any moment opened
with patience.*
—Noah benShea

Remember the story of the monk, the tigers, and the strawberry I recounted in the Introduction? I told it in class the other day and was met by the following objection:

"The monk was simply denying," a student said. "He wanted to shut his eyes to what lay above and below, so he concentrated on the strawberry."

But the parable is not about blindness and denial: The monk is well aware of his predicament. Precisely *because* of his situation, he is more able to savor the fullness of the moment. If something anxiety-provoking is about to happen, the story asks, can we live it once, when it actually happens, rather than impotently rehearsing it again and again before anything has occurred?

No matter what has just happened or will come in the future, why miss the full experience of the present? Even if you're about to slip into the void, why miss the strawberries?

This might sound trite, yet its relevance to our everyday life is profound. Whether stuck in a traffic jam beyond our control, or anxious about a future meeting or deadline, unless we can learn to open up each moment and be fully present for it, our life will go speeding by and we will miss it. But we often opt for *shortening* the present moment, rather than expanding it. Dr. Larry Dossey, the author of *Space, Time and Medicine,* asked a group of business executives to sit still for a moment with their eyes closed and tell him when a minute was up without counting (you might try this yourself). Most of his subjects called "time's up" after about fifteen seconds; one made it only to six.

If a subjective "minute" is fifteen seconds, how long is a "moment"? The eight to ten seconds of a sound bite?

Unless we learn to open up each moment and squarely face what it presents to us, our life simply hurtles toward its certain conclusion. To be able to inhabit emotional/feeling time, we need to *expand* our moment, to wedge it open so we can step inside, linger without fidgeting, and experience what's going on within it.

Most of us are afraid of what the moment might hold for us, and thus we avoid it. *The tigers* in the Introduction inspire so much stress and anxiety that we busy ourselves to forget them or deny them. Accepting that they are there means accepting ourselves as we are, and accepting the inevitability of our death.

Many of us believe that when the tigers run away—"when things calm down"—*then* we'll eat the strawberries. When the next crisis ebbs, we'll take time to relax, "enjoy" life, start the diet, begin to exercise, or take our dream vacation.

But when the tigers finally disappear, lions may take their place. If we let them, the past and future will exert so much pull on us that we won't be aware of what's right before us right now.

So slow down. Stop. Pay attention.

Obviously it's not easy to just be in the moment; if it were, we'd be comfortable and at ease in the present all the time. In fact, it takes courage and effort to reverse the trends in our lives, the impact of entrainment, and those around us who urge us to go faster. It means we must accept both our predicament, and ourselves.

Unfortunately, many of us only recognize the importance and the singular reality of the now when we're faced with a terminal or catastrophic illness. Confronting our own mortality can produce a full experience of the present which we simply did not appreciate before.

Over the years, I've worked extensively with AIDS and cancer patients, among other clients faced with catastrophic or terminal illness, and I have often been deeply moved by their courage and the extraordinary transformation that takes place in them. Here is what Betty, a woman with end-stage breast cancer, told me:

> This disease is the best thing that's ever happened to me. My marriage was strained; I was estranged from my only son; I was anxious all the time. But because of the cancer, I know that if I were ever going to change things, I'd have to do it *now*. So I've gotten to know my husband in a way I never did before, and I've developed a wonderful relationship with my son.

This newfound value in life extends beyond human relationships to the most mundane matters: a meal, a walk in the grass, the beauty of a twilight, or a chance meeting with a stranger.

These simple wonders abound in every moment of every day; they are available to all of us, in health as well as in sickness. We shouldn't wait until the eleventh hour to appreciate them.

There's a word for the conscious focus in the present moment: "mindfulness." It is drawn from Buddhist meditation practices and encourages the state of attending to the moment.

The word is a bit confusing. It does *not* refer to living only in the mind, or analyzing everything, or staying in mental time. It means conscious awareness of the present, using all our faculties, all our senses—being aware of what's going on around us and within us as well. Mindfulness is a state of being that we can experience at any moment of our life. Attention and awareness are all that is required.

When we enter a state of mindful attention, the present moment, the now, eases open. And when it does, life pours in. The more we are mindful in simple, everyday situations, the better we get at it. The more we learn to pay attention on a daily basis, the more we are able to bring true awareness to everything we do. It is something we can learn, just like riding a bicycle or reading. The difference is that here the learning process involves slowing down first and emptying ourselves of busyness, to allow ourselves to "do nothing," despite the inclination to resist this notion at all costs.

Mindfulness is almost automatic when we experience either great crisis or great joy. A car crash, for example, will catapult us into a state of full attention and awareness. If you've ever experienced a sudden, serious accident, you know that any thoughts of the past or future vanish immediately, and that later you can likely recall with amazing vividness every minute detail of what happened.

After a wonderfully intimate evening of lovemaking, or a fine meal shared with a special friend, we remember details of sound, smell, and color. We remember because we were mindful when the event happened—all our faculties were involved in the moment.

There is no question that we all experience mindfulness. We must learn to experience it in the more mundane parts of life; indeed, in everything we do.

At this point in my classes, someone always says, "It's fine to be mindful when it's something I like to do, like lovemaking or playing tennis. But why bother with being aware when I'm doing the dishes?"

The answer is that, each time we push away the present moment and resist being aware, we cease to be alive. It's fine to decide you never want to do the dishes again, but while you're doing them, pretending that you aren't, or rushing the whole time so you can get to something "important," means living in the denial of your life. Mindfulness is about embracing *all* of our life, every moment, the 89 percent that's mundane along with the extraordinary remainder.

The door to a deeper appreciation and awareness of life is the simplicity of the everyday. To be mindful of an intense event is easy; we almost can't help it. But being consciously awake and alive while sweeping the floor, driving in a car, or walking along a city street is to expand the ordinary moment and to make life more full.

Anne, a participant in a wellness class I was conducting, described her own experience of discovering the practice of mindfulness. After a deeply relaxing bodywork session, she felt herself perceptibly slowing down and becoming more aware:

I saw a leaf on a tree near the walkway to my cabin, and I went over to look at it. It was a beautiful, rich, sentient green. "This is the most fascinating leaf I've ever seen," I remember thinking. I took it in my hands and stood there and stared at it—feeling its texture, tracing its veins, seeing how the veins looked like rivers from way above the earth, splitting and merging. I lost all track of time. When I got to my cabin, I realized I'd probably stared at that one leaf for twenty minutes.

Clearly, this leaf was no different from billions of others Anne had passed by in her lifetime. It was the most fascinating leaf because it was the only one she had ever really looked at. Usually, we don't differentiate one leaf from another, let alone one tree from another; when we walk through a forest, we have a general sense of greenery, and that's about all. Yet when we think about it, the potential for a deep and memorable experience lies everywhere. All we need do is notice.

It's like driving your car past a familiar stretch of road, and then one day walking the same route. It seems like someone has planted a new tree or built a house we never noticed before. When we slow down, we become aware of what surrounds us all the time.

Don't fear the slowing down.

When I go to a Caribbean island for two months each year, it is always an opportunity for me to slow down and therefore feel more connected with myself. There is a deeper rhythm in operation, arising from inside me, a basic rhythm that, too often, my work at the Institute compels me to reject.

Recently I stopped at the top of a hill to watch the sun set and a full moon rise. In the distance, I could see many islands in the dark emerald sea, each a slightly different hue, and I sat quietly on a stone wall off the road, drinking in the magic of the sight. Soon a couple drove up in a car. She jumped out to get a quick picture, while he stayed in the car with the motor running—they were gone in a flash.

She would show it to her friends back home, tell them of the beautiful spot they had visited. But I wondered whether they had taken the time themselves to see or feel the beauty before them.

Next, a car with three or four people inside slowed briefly. A man called to me, "Hey, this is one of the most beautiful spots in the world, heh?" and, without stopping, they were off.

There's so much more to life if we can slow down long enough to be aware of it and appreciate it. Mindfulness doesn't "take" time; it gives it.

Our resistance to doing things more slowly arises from old habits that have not served us well enough. Indeed, when I first mention slowing down to my students, they look exasperated—they think, "I have so much going on in my life, the last thing I need is to slow down!"

I'm *not* suggesting we discard the skills of efficiency and productivity. There's nothing wrong with driving instead of walking to work; I don't advocate living in a tipi; and becoming a sloth at your job will certainly endanger it. And I'm not talking about meditating or being quiet and serious all the time. A critical part of being alive is our ability to have fun, and having fun often means going fast.

What I'm urging is *balance,* a mindfulness that allows us to bring a different rhythm to our days. When we give it a chance, we'll discover a surprising truth: It's when we slow down that we show up.

There are many ways we can practice consciously expanding the moment—creating the time we need to fully open up to life. Methods range from just sitting and breathing, to paying attention while we do something we enjoy, to spiritual practices. We can do these for a few minutes to a half hour a day; or take occasional intensive weeklong mindfulness retreats. Best of all, we can do both.

One of the simplest and most effective ways to become present in our life is to pay attention to our breathing. Breathing is a way of bringing us mentally and emotionally back to center, as though we were resetting our internal-clock mechanism; it is a deep and inte-grating rhythm of the body. By allowing ourselves to become conscious of our breathing, we begin to slow down into the breath and allow ourselves to set a rhythm for the body that is peaceful, calm, and healthy.

Try it now! Even as you've been reading you've been breathing, but now become aware of your breath and really experience it. Fill your lungs completely, slowly, and let the air out slowly, deliberately. Do it a few times. "Watch" your breath as it comes in, watch it as it goes out. Feels good, doesn't it?

You may want to put this book down for a few minutes, just to breathe. Sit with both feet on the ground in a comfortable chair— or lie down if that's more comfortable. Begin to notice what your body feels like, whether you're cramped or relaxed. Do you feel tension in your back or tightness in your neck? Relax. Feel loose. What does the room smell like? What do you hear when you get still?

Closing your eyes is particularly helpful. Our eyes scan the world, mirroring the flitting and skimming of our mind, and shutting them draws us out of the automatic, almost robotic, rhythm to which we entrain without realizing it.

Turn your attention to your breath, putting your hand on your lower belly and breathing in easily, sending the air all the way down to the bottom of your lungs. You'll know it's there when your lower abdomen pushes your hand out. Take a few seconds, to breathe in fully, easily. As your lungs fill up, move your hand higher on your abdomen and feel that. Last of all, the area around your collarbone will rise. Let the breathing feel smooth, silent, unrestrained. Keep your shoulders down and your face muscles relaxed. After just a few breaths, you'll begin to feel a sense of ease.

Let breathing help you feel more centered. After all, we're breathing all the time anyway, so being conscious of it simply allows us to come in to the present. It only takes a few moments, and then you can jump back into your activities refreshed, and go once more into a fast rhythm.

This simple practice of stopping, closing my eyes, and taking a few minutes to breathe fully is very important to my daily life. Often in the midst of tumult, when I'm experiencing a painful period or a joyous one, I'm amazed that when I tune in to my breathing, it's always the same. It's like coming home to myself.

Despite the uproar, there is peace within me. Meditation teacher Gunilla Norris writes:

> When we sit in stillness we are profoundly active.
> Keeping silent, we can hear the roar of existence.

Typically, when you begin a consciousness exercise like this, you'll find that your mind races—"itching, twitching, and bitching" as one mindfulness teacher at Omega put it. But, just as with an emotional wave, any discomfort associated with watching the breath will soon recede. If thoughts race through your mind, just notice them and breathe them gently away on your next exhalation. You'll find that the more you do this, the quieter your mind will become. The ability to follow your breathing can profoundly strengthen your concentration. The quietness produced in your mind will become a profound peacefulness, yours to summon in any situation.

I like using a simple technique brought to the West by Thich Nhat Hanh, which involves repeating phrases slowly in rhythm with the breath:

> Breathing in, I am calm,
> Breathing out, I smile.

Breathing. It's something we normally do without thinking about it, yet it keeps us alive. There is a Zen story of a young student monk who complained that following his breathing was boring. His master asked the student to put his head into a pail of water and hold it there for a while. When the student finally came up gasping for air, the master said, "Do you still find breathing boring?"

Another effective way to deepen the sense of presence is through one of the many forms of meditation. As author Stephen Levine notes, "Meditation is a means to an endlessness."

Meditation encourages us to tune in to our surroundings and to sink into whatever's going on within our skin. In other words, it trains us to be more aware, and to concentrate.

As with any form of art, it's not what we do but how we do it that counts in meditation. In the West, unfortunately, teachers and students often adapt meditation to a model of achievement: If I meditate two hours a day, and get it right, I'll attain enlightenment. Meditation doesn't work that way. We'll explore the subject more in the chapter on Self, but now share with Teresa, a Kentucky woman in her seventies with no formal experience of meditation, her description of her daily ritual:

Every morning, before anyone else is up, I get myself a cup of tea and then sit in my rocking chair on the porch and muse. I'm not *doing* anything. I don't think of all the things I have to do, or anything in particular. If I'm worried about something, or if I'm angry with someone, I just let it come up and then it passes.

Mostly I just rock and rock, look at the sunrise, and—My! how wonderful it is to be alive, to breathe, to smell the pine in the air. How lucky I am to be here! I need do nothing but rock, and I'm happy. Sometimes I miss my musing, and then I feel out of sorts all day.

"Musing" is a word I had heard used by another special person I had the privilege of meeting on the other side of the world.

In the mid-seventies, I chose to finish my medical school training in a hospital in northern India. There I heard about a Hindu mystic, known as Shri Bhagwan, who lived in a nearby temple, and I immediately went to find him.

I spent the next four months working at the hospital in the morning and spending the rest of the day with Shri Bhagwan, talking about—and experiencing—life from a perspective I had never before encountered. I'd spend hours a day sitting with him in silence—musing—or taking slow walks into town with no destination in mind, and he'd tell me about his earlier life.

When I met him in his early 80s, Shri Bhagwan had already renounced the active intellectual and political life he had lived years before. (He had worked with Mahatma Gandhi, with whom he had spent time in prison during India's independence movement.) He spoke many languages, was obviously well read, yet had chosen a life of utter simplicity.

Now he lived like a nomad, camping out in the first-class waiting room of the New Delhi train station during winter, moving to the hills, where he lived on the floor of the temple, during warmer weather. He had almost no possessions and gave himself severe restrictions: He wouldn't use money, write, read, sit in a chair, touch another person—or do hundreds of other things.

I experienced him as the freest human being I had ever met.

In his presence it seemed that time would cease. Nothing in particular would happen; there seemed to be nowhere to go and nothing to do. Yet I felt happy and fulfilled.

Initially, this newfound contentment caused me great alarm. I was on a mission to help at the hospital, and envisioned myself doing many important things, yet I was aware that the time I spent with Bhagwan seemed magical and charged. I felt fully alive in the present moment, which was very new to me.

Before my trip, I had been studying Zen Buddhism in the States in a typically Western way, hoping to attain enlightenment by reaching some state of consciousness I couldn't define and had clearly not yet experienced. Bhagwan liked to poke fun at my "Zenism" meditation. He told me to forget about such ideas and just settle into a fuller experience of the present. There were no other states of consciousness to attain, nothing else I needed to be doing. The answer was simply to pry open the door to a fully conscious experience of now.

I still recognize the grace I experienced with Bhagwan. During the musings, our walks, and our visits to the local sweet shop (where he would insist I eat pastry, but would never eat himself) he modeled for me the possibility of being fully present, and the remarkable sense of freedom and peacefulness that ensues.

I haven't chosen to live like him, nor do I recommend it for you, but Shri Bhagwan's presence has inspired me, and meditation is still a vital part of my life. Meditation has shown me that it's possible to expand the moment into a sense of time freedom so luxurious that we are conscious on all the levels of our being.

Roshi Philip Kapleau, a Zen master, described meditation to me as "the dance of death." To face oneself stripped of all busyness is to look within at the very essence of who we each are. Often when I'm sitting doing meditation practice, I can feel my internal motor revving, my mind informing me of everything else I should be doing right now. Being able to just sit with this, letting the thoughts come and go and allowing a calmness to overcome the agitation of daily life, can be profound.

Yet after a time I feel the pull of life around me, urging me to get going. It's not that I love to meditate; in truth, I sometimes find it difficult. And I don't automatically feel wonderful, or even better, after I get up. But I do notice the difference in my life when I'm meditating regularly—life seems to be more peaceful, to flow more easily. I believe that on a deep level, I am entraining myself to a rhythm of peace and harmony that is essentially healing.

In many different spiritual practices there is a reference to an enlightened state of being, one of full awareness without differentiation between subject and object, but with a sense of the oneness of existence. His Holiness the Dalai Lama has said that time only exists if there is impermanence—and life as we know it and live it is subject to continual change.

Time is thus a measure of transformation. It exists because there is change; in fact, the more there is change, the more we have the perception of time speeding by. Time appears to slow when nothing seems to be happening, and seems to stop altogether when there is no change, when we enter the place beyond that which comes and goes, beyond all that is transient. Timelessness is experienced as a pure awareness of existence beyond any change. *This* constitutes enlightenment: an awakening from that which is continually changing.

At its heart, enlightenment means becoming so fully immersed in the present that nothing else exists. Developing the ability to focus more fully, to become ever more present, is the path. This means fully letting go. We must stop pushing forward and allow ourselves the grace that occurs when we drop into the present moment.

★ ★ ★

Another way to bring us back to the present—to the strawberries before us—is by listening to slow, beautiful music. Because we entrain so naturally to our surroundings, we can easily allow the length of our moment—our tempo—to be shifted by music. Consider the recent surprising popularity of Gregorian music; much New Age music can have a similar effect. (If that's not your style, try Mozart—anything that will slow you down.)

Mostly we use music as background, like Muzak in stores, or as sound to accompany mundane chores so we don't have to feel. What a difference it makes when we actually *listen* to music instead of just "putting it on." See how you feel after twenty minutes of actually attending to a favorite slow piece—Allow yourself to move your body, dancing or swaying, to the rhythm.

It's a common practice in spiritual traditions to ring a bell during ceremonies and times of meditation. A good, resonant bell will extend its tone for a long time after you strike it—and the effect of that tone, like slow music, is to expand the moment. The bell tunes us to a different, deeper rhythm from the staccato sounds of society. It's long and generous, languorous, and it helps to stretch out our length of focus.

In my classes we choose a designated bell-ringer to help bring us all into the present moment. Several times a session, without announcing it, this person will hit the bell. No matter what we're doing or saying, all of us stop until the reverberations fade, close our eyes, and take three luscious, slow breaths, then return to the discussion a little clearer and more centered than before.

Incense is also used in spiritual practice; a strong smell has a way of widening the moment. We have all had the experience, the olfactory equivalent of a *déjà-vu*, when we vividly remember a past event through the sense of smell. It is always an event for which we were fully present at the time.

Our more primitive or earlier evolved senses—smell and touch and hearing—are slower than our visual sense, which is more connected to our thinking, and are thus more closely allied with our feelings. Because these senses are slower, we are more easily able to expand the present moment when we use them. We have seen how music can set the rhythm of the moment. When we receive a massage or someone touches us on the back or caresses our cheek— these bring our focus into the moment. And if you notice when you are most aware of smell, you begin to see that it is usually associated with moments strongly rooted in the present, when food is placed before us, for example, or when we enter a flower garden. We associate heightened smells, from perfume to the smells of the body, with sexuality, and in sex we are supremely in the present moment.

I'm sure you've noticed that we're borrowing tools from some of the great religious traditions to help us become present. This is because spiritual traditions use methods designed to slow us down to the point that we *notice*—so that we can cultivate a reverence for life. The magic is in the attention.

There is nothing mystical about being truly present, and yet it is what mysticism is all about.

Watch a young child. She is totally focused on what she's doing, without concern for the future or regrets for the past. In a real sense, this is time freedom. But we're socialized out of this natural sense of awareness and wonder early on. Jocelyn, a workshop participant in her thirties, describes how she felt in time freedom as a child, and what it was like being trained to leave it behind:

Early one morning before school, I was outside blowing bubbles—using one of those contraptions that makes huge, beautiful, iridescent bubbles that fly and bounce. I was completely focused, watching the light create shifting colors on these things as they wafted around—I was totally fascinated and totally immersed . . .

Suddenly my mom stuck her head out the door and yelled, "Jocelyn, what are you doing? Come in, you'll be late for school!"

I had the clear sense that what I was doing was in fact very important, although I couldn't explain why. I felt like my mom literally yanked me out of the present that I was rooted in. And I've felt that people and things have been yanking me out of the present ever since.

We *are* yanked—or, as adults, we yank ourselves—out of the current moment, and the current moment is all we have. Indeed, the Buddha taught that life is lived only in the present.

I worry that we've forgotten this wisdom. If we miss the present moment, we miss life itself.

CHAPTER SIX

TIMESHIFTING

———

The simple ability to pay attention to the
world as we find it may be at the heart of a
soulful life worth living.
—DAVID WHYTE

EVERY INSTANCE OF timeshifting begins with a two-step process of changing the focus of our attention, and thus our *perception*.

First, we simply become *aware of the present*.

This may seem superfluous: Aren't we always "aware" of the present? In fact, we're not. In previous chapters we've seen how distracted we almost always are—by anxiety, stress, or negative entrainment. A thousand and one influences pull us away from direct experience of ourselves and the world around us. We spend the greater part of our days more or less in this state of distraction. We cannot possibly timeshift, unless we stop, take notice, and have a clear perception of the very existence of this present moment.

Second, we sense the particular *rhythm and flow* of the present moment.

Timeshifting is a conscious effort, a decision to somehow alter our relationship to a particular rhythm or set of rhythms we find going on within us or outside of us. Usually we timeshift when these rhythms are wrong for us—we're being negatively entrained—and then we want to set a new rhythm, a different basis for entrainment. On the other hand, we can sometimes find that we're having difficulty entraining with a very positive rhythm. (I remember sitting in a concert hall, listening to a particularly beautiful symphony, reveling in the music and aware of its beauty—yet nevertheless vaguely uncomfortable because I couldn't stop thinking of the outside world.) In either case, we need to open ourselves to feeling and understanding the moment's actual rhythm, or we won't be able to decide how we should respond to it.

Each of these preliminary steps is necessary if we're going to be able to timeshift with ease and grace, and do it effectively. They are how we establish a kernel of mindfulness out of which a more extensive mindfulness can grow.

Characterizing the process of timeshifting, I've used the analogy of shifting gears on a bicycle. You might say that timeshifting without this foundation of simple, clear awareness of what *is actually going on* is like shifting the gears, but while riding with our eyes closed.

Riding a bicycle, we are consciously deciding when to shift gears—but we're able to ride because we've learned how to handle most of the process unconsciously. We all remember what it was like when we first tried it: staring down at the handlebars and the pedals, wobbling along because we were paying so much attention to the process itself that we couldn't fall into the rhythm that would give us our balance. It was only when our bodies and unconscious minds took over that we really "knew" how to ride a bike.

Timeshifting works the opposite way, because it involves directing and heightening our awareness through a conscious process, which I call "conscious awareness." You may eventually arrive at a point where you no longer have to "think about" being mindful; but until then, we must deliberately train ourselves into mindfulness by timeshifting—just as the monk uses meditation practice in order to achieve enlightenment.

Basically, timeshifting leads us to shifting our rhythm to join the external rhythm of the moment, or to tuning into our own rhythm and choosing to stay with it. Unfortunately, most of the time, without awareness of the rhythm of the moment, we are just swept along, marching to the beat around us. It's as though we're constantly in that first moment after the alarm clock goes off in the morning: For a second, we're befuddled and not quite sure of where or even who we are, but we're already responding to a command.

We must recognize the need of each moment. This one may need an urgent response at a fast speed. If so, then we respond without resisting, or wishing we could go more slowly. We respond in the present, urgently. The next moment may hold an interaction with someone wanting our understanding or support. A slower moment is required, so realizing this, we slow down and become present. Or having worked all day, we become aware of our internal yearning to slow down and relax, and we let the external rhythms of the world fade as we come into sync with ourselves.

As a physician, my daily practice required rushing through certain parts of the day—writing in patient charts, catching up on phone calls, seeing acute problem patients with traumas needing immediate attention. During these times I would be highly focused, and I felt great as well as effective in what I was doing.

Then I would sit down in my office with a patient who had pains in her stomach, or a man with breathing problems. Such situations required that I shift into a slower, more caring rhythm in the present moment. When I did, a deeper level of communication occurred, the patient felt heard and cared for, the root cause of the problem was more easily discovered, and fears about treatment were considered and discussed.

But this took a conscious timeshift; otherwise I would continue at a rushed, urgent pace, quickly assessing the problem, never making real contact, prescribing some drug, and moving on to my next task. The result was satisfying neither to the patient nor myself. Underlying causes and stresses were never revealed, and the patient left frustrated as well as still fearful about a potentially serious problem. We had not shifted into a rhythm that promoted healing.

During all of this, as I felt the pressures and demands of my work, I found the greatest relief was to simply take a few moments to shut my office door, close my eyes, take a few breaths, and allow myself to feel my own rhythm and just relax. Doing this made it much easier to then shift speeds at other times of the day.

Timeshifting, like shifting the gears on a bicycle, is finding the pace of everyday life most deeply nourishing to our soul as well as completing the myriad tasks and responsibilities at hand. In order to live well in modern society, we must be able to switch rhythms effectively throughout the day. Conscious awareness and the use of rituals are essential if we are to succeed.

Perhaps the most effective way to shift rhythm is through ritual. Historically, all religions have been aware of the need to shift time, and have used ritual to clearly differentiate sacred from profane time. As part of their ritual, people have used the various means I mentioned in the previous chapter—incantation and sacred song, bells and other sounds, prayer, images, incense—in order to bring their followers *into* sacred time, shifting them from activity to contemplation, from the everyday to the universal.

But ritual does not have to be connected to religion. We can devise rituals of our own choosing to help put us into the present moment, to help us shift from one kind of rhythm to another.

Workers in the field used song to change rhythms; ancient societies provided festivals and celebrations to alter the pace of their citizens' lives.

Today, in the modern world, there are innumerable opportunities to create our own timeshifting rituals. We only need to be aware that they exist, and then to use them consciously. Use the ring of the telephone or school bell, or the starting sound of a computer to take a few breaths. Before each meal, stop and be conscious in whatever form of grace you use. Washing the dishes or walking the dog or folding the laundry are all ways to become present. Sitting in a car for a few minutes before entering the house after work, or exercising before leaving the house in the morning, can create a shift of rhythm. Pausing to get centered before a meeting is such a ritual, just as a basketball player will always stop, concentrate, breathe out, feel centered, and then shoot.

During my busy days practicing medicine, I always found there was more to do than I could fit into the schedule of my day. By the time lunchtime arrived, I was already behind on appointments, hadn't had the chance to finish writing in the charts for the morning patients, and was faced with several phone calls to be returned or patients with acute problems who needed to be squeezed in somehow. In those days, if you'd asked me what I'd had for lunch an hour after I'd eaten, I couldn't have told you; invariably, I'd been gulping down my food while attending to something else. I remember wishing that I could take lunch from an IV bottle, without having to occupy my hands or waste any time.

Today I understand that eating is an important occasion for changing pace, and how essential it is for us to shift our rhythm at the beginning of the meal. The ritual of saying grace before a meal, stopping to take a few conscious breaths, or simply pausing for a moment, allows us to shift from the rhythm of the previous activity, relax for a moment, become present, and then actually enjoy our meal. Whether or not one views this as an homage to God, the Creator, or Nature, or more simply as a moment to come into harmony with oneself, doesn't matter. For me, it has become a regular opportunity to be present once again in my life.

Consider the concept of the "power lunch." Don't waste time over the food itself: Concentrate on business. Don't let anything so mundane as eating (even when the food's delicious, as it tends to be at power lunches) interfere with the real goal of the day: making money. No time for contemplation here, much less simple enjoyment. No time for the present.

A friend of mine was recently traveling in the Italian countryside. He'd stopped to buy something and found that he'd done so at the time when everyone had stopped working to have a leisurely meal and rest. He couldn't get *anyone* to stay even a few extra minutes to sell him what he wanted—their ritual time off mattered more to them than his money did. In the following days, he noted that everyone did the same, always at a certain hour in the afternoon. For the entire community, the priority was in living life; there was simply no question of staying busy just to "buy" leisure time later.

* * *

There are many different rituals that we already use regularly to shift time throughout our day. We would do well to become aware of these rituals—to at least recognize that we perform them, without necessarily recognizing why—because this awareness can allow us to give them priority rather than rushing through them. It also helps those around us to realize their importance for us.

Many people, immediately when they get home from work, change their clothes, walk the dog, putter in the garden, play with their children, meditate, exercise, talk quietly to their spouse: All of these are rituals. Nancy, in one of my classes, mentioned that, upon returning home, she always sat in her favorite lounge chair. Her cat would immediately come bounding in and settle on her lap to receive its daily massage, with much affectionate purring. In return, Nancy received the gift of a daily, ritual occasion for relaxing into a slow and caring rhythm.

My father practiced a consistent ritual for shifting from work time to family time when he came home each night. No matter the hour, after saying hello to my mother and the kids, he would take a shower. I remember sitting at the table along with my mother and siblings, dinner prepared, waiting for him to come downstairs. My mother would often be exasperated or furious at his lateness—with us kids generally siding with her, eager to start eating—yet nothing could make him abandon his personal ritual. He was not truly home, he used to say, until he'd "washed off the day"; for that, he needed his shower.

Looking back, I realize that if my mother and father had been aware of the role of ritual, and had communicated about it, she would have been more understanding. She might have accepted and respected his ritual in general—but suggested that, if dinner had been ready for a half hour or so, he might relinquish his timeshifting and join us immediately. With both points of view acknowledged and understood, the friction could have been avoided.

I know several people who immediately turn on the television to watch the news when they get home from work. I believe this is a habit, not a ritual: It's a simple switching on of image and sound that does not alter the basic rhythm of society they've brought home with them.

Distinguishing habit from ritual is fairly easy. Ask yourself, about any activity, "If I were consciously trying to change my rhythm, would I do this?" You'll see that your rituals actually do shift time, while the habits tend to reinforce a sameness of rhythm.

However, through conscious awareness, we can make rituals out of habits. If, for example, you always turn on the television set when you get home not because you're interested in any program but because you "need" noise, you can be consciously aware of that need and put on music instead of television and slow down to really listen.

Chores, too, can become conscious rituals. For instance, I wash the dishes every night, and I consciously use it as a way of settling in. For me, it's a wonderful way to practice mindfulness. In fact, I've come to realize that I really enjoy washing the dishes. In my busy day, it's one of the things I know I will get completed, I can do it without struggling against it, and it won't make me feel stressed. Why should I rush it? To show myself how efficiently I can get it done? I simply do the dishes and breathe. It's not my greatest joy, or in any way earth-shattering—but becoming present through just this sort of mundane ritual is the foundation of the rhythm and flow that can create well-being and harmony in my life.

There are hundreds of other possible rituals, ones you may already do, or ones you can adopt. I've already noted how powerfully music can change our rhythm; why not use it ritualistically? As I drive to my weekly basketball game, for example, I always play fast music as a way of pumping myself up.

Cultivate hobbies, or other "unproductive" activities. Phil, a student of mine, spent months rebuilding an old Wurlitzer jukebox every evening when he came home from work. "In our era of high tech," he told me, "it was my way of going back to the past. Here was a creaking arm in a time of CDs. Working on it was like meditation."

John Stokes, a consummate wildlife tracker who has studied with the Aborigines of Australia and now teaches at Omega, recommends consciously greeting the first animal you see in the morning, even an ant, as a way of becoming present with nature. In our mechanical and electronic world we have tuned out nature, yet, when we really notice what's around us, it becomes amazingly important. When you realize that it's the same bird by your window every morning, then it begins to have a personality, a quality of individual being—and becomes a representative of the entire natural world, with which you now have a kind of relationship.

If you have a pet, set aside a few times every day for spending conscious time with it. Instead of absently stroking it, really concentrate on its reactions—and yours. You'll find yourself settling into a tranquil present.

If you have a child, take time each day to really pay attention to and be with him or her. If you have more than one child, try to have private time with each one individually. Not only will you be able to entrain with that wonderful childhood rhythm, but also you may get to know your child in a whole new way.

Honor the mundane ritual by leaving time for it. I wake up early, to have time for meditation and tuning in to the day. Try setting your alarm a little earlier than you are used to, so you can perform whatever ritual you choose to enable you to enter into the day in your own individual rhythm, rather than plunging at once into that of the world's.

A friend of mine makes sure she gets to the office fifteen minutes early every day. Years ago, she never would have considered coming in early voluntarily—and would have balked if it had been suggested that she should. But now she says that doing this has literally changed her life, because it's subtly and profoundly affected her approach to work. Simply by giving herself time to sort through her papers and do some quiet thinking, she starts the day at her own pace, and is able to continue in it throughout her day—instead of feeling rushed and always behind, as she previously felt.

Another friend takes a meditation break at work in lieu of coffee or a cigarette. A third always sits in her car for at least five minutes after driving home from work before she enters her house to join her husband and three children.

All these are means of shifting time. Use them, or use your own (you already have some; find more). And *know* you are doing it.

In the next chapter, I'm going to look at a number of aspects of our lives to discover the opportunities for timeshifting that they present to us. Most of my practical suggestions are for rituals that you can incorporate into your day, and they roughly fall into one of the following six categories:

Being in the moment
Creating time boundaries
Honoring the mundane
Creating spontaneous time
Doing what we like to do
Creating time retreats

Let's look at each of these techniques for timeshifting in turn.

CHAPTER SEVEN

EXERCISES IN TIMESHIFTING

—

*The miracle is not to walk on water. The
miracle is to walk on the green earth in the
present moment, to appreciate peace and
beauty that are available now. . . . We need
only to find ways to bring our body and mind
back to the present moment so we can touch
what is refreshing, healing and wondrous.*
—THICH NHAT HANH

Timeshifting to Be in the Moment

DURING TIMES OF stress or urgency in everyday life, it is
especially important to be able to timeshift. You may feel as if your
head or heart will burst; that you are going even faster than the
chaos around you; that your pulse has accelerated. You may feel as if
you're in a race where everyone is overtaking you. It's precisely at
these times that it's vital for each of us to have a ritual or process we
can invoke to help us to "come home" to ourselves.

Computer keyboards have "pause" buttons; establish your own.
If you use your own individual method for slowing down and entering the present every time you feel your anxiety build, you'll find
that you're now applying your own rhythm to the situation rather
than succumbing to the outside force that caused the stress in the
first place.

As I mentioned in the previous chapter, I have someone strike a bell during my workshops at irregular intervals, and we all stop, close our eyes, and take three deep breaths. You need to create a "bell" for yourself that you can invoke to help you change your pace.

Our lives are, in fact, constantly being interrupted—not by bells, but by things that urgently demand our immediate attention. When such interruptions occur, instead of responding immediately, we can take the opportunity to pause and come into the moment.

There's a literal bell that each of us can use every day as our signal to pause: Thich Nhat Hanh says to let the telephone be a bell of awakening. When it rings, stop and take a deep breath instead of snatching it off the hook. You'll find yourself slowing down, becoming calmer, and better able to respond to the call.

Teachers can use the period bell to take a breath and come into the present before the next class. All of us have repeated occurrences in our day that we can use for our bell. Whenever they come up, simply relax for a minute—and then move on to what needs to be done, without feeling rushed.

In addition to the bell, become conscious of your breathing whenever you think of it. Take a deep breath—and another. Take as many as you need to feel the acceleration reverse, your inner engine slow. I've talked about the importance of breathing earlier. While most other means of entering the moment are individual and often idiosyncratic, breathing is universal.

Often, in the midst of a heated business meeting, I've excused myself for a "bathroom break." What I'm actually doing is using an excuse to leave the room, to give myself a space of time to breathe in private.

A friend of mine, when he finds himself getting agitated at work, will close his office door and simply stare at a picture of a beautiful sunset he took on his last vacation. His teenage daughter, he tells me, will "commune" with her teddy bear until her agitation ceases.

One workshop participant told us she keeps a jar of Tiger Balm on her desk, which from time to time she rubs into her temples. She feels its effects for minutes afterward, further expanding the moment in which she slowed down. Another friend listens to a relaxation tape for three minutes when she gets to her office.

One student told me she counts to ten before committing herself to any action or argument. Another keeps a prism on her desk, and spends a moment regarding the way it refracts the light, before turning to her next task. A third student, a pianist, drinks a glass of water, whether he's thirsty or not, just before he goes onstage. A mother I know with a three-year-old daughter carves out "mommy time" whenever the child throws a tantrum; she disappears into her room, locking the door behind her for five minutes.

"That sounds almost like child abuse," someone said to her in class.

"Not at all," she replied. "The only thing that happens is that she stops crying, and we both get more relaxed and can find a rhythm in which we can communicate instead of being 'on it' all the time. And now, from time to time when she's mad at me, she tells me, 'Go take mommy time.'"

The point, as always, lies not so much in the specific exercise but in the awareness that the exercise is a tool, specifically and consciously created to counteract stress, anxiety, or imagined crisis. Without these tools, the stress intensifies; by using them, it disappears. Remember: *In the present moment, there is no stress.*

Timeshifting to Create Time Boundaries

Each of us needs some time that is strictly and entirely our own, and we should experience it daily. Preferably, it should be the same time every day—a half hour after dinner, perhaps; fifteen minutes just before the start of work (anything less than fifteen is inadequate); or an hour in the afternoon uninterrupted by meetings, phone calls, or chats.

This is a time to adhere to boundaries that keep the never-ending interruptions out. It's a time dedicated to being in process with ourselves: no achievements or goals, no catching up on past obligations. This is time for ourselves, for doing what *we* want; it belongs to us, not to society, our boss, or our family. Of course, it's not necessary to "do" anything; this is our time to "be," not "do." All that's necessary is taking some quiet time, free from the issues of the day.

Make this a time for meditation, for contemplation, or for enjoyment of the things around you. Such time is often labeled "nonproductive." I see it instead as a way of being present in the process of life, not as an end result or an endeavor.

People who take this time first thing in the morning notice the most positive effect. Starting the day tuned in to your own rhythm sets up a pattern that you can continue throughout the day. Walking your dog, walking in nature, jogging, puttering about the house, taking a bath, meditating, just listening to music, reading poetry or reflective prose—these all allow us to feel our inner rhythm, and strengthen it, so it can stay with us.

While the importance of such time has long been acknowledged, charting it out and sticking to it is difficult. Among other things, it requires developing the ability to say "no" in order to maintain that boundary around your own time—and we do need to set up some formal boundaries in order to ensure that we, and others, honor this time with ourselves.

The boundaries should not be too flexible. The benefits are only obtainable if you insist on the time for yourself alone. To let in a coworker, a child, a spouse, or a friend, will deprive you of the timeshift you need. The no is for this moment; in the next, you can say "yes."

Nora, a student of mine, agrees on the necessity of boundaried time wholeheartedly. When she first gets up in the morning, her husband knows that he should let her have some time with herself—because she asked him to, and explained how important it is to her. Meanwhile, she "putters," concentrating wholly on the smallest tasks. She particularly enjoys making the morning coffee. "It's beautiful, the way it drips and steams," she says. "I like to listen to it, to watch it. While I'm making coffee I'm doing nothing else." When the coffee's on the table, then her husband knows that Nora's boundaried time is over, and they can start their day together with a relaxed, easy rhythm.

Of course, one of the hardest interruptions of boundaried time to avoid is self-interruption. There are the bills to pay, the lawn to be mowed, the important phone call, the letter waiting for an answer. There's always something to do—and the more you do, the more there is to do: You never get to the end of the pile.

But there must be some block of time in your day when you simply won't allow yourself these self-interruptions. Try cutting just a half hour out of your busy schedule to do something you find compelling *in itself,* not as progress toward some productive goal. If God could take the seventh day off to rest, then a half hour a day doesn't seem much to ask of ourselves.

Boundaried time should be like the beauty of a flower: It doesn't have any purpose; it's just there. And, like a flower, it refreshes us and brings us to an awareness of the glory of the world.

Take a walk in the park. Go for a swim (not for its aerobic benefits, but because swimming is fun). Ride a bike, take a leisurely bath, drink a cup of tea, meditate.

Ginnie, an advertising executive, expressed with great vividness the effect of creating boundaried time. She used to just roll out of bed and dash off to work.

I felt like I was stuck on a whirling Ferris wheel. There was no in-between time, no down time, except when I was unconscious. It felt relentless, even brutal. But I've learned to take time. I now get up early enough so that I have at least an hour between getting dressed and the time I need to leave. It's so worth it! I sit and do nothing. Or think about my dreams. Sometimes I'll read the paper, sometimes I'll go for a walk— but that one hour has literally changed my life. It stuns me, how simple this is. Yet I feel like it's a major discovery, the key to my life being *my life*—as opposed to being a person who just recharges the battery for the executive who goes to work.

Timeshifting to Honor the Mundane

All aspects of life are potentially rich and full. Most of us, though, treat our days as composed of highlights—the big meeting, a good meal, a session of lovemaking, an outing with the kids—with the in-between times merely connecting the "important" events, not intrinsically valuable in themselves. In these mundane times, however, lie treasures for the soul, if only we can learn to find them.

There are, for example, two ways to sweep a floor. I can sweep it to get it clean, or I can sweep it *to sweep it*.

In other words, I can swish the broom around, thinking of all I have to do in the "important" parts of my life, or I can bring my full attention to the act: the play of my muscles, the look of the floor, the sound of the broom against it.

The result is the same: The floor gets swept. But, as a dance teacher I know likes to say, "It's not what you do but how you do it that counts." And if I sweep the floor to *sweep the floor*—as a kind of dance, even—then I experience the act of sweeping itself, and therefore experience the moment.

Brenda, a financial analyst who works at home, told a timeshifting seminar that what she likes to do when she gets frustrated is iron laundry.

Everyone laughed. "You *like* to iron? I'll send you mine!" She laughed with them. "I have enough, thank you. But I *do* keep an ironing board outside my home office." She described her ritual:

I take a blouse out of the to-be-ironed bag. I sprinkle some water and put it on the board. It smells really clean, and when the iron hits it, it hisses. As I pass the iron over the blouse, the floral patterns in the fabric start to leap out—the colors become more vivid than they were when they were dry. Bit by bit, I smooth the wrinkles and the fabric feels warm and comforting under my hand. You can't rush a wrinkle; if you do, you get a crease. So I just keep at it, again, watching, smelling the steam. By the time I'm done, it's all smooth and restored.

We could feel the strength of her presence in her ironing. She was giving us a lesson in "the Zen of Ironing."

And what would she do if, after she had finished ironing, she still felt anxious or frustrated?

"Iron again."

Too often we act like children who feel they "have to" do their homework. It's OK if we want to live that way—but suppose instead we forgot about rushing, forgot for a while about everything else we have to do, put on some beautiful music, and just allowed ourselves to feel the rhythm and sweep to the music? In fact, it can become fun. Since we need to do these everyday things that make up a significant part of our lives anyway, why treat them as drudgery?

After all, it's our life, and it's our choice.

Thich Nhat Hanh put it this way:

If I am incapable of washing dishes joyfully, if I want to finish them quickly so I can go and have dessert, I will be equally incapable of enjoying my dessert. With the fork in my hand, I will be thinking about what to do next, and the texture and flavor of the dessert, together with the pleasure of eating it, will be lost. I will always be dragged into the future, never able to live in the present moment.

If we push away the mundane, we push away the present. And when pushing away becomes our habitual pattern, we're likely to push away the extraordinary moments, too, unable to fully savor them in our rush to "get on."

But by developing the ability to be present in the mundane parts of our lives, we begin to value life itself, the everyday living of it. The true "adventures," then, begin to resonate more profoundly, for we have learned how to awaken ourselves to the present in all things.

Timeshifting to Create
Spontaneous Time

Remember snow days? As a child, when it snowed, I would get up in the morning and immediately turn on the radio to see if school was going to be closed—and how I rejoiced when it was! A free day, completely unplanned, in which I could do anything I wanted! It seemed like a present from God.

When I mention this in my classes, I can always see the recognition in the room. We sigh with nostalgia, remembering the unexpected pleasure of such days.

As adults, we need to create our own snow days, or at least snow time—a time for unplanned, unexpected events. We should offer this gift to ourselves. And why wait for snow?

Most of us lead lives of routinization. The weekdays are for work, the weekends for chores and social and personal commitments. Family matters are to be taken up after dinner; vacations are enjoyed in a "favorite" spot. There is little difference between what we do on a Friday in September, say, and a Tuesday in May.

In our lives we can expect variety, but we tend to get sameness. We want to fill our lives with the "new," but somehow we don't have the knack for it. We're comfortable with how we live, so although the idea of change is alluring, the actuality of it is frightening.

But routine leads to internal passivity, and repetition can lead to a state in which we rarely experience the present, but simply glide through it without being aware of our surroundings or, essentially, ourselves.

Of course, we build the anticipation of pleasure into our routine: We look forward to vacation in the summer, a picnic on the weekend, or a movie on Friday night. But often what we have anticipated with such optimism turns out to be disappointing (the weather's lousy, the movie isn't very good), or it never happens at all because something intercedes (the boss insists you work through your vacation time, the kids get the measles). Somehow, life never seems to live up to our expectations.

Spontaneous time allows us to break "set" and come freshly, without expectation, into a truly new experience. We may fear the uncertainty of this, or be afraid that we'll be bored, but it is an opportunity to be truly present, rather than measuring the experience against what we thought it should have been.

My dear friend Rob, an ever-adventurous lawyer, needed a winter vacation, so he went to the airport and took the first plane leaving for the far south. He ended up on an island in the tropics he'd never heard of—and he had the most wonderful time of any vacation he had ever taken. Everything was new, an adventure to be discovered and, as it turned out, completely delightful.

He acknowledged that he had taken an enormous risk: The trip might have been a dud, there might have been no hotel rooms, etc. But taking the risk of such freedom in our lives allows us to experience the present in a way we often shut ourselves off from when we are merely going through the same motions we always do.

It was precisely the *spontaneity,* he emphasized, that had made the trip such fun. He had felt most alive at the moment when the plane had lifted off, and he'd had no idea what the outcome would be.

Similarly, I once arrived at an airport in India, to take a flight from New Delhi to Bombay. But there was no flight that day, I was told. Yes, I had a ticket, and yes, the flight had been confirmed the day before. Nevertheless, there would be no plane going to Bombay.

"Ugly American" that I was, I shouted and protested, all to no avail. My own wind would not lift the plane off the ground. I was stuck.

Not stuck, though, I quickly discovered: rather, in spontaneous time that provided me with one of the most exhilarating days of my life. I felt like a leaf in the breeze, with no responsibilities and no goal, in a time free from time. Nothing particular *happened* that day, but I still remember it as a magical one—and I have tried to give myself the gift of spontaneous time whenever I can.

I'm not advocating that you never plan your vacations, or that you simply wander off whenever you feel like it. (Although the latter idea has merit; I know someone who purposely gets himself lost every once in a while to experience the special quality of seeing everything as new to him.) I'm merely urging that you work spontaneous time into your life.

In my own life, I try to *create* spontaneous time. Paradoxically, I actually try to *schedule* it.

Pick a Wednesday afternoon three weeks from now, write your own name into your appointment book, and leave work at one o'clock for an unplanned afternoon, going wherever your whim takes you. Or pick a Saturday to drive . . . anywhere. You can do anything you want, as long as it isn't planned. If your "Spontaneous Saturday" means simply a day lying in bed reading, so be it. The only rule and guide is that spontaneous time is *your* time and is *unplanned* time.

Many people say they don't have enough time to do this. I know someone who tried to set up his spontaneous time—but would write it into his calendar in pencil. Inevitably, something would come up, and he would erase it. Then he tried a pen, only to cross it out. Finally, he simply cut the page from his calender—the only way to make sure it was "his."

Deciding we don't have enough time—or allowing someone or something else to decide for us—is just resistance. Any of us can do this, no matter how busy we are or how compulsively we fill our days.

So start by picking a Saturday in the near future. Write your spontaneous time in your calendar—and when someone wants to make plans, tell them you're already booked.

Timeshifting to Do What
We Like to Do

When I asked the people in one workshop what they liked to do, one man, a real estate executive, said, "I like to color in coloring books with crayons."

"What a brave thing to admit!" I thought. The man was no budding Rembrandt, preparing for a career change. He simply colored because he liked it; the child's diversion had become the man's.

I think about him a lot. All of us need to do something simply for the fun of it, without any motive of gain, self-enhancement, or reward, beyond the pleasure of the activity.

My own passion is basketball. I don't play because the exercise is "good" for me (although I enjoy feeling fit), or because I "have to win" (although I like winning). I play basketball for the fun of it, and I make sure I play it regularly.

In the summer at Omega, I play at 5:00 in the afternoon Mondays, Thursdays, and Saturdays. I do it religiously, arriving promptly on the hour—it's one of the few things for which I'm always on time. The staff and my friends know I'm unavailable during that time; strangers with urgent business just have to wait.

A few years ago, I was working regularly with a business partner whose office was about an hour away from the court where I play. So, every Monday and Thursday afternoon at 3:30, I'd say to him, "I have to go."

He'd glare at me. "But you're *just* going to play basketball!"

I'd smile. "But we were *just* sitting here doing business."

To me, each was equally important. I was lucky to be able to do both.

In our society, you're not "supposed" to have fun at the expense of business. Relaxation is evidently only permissible when work is done.

I say, we must try to mix the two—they're equally important.

You might object that if you take time from work to do what you like, you'll be fired. Yet, if you can get time off from work for a doctor's appointment, why can't you take time to go for a walk (which will probably do as much for your health)—or to color in a coloring book?

My advice is to sneak the time in, if you have to, but make sure at least *some* time is available. We have to take the need for our own time seriously, or we'll become machines in the service of our bosses, our families, and linear time.

And life will pass us by without our realizing it.

Timeshifting to Create
Time Retreats

We've seen the necessity for bursts of time—days, hours, minutes, moments—devoted to bringing us into the present. But once a year or so, a longer period of a week or more should be spent doing something out of the ordinary—something that allows us to shift into a slower, less world-dictated rhythm.

For many, this means going into nature or to the sea, into the mountains or the woods, because the wilderness plays a vital role in our psychological and physiological lives. After all, we've evolved from the rhythms of nature into the rhythms of the electronic age, and a return to a slower, more natural rhythm is a life-affirming act.

I once sailed with two other men in a small boat across the Gulf of Mexico. I remember one nighttime watch in particular: As the others slept, I entrained with the rhythm of the sea. A few years later, I went with a friend on a camping trip in Utah, where I spent daylong moments alone in the untouched wilderness. (My friend and I would simply leave a daily signal that we were all right, then go off by ourselves.) Here I felt I was as one with the mountains and the sky, part of the primordial, eternal existence of the earth.

Some of you undoubtedly have had similar experiences, and others will prefer a milder sort of entrainment, as I usually do. I love going to the Caribbean, where events occur in "Island Time." It's a slow-paced rhythm that usually infuriates Americans—until they succumb to its spell and begin to loathe the idea of going back to the pace of their "working" lives.

You'll notice that I haven't used the word "vacation." For too many people, this means plunging into Disneyland with the kids, or racing through six European cities in ten days—"vacations" that maintain the frenetic rhythm of the rest of the year. The word "vacation" comes from the Latin word *vacare,* meaning "to be empty." Used in that sense, it *is* appropriate—an extended period when you empty your life of your habitual work, routines, and rhythms.

A Zen story illustrates when I mean:

A Western professor, anxious for enlightenment, visits a Zen master and is ushered into the master's home. During their talk, the Zen master pours tea for the professor, pouring and pouring until the tea overflows the cup, spilling onto the table and flooding the floor.

"Can't you see, you idiot, that there's tea all over the place?" the professor asks in exasperation.

"You come expecting to learn from me," the master replies. "But you're so filled with your own knowledge that there's no room for any other."

In our own lives, when we're preoccupied with work, worries, relationships, and stress, we're too "full" for reflection. Yet reflection is deeply healing, and we need it in order to assess where we are and where we want to be.

We can only reflect when our pace has sufficiently slowed to allow us to think and feel, undistracted by events or other people. With time retreats, we can shift our rhythm to embrace long periods of peace, and return to the natural rhythm that was engrained in us at birth, and which is frequently blocked for us by the events of daily life.

Creating a time retreat is not simple. Many people are more jittery at the beginning of a vacation than they are in their work lives, since they feel enormous anxiety about packing in as much fun as possible in a prescribed number of days.

When Noah, a man in his sixties, came to Omega's Caribbean program a few years ago, he was tremendously uptight: His cabin wasn't right, there were lizards, and he didn't like his roommate. At the end of our stay, when we got to the airport, he sheepishly admitted to me that he had forgotten his ticket—in fact, his wallet. I told him I'd put a new ticket on his charges for the seminar, and we'd work out the finances when we got back to the States.

"I forgot my luggage, too," he said. It was only when I stared at him in amazement that I realized he was wearing sandals, a T-shirt, and shorts—hardly the most appropriate attire for the return to an Albany snowstorm.

Noah made it back home. But I'll bet it took a long time—if ever—for him to fall back exclusively into his pre-Caribbean rhythms. And I wonder if he "forgot" almost everything he'd brought with him because he realized he'd found something much more valuable.

It takes time to "make" time, which is why I strongly advise against summers spent with only "long weekends" for breaks, let alone years at work when you're "too busy" for vacations. There are no exercises to get you into time retreats, but you must be aware that the retreats are there to be taken, and you need to consciously plan your life so that they are available to you.

And you don't have to go to the Caribbean to find them. One couple I know rented a house in the country for a week with two friends. At the last minute, the other couple cancelled. My friends couldn't afford to take the house by themselves, so, since they had told everybody they would be out of town, they took their retreat at home—sleeping when they felt like it, going to afternoon movies, making love in the morning: In other words, living in their own rhythms. It was the best vacation they'd ever had.

PART TWO

To enter into our healing self as world, let us move
into Deep Time. Let the reaches of time that we
inhabit with our ancestors and those to come become
real to us, as our birthright and wider home. Let us
step out of the tiny, hurried compartment of time,
where our culture and habits would enclose us. Let us
breathe deep and ease into the vaster horizons of our
larger story and our true, shared being.

—JOANNA MACY

CHAPTER EIGHT

SELF

—

*Dwell as near as possible to the channel in
which your life flows.*
—HENRY DAVID THOREAU

THE TROUBLE WITH those of us in the West is that we're
always busy, always doing, always on the go. True, we're alone a
great deal of the time, but even when we're by ourselves we're busy.
Indeed, our society proclaims that being busy is a virtue, and we
feel vaguely guilty when we're not.

There is a need for more time for *solitude,* a time for contemplation and meditation, when the mind is quiescent and feelings are at
ease. Getting to that time is one of the principal aims of timeshifting.

Yet we're afraid of solitude because we're afraid of the feelings
that will rise before we can be at ease, afraid to confront who we are
when stripped of our "doing" nature. I'm a doctor, a father, a
lecturer, always in one role or another—yet who am I without all of
this?

And so, when we're alone, we straighten the house, pay the bills,
cook the dinner, watch television, surround ourselves with the
canned noise of a radio or Walkman; in effect, we are seeking
companionship even when there is no other human being around.

There is a difference between being alone and being lonely. When we're alone, we can be in any sort of mood, happy or sad. angry or calm; but loneliness invariably *hurts*—and so, quite naturally, we run from it.

How many times, for instance, have we entered someone's house when a television set is on although there is no one in the room watching it? Why, when we're alone, do we talk aloud to ourselves or suddenly pick up the phone to call a friend?

We feel a need to be surrounded by people, by activity; to entrain with another's rhythm—anything *but* solitude, for that's where loneliness lurks.

I remember vividly a time when my life was full of emotional turmoil and I could not turn to family for solace since they were part of the problem. I didn't turn to friends, either, because I did not want them to know there *was* a problem.

So I stayed by myself in a small cabin on the shore of a lake near the Omega property. One morning, after a troubled sleep, I sat in a chair on the porch, looking at the still water, and was suddenly overwhelmed by a feeling of loneliness. I was sure that nobody loved me or cared whether I lived or died, that I was naked, defenseless. I was certain that nobody would ever visit me again.

My initial urge was to get out of the chair and do something—anything—to relieve the pain. But I *forced* myself to sit where I was and I opened myself up to the feeling. My feeling of loneliness shifted to that of rage and then to sadness, all uncomfortable and painful. I can still feel the enormous effort it took to stay with those feelings—and their profound effect.

I noticed an oak tree on the shore of the lake and focused my attention on it, all the while awash in feeling. I remember thinking that the oak tree didn't seem lonely where it stood, it was just playing out its part in the world as an oak tree. It seemed majestic, a beautiful solitary figure against the horizon.

Suddenly I felt myself like that oak, solitary, alone, simply being myself, with an immense feeling of freedom—I no longer felt lonely, merely alone.

I had reached the depth of my feeling, and when I did, it vanished. I had merged with the rhythm of nature, with the almost motionless rhythm of the oak.

I could feel a shifting of time.

It was a profound experience, one I recall in those moments that again bring up the fear of being alone. It has changed my relationship with simply being by myself, with whatever comes up, just being, without anything to *do*.

From time to time, all of us, like Garbo, "want to be alone." What a relief, we think, to get away from the spouse and kids, or from work, or even from well-meaning friends, and have some time to ourselves. How happy we are if we can take a solitary shower, shut ourselves in our workroom, stay indoors when the rest of the family is frolicking outside, eat a meal by ourselves, or go on a business trip and spend the night alone. No noise. No interruptions. No obligations. Peace: It's wonderful!

If we can somehow manage to find a long-term period of solitude, a strange thing happens: We get lonely or afraid, and we wish we were securely back with our family, or our friends, or our coworkers. Their "sins" are forgotten (or at least forgiven); we actually miss them!

All of this is about our resistance to being in the present, for in the present we experience this emotional discomfort, and then we want to be busy in our common environs with others. But we miss the present when we are with them, for they are the means of avoiding our discomfort. Other people provide our escape.

A client named Joan tells me that when she retired, friends hoped "she'd be able to keep busy." Indeed, so ingrained was the sentiment that when it turned out she was *not* busy, *and that she was enjoying it,* she felt anxious, as though she had somehow transgressed.

"You're going to feel bad if you're not busy," she was warned, and when she felt good she imagined there was something wrong with her. She was responding to what she was "supposed" to feel, not her authentic feeling. Society (and tradition, family, doctors, ministers, government) is always telling us what our response should be, and we are somehow queasy if our genuine response is something altogether different.

A tennis-loving friend quit his corporate job to go into business for himself. He could structure his own hours, and he promised himself that when it was time for the U.S. Open, he would watch it all on television and do his work in the early mornings and late evenings.

At noon on the first day of last year's Open, he found himself suddenly jumping from his couch, overcome by guilt. "I should be doing something else," he thought. "I should be working."

He was laughing at himself when he told me the story.

"Would you have felt guilty if you had actually been at the matches," I asked him, "instead of just watching them on television?"

He paused, considering. "Absolutely not."

"When you listen to music at home, do you find you can sit through an entire symphony?"

"Rarely, if ever."

"But if you're at a concert?"

"No trouble at all. A symphony *and* a concerto, with enormous pleasure."

It was, I told him, a matter of entrainment. When he was alone, he was entrained with society's inculcated rhythm, and his guilt was society's reprimand for "wasting time."

But when he was at the tennis stadium or concert hall, he was entraining not only with the sport or the music, but also with the audience, all of whom (having paid their good money for the event) were "permitted" to enjoy themselves, and therefore so was he.

The same event. The same "free" time. Yet in one instance anxiety, in the other, pleasure.

Society allows us to go to a game or a concert with others, but frowns when we watch or listen by ourselves.

It is very important to give yourself time to be alone doing something you really like, no matter what anybody says. It's okay to not take your kids to the ballgame, okay to not spend each evening with your spouse; okay to skip the family picnic, or to go left when everybody else insists you go right. The point again is to achieve a *balance*. It's your time. Make sure you give it to yourself, and don't allow interruptions or other activities to take precedence.

Listening to music, taking a hike in nature, reading fiction or poetry, woodworking or quilting, or lying on a lawn in the evening looking at the stars are all activities we can do quietly and alone, as long as we remember to be "present," and not do them just to busy our hands or to escape feeling. Many of us don't know what we like to do by ourselves because we haven't spent enough quiet time alone. When we're alone, we get bored or restless. So it's back to busyness as quickly as possible.

Why is it that time for ourselves is so low on our list of priorities? I think it's because so many of us feel ourselves "unworthy" of this "indulgence"—and society agrees with us. Our parents complain of our "loafing" when we're not engaged in an activity; our bosses scream at us when we stare into space; our spouses criticize us if we're "not there for them."

Where does that leave us when we're alone? Feeling guilty.

Yet Thoreau has eloquently shown us how vital solitude is, and Rilke says, "A good marriage is that in which each appoints the other guardian of his solitude, and shows him this confidence, the greatest in his power to bestow."

"I need some space" is an argument often heard in domestic battles; I believe "I need some time" is just as valid, and in many ways less threatening.

Most of us don't know how to use time alone and run from solitude. But care of the self is the groundwork for any relationship, and self-esteem comes not from others but from within.

Solitude takes practice. It requires facing down loneliness and realizing that there is nothing more important you can do. Far from being an "indulgence," quiet, solitary contemplation—"doing nothing"—is as restorative as any elixir. Solitary time leads to health. Without it, time spent with others is less full.

Solitary time is the doorway to our spirituality, when the self opens up to a place both timeless and time-full. The key to finding it is contemplation.

We have discussed the rhythms of time to which we entrain, and the process of expanding the moment. Exploration of feeling and understanding the self (which is necessary to feeling comfortable with oneself, in solitude or at any time) are best reached through the practice of meditation.

Meditation encourages this expansion and brings us into a more profound experience of the moment, as we entrain to a universal rhythm found deeply within. It requires practice to develop the sense of just being present in the unfolding rhythm of the universe. Often there is concern about "doing it right," but this is usually just the mind creating resistance with thoughts, instead of allowing us to ease into the moment.

Meditation enables each of us, alone, in solitude, to decompress from the societal and individual rhythms that keep us moving so quickly. It is about slowing down until there is really nothing happening, nothing to be doing—just watching the breath rise and fall, watching our thoughts come and go. Experiencing just being, without any need for doing.

Meditation is a difficult task for those of us who are focused on the everyday working of the modern world. We rely on a quick and attentive mind and feel uncomfortable trying to turn off or not react to our thoughts.

So when we begin to meditate, the mind resists and demands our attention. One thought after another arises. We start to think about where we have to be in an hour, and before we realize it, we have developed a whole story line about what will take place, what might go wrong, why we're upset with someone, etc. And all the while we're just sitting, unable to be present because the mind is off in the future, or back in the past. Practice is surely necessary. Time is needed.

Remember that meditation is not about reaching some altered state of consciousness or having visions or becoming someone other than yourself. It is simply about being present in this moment.

The Sufis use the word "remembrance" to mean a return to an earlier state of being that is without the rush and judgmental mind that is usually operating. Watch infants when they nurse or play. You can sense their bliss. It comes from simply being present in this moment. Nowhere to go, not trying to be anything else, simply present.

Meditation becomes less difficult if we allow ourselves to relax into the moment, because there is nothing to do. To start, all that's needed is giving yourself some time alone. Simply focusing on the breath as it rises and falls is sufficient. When we react by thinking we're "wasting time" or if we feel bored, we are simply experiencing the entrainment patterns to which we have become habituated.

Give yourself fifteen to twenty minutes each day for meditation. It will significantly affect how you feel. I find that it is like sounding a beautiful tone each morning, which sets up a rhythm that persists throughout the day. Sure, my mind sometimes races or I long to get busy. For me, meditation can be easy; often it's a struggle. Yet I never doubt the worth of the struggle. I am always aware that when I am meditating regularly, the rhythmic pattern of my life flows more smoothly.

Begin meditation on your own simply by sitting in a chair or on a cushion. It's best to sit upright with your back straight so that you stay alert and don't succumb to sleepiness. Simply watch the breath and silently repeat the word "rising" with the in-breath, and the word "falling" with the out-breath. Or you can count each breath until ten, then repeat the process over and over. The method is less important than the committment to time in your life for stillness.

Don't worry about getting it right. Theresa, whose story I told in Chapter Six, had never heard of meditation, yet her daily ritual of sitting with herself opened a sense of presence and grace that was as deep as any other kind of meditation.

To develop regular meditation practice, it is often helpful to find a group or class that meditates (while meditating, you'll be both alone and with others). The group sets up a rhythmic entrainment field that can support developing this practice.

Meditation is as profound as any teacher, and if you can get comfortable with it, you will find your life dramatically affected, as mine has been.

"Be like a flower," Thich Nhat Hanh advises. "Be there. Smile."

Sit quietly, I tell my class. Breathe deeply. Watch your breath. Count your breath. Experience it. Come home to it. Sit and breathe and let time flow, with no engagement of your mind, no thought—just awareness.

The question "Awareness of *what?*"—as Ram Dass explains—is

the wrong question. Just awareness, the way "mindfulness" means being away from mind.

We're describing being in the present. Let joy and pain and fear and life and death commingle in you, as it does in all presents.

Take your time. Don't run. Impatience signifies denial, boredom signals fear.

You will stop when it is time.

Many people I know find that journal writing each day can be a remarkable exploration of the self. The journal is shown to no one; there are no rules to what you write.

Each day, at a regular time (first thing in the morning or just before bed), write up your experiences of the day, how you feel, or any thoughts that arise. This can be an extremely profound way to reach within, to help sort through and clear the issues in our life.

Elizabeth, a friend, says that she has been doing this for over twenty years and would never miss a day. It's like making a date to come into rhythm with yourself, she says, to be present as a listener to what's going on beneath the surface.

Some people feel they need help in understanding themselves. They are anxious about time spent alone or unstructured time. Journal writing or meditation seems too difficult because they find their mind too active with troubling and perplexing thoughts. There is no sense of quieting the mind, only continued mental chatter and relentless waves of emotion.

Psychotherapy and psychoanalysis are methods of getting in touch with ourselves, overcoming our fears, and understanding our motivations, but the trouble with such therapy is that it describes our psychological patterns based on what happened in the past, and we tend to use this as a crutch in the present. Therapy labels us as withdrawers, reactors, or obsessives. It shows us how our parents' treatment of us when we were children shaped the way we are as adults, and we can legitimately rationalize that, because we were unloved as children, we are now incapable of love; or that because we were emotionally or physically abandoned in the past, we are afraid of close relationships in the present.

There is no question that therapy is a tremendously valuable and true way to understand our behavior. We gain great insight into our inner nature in ways that help us deal with the issues that life presents to us, and the way we interact with them. I have always found that in working with clients, therapy often plays a critical role in dealing with stress and many core life issues.

But while most of the common forms of psychological therapy can profoundly affect the way we behave in our lives, I think it can be a convenient way of avoiding what we are really feeling in the present moment. We blame what we feel on our ingrained psychological patterns, and so avoid the feelings in the present. Once again, we are lost in the story line or drama of our life instead of showing up in the authenticity of present feelings.

I've seen many clients under a great deal of stress go to psychotherapists, yet their stress seems to remain. They know *why* they are stressed, and in many ways that makes the stress easier to incorporate into their lives, but it continues. If there is a crisis, then the old patterns emerge, and they react as they would have before the therapy began.

We need to make sure that all forms of therapy incorporate the past and the present, as many already have. We must come to a place when we can feel this moment only and fully, when we are mindful of our state of being in the present, not of past wounds or past patterns.

The key is to become slowed down enough to be *here,* where we can act rather than react, feel the present without being consumed by the past, and not run from the present into the old psychological patterns and modes of behavior that have crippled us before.

When we slow down enough to stay in our present emotion, then, and only then, will we be able to break old patterns and form a new self, a new authenticity. We will learn to react in new ways to situations that therapy caused us to predict from old patterns of behavior.

By being authentic in this moment, we will gain a new mastery of life—we will own the past rather than be owned by it, we can control the present rather than let the past be superimposed upon us. We will have the capacity to approach each new situation—indeed, life itself—however we choose, free from past chains and the fear of the future.

During my seminars given in a country setting, I often suggest that people spend an hour just sitting within a six-foot-diameter circle. No props. No talking. Just being. Initially, people experience boredom, chafe at wasting all that time, or feel their fears rising.

Inevitably, though, people have wonderful experiences as time slows down. Long forgotten memories of childhood surface. There is deep relaxation, a feeling of being free in time.

Try it. Sit with your back against a tree or find some spot in nature where you can be alone for a bit. An hour can work wonders. So can many hours, spent on wilderness journeys (with other people, though with lots of time alone), camping, or taking day long hikes around a lake or by the sea. "Dwell as near as possible to the channel in which your life flows," says Thoreau.

Nature is that channel. In nature is the preservation of our soul.

There are other ways to be alone that, while not as profound as meditation or hours spent in nature, also offer enormous rewards to the soul:

Take a bubble bath.
Exercise.
Go somewhere by yourself. (Where? Anywhere.)
Listen to music. Play music yourself.
Go for a walk in the woods.
Go for a walk in the city.
Sit on a porch and watch the sky.
Lie in bed and watch the light from outside play on the ceiling.
Read a novel. You might try a novel by John Yount called *Toots in Solitude,* a glorious analysis of our twin needs for aloneness and for love.

Read poetry. Here you will entrain with the poet's rhythm, quite a different one from prose.

Write in a journal, knowing you will not show it to anyone else.

Being alone "doing nothing" is an art, and like all art you need to practice it to reach your highest potential.

Do not stint. Do not consider it a waste of time. Do not feel unworthy.

The self is sacred, both as individual and as part of the flow of the universe in and out of time.

CHAPTER NINE

RELATIONSHIPS

———

There is an old story that, if we were to treat
every person we met as if they were the
Messiah, then it wouldn't make any difference
if they weren't.
—NOAH BENSHEA

WHEN TWO PEOPLE are in the same rhythm, the relationship is good. When they're not, arguments or worse can ensue.

In order to have a truly clear and full communication with another person, we must take the time to be with that person, for time is the core element in any relationship. This sharing of concentrated, focused time is the only way to reach a shared rhythm. Once we find it, we entrain into the rhythm, knowing instinctively that our partner is with us.

But too many times we just connect with the most superficial aspects of another person—their looks, charm, or title—realizing too late that these are masks behind which lies the true self: Handsome may not be what handsome is; charm can hide enormous insecurity or rage; a title says little or nothing about a person's inner worth.

The mask often appears as the role we play in society: doctor, lawyer, teacher, policeman, mother, father, CEO. Yet if we don't take the time to look beneath the mask, the rhythms we encounter are society's rhythms, not the authentic rhythms of the inner person.

A few years ago, a toy manufacturer making dolls that looked like Miss America was sued by the manufacturer of the Barbie doll for copying that beloved image. A news commentator suggested that the problem was the other way round: Miss America contestants were trying to look like Barbie dolls! Too often in our society we try to impose a superficial look on our role models that has no relation to their natural appearance.

A CEO, tough and authoritative in the boardroom, actually masks deep insecurity; "the life of the party," when faced with a potentially deep relationship, becomes tongue-tied; the bumbling worker is superb in a crisis.

In order to find out where someone is "coming from," we need to harmonize our rhythm with his—and again, for that we need time.

Rhythm is the great communicator, as is easily seen in dancing; a couple dancing together is drawn closer, and their coming into sync helps ignite sexual passion, or a rapprochement when the relationship is going through difficult times. And nowhere is harmony more important than in marriage—or indeed in any intimate relationship.

The Greeks know that, which is why their weddings last for days. There is dancing every day; and the entrainment of the community—everyone joined in rhythm—supports the couple in their own entrainment. Many societies use music and dance as a regular part of community gatherings. Our society is out of touch with this; our current form of music and dance is so chaotic, it often doesn't bring us into rhythm with another person, but rather reflects the frenzy and alienation of modern life.

Sex, of course, is the ultimate coming together of rhythms (and how frustrating and bitter it can be when the rhythms don't mesh!), but even so simple a thing as a bridge game can show you the benefits of entrainment. In tennis, a friend tells me, when he and his wife are equally concentrated on the game, they share a special closeness, even though they're separated by the net!

* * *

Yet how we run from shared rhythm! How afraid we seem to be of truly entraining with another!

Usually, early in a relationship, the excitement—the turn-on—compels us, and we don't investigate the everyday rhythms that can bind us into a profound partnership. It's the thrill of the chase, the conquest, the climax that initially brings us together.

But relationships based on sex are bound to fail if we're bent on conquering the object of our love, rather than striving for a true union, a communion that can only exist when "I" and "you" disappear and we become, truly, "we."

I believe the reason we run from deep relationships is that we're uncomfortable with the process of investigating the deep, inner, everyday rhythms in ourselves. We don't want to slow for fear of what we may find within ourselves.

Introspection, we tell ourselves, is nonproductive, particularly when work is going well, we're making enough money, and one sex partner is as good as another.

When the sexual excitement dies down, however, a different and more essential excitement can take its place: the excitement of really getting to know your partner—in thought, in soul, in heart, in feeling, in *humanness*.

Such excitement comes in time—in *spending* time.

One of the great myths about marriage is that a union founded in genuine love will overcome all obstacles; that such a relationship will "take care of itself."

Not so. In my own first marriage, I found that wasn't true. Work, study, helping others, making money—all came between me and my wife, and I thought that since we loved each other, there was no need to *be* with each other. And so we weren't together, even when we were in each other's presence. We were self-involved, in different rhythms. We just didn't take time to slow down, to investigate, to work with each other and for each other toward harmony. Creating time together was low on our priority list. It should have come first if the marriage was to last.

Our focus became the children; we believed that commitment to them would sustain the marriage. But commitment to each other and time with each other are the true elements that are needed for a healthy relationship.

Slowing down enough to feel someone else's rhythm as well as your own is what timeshifting is all about. One must start, I think, by realizing that relationships, like time itself, are cyclical, and must be viewed on a long scale. Eros ends and is rekindled; traumas occur and pass away; affection is sublimated to outside activities, then once again becomes predominant. Love ebbs and flows, not necessarily for one at the same time as for the other.

Looking at a relationship as long-term and cyclical means knowing that problems will inevitably occur and you will be able to navigate *(not* circumnavigate) the pitfalls. It means accepting differences, recognizing discordant rhythms, and attempting always to get back into sync with each other—even when entraining seems impossible.

Some events are particularly fractious. Doing a budget, for example, packing up the summer house, deciding on the use of leisure time, disciplining the kids, putting together toys for Christmas, even deciding when and where to make love.

Arguments flare when rhythms don't mesh. When we get angry, we tend to go up-tempo to get our point across, almost always making things worse instead of better. We shout, scream, slam doors, stomp away, even hurl things.

Our rhythms clash; we clash. And sometimes, to avoid these fights, we turn instead to a kind of distant politeness, as though we were strangers, not longtime lovers, husband and wife.

When this happens, there is no presence. Even though we may be sitting side by side, we are as far apart as people separated by an ocean, and we work so hard at avoiding each other that inevitably we avoid life, and live in a kind of remoteness where everything is dim and gray, a half-world.

Half-worlds are boring, and boredom leads to the death of any relationship. Sometimes this comes about because we are trying to avoid conflict; at other times, it happens because of inertia—an unvaried routine where sameness is as fatal as poison. The same conversations, the same TV shows, the same pattern of the days, the same regimen in lovemaking.

Boredom puts us into a contracted state when moments become shorter, not longer, and then we need outside experience (or drugs like cocaine or television) to provide our kicks. Emotional hurt can do this, too. In a long-term relationship, when we know each other well enough to know what really hurts our partner and we use it as a weapon, the injured party will often flee into new experience rather than work through the old.

So we start looking for high-intensity experiences, like a love affair, where the excitement is in itself our gratification. In the vast majority of cases where a marriage is broken up by an affair, the "straying" spouse does not end up with the affair partner, for the spouse brings with him/her all the dissatisfactions that made him/her cheat in the first place. We tend to wander from experience to experience, looking for ever more intense highs. But when we find them, they are usually fleeting and emotionally unfulfilling.

I don't mean to sound like a preacher here, particularly when it comes to affairs, because I don't believe there is any "right" way a relationship should be—monogamy, serial monogamy, multiple relationships, or no relationships at all. I am simply saying that a relationship is genuine only when it is not part of a fantasy, when we are present with the other person and know who he or she is.

When I'm in a contracted state (and we all enter them from time to time), I generally avoid intimate contact. I feel uninspired, down on myself, frustrated by life. Yet instead of letting myself feel this, I turn to fantasy (generally television-inspired fantasy) and I want a "television woman" or a feat of daring-do to turn me on.

When I'm able to slow down, to let my emotions quiet, the place in which I find myself is painful, but when I can allow myself to experience those feelings of boredom, frustration, unworthiness, anger, etc., the feelings pass and I get into a state that is deeper and more authentic.

It's at this point that I can feel most blessed in my relationships, and my life. It's then that moments seem long again. It's then I am at peace.

Couples who want to stay together, but who cannot seem to get in rhythm, who continue to fight, who wish to "spend the time" but don't know where to find it, can turn to a number of remedies.

Psychologists Gay and Kathlyn Hendricks have worked extensively with couples, getting them simply to breathe in sync together as a first step toward entrainment, a first step toward communication. Remember, we need to find a shared rhythm with our partner.

Stephen and Ondrea Levine have taken this further by asking one person to lie down and breathe, and his partner to just sit next to him and observe the breathing. Next she puts a hand on his stomach to *feel* the breathing, and tries to match it in herself, breathing at the same rhythm. The Levines have found that the bonding that ensues is enormously beneficial. It helps the couple begin to work on deeper issues that result from being out of sync with your partner.

Harville Hendrix, founder of the Institute of Relationship Therapy and author of *Getting the Love You Want,* has developed a process he calls Imago Therapy. I believe his approach to be the best in working with relationships.

It is a process of mirroring conversation, to have each party *listen* to what the other is saying; and when they listen, they slow down, instead of letting the pace escalate into an argument.

It works like this:

Wife: "Next time we go out together on one of our 'dates,' I'd like it if you'd bring flowers and show up on time."

Husband: "What you're saying is, you want me to bring flowers. Is that what you said?"

Wife: "No. I also said you should show up on time."

Husband: "So you want me to bring flowers and make sure we go out to somewhere you like?"

Wife: "No. I also want you to show up on time."

It may seem too obvious that the couple is miscommunicating, but remarkably, after listening to couples go through the process with Dr. Hendrix, it's apparent that the process repeats itself over and over again.

The husband, though trying to listen, has heard some but not all of what the wife was saying. Usually, the part he hasn't heard is about the issue over which they often disagree. The wife is able to correct him, and he has slowed himself down enough by listening to let some of his own anger dissipate. He knows that when he has fully understood his wife, it will be his turn to speak, and his wife's turn to mirror what he has said.

This example only begins to touch on the work of Imago Therapy, and there are many other methods used to help in the process of creating understanding through enhanced communication.

When our communication is clear and smooth, we are in rhythm with each other, and it's obvious there is no problem. Yet in the continual arguments couples have, the pattern of discord usually repeats itself, and the arguments sound alike. "Here we go again," is a common plaint of one partner or the other.

Miscommunication requires that you slow down to find a shared rhythm upon which to build harmony and understanding. You need to fight the inclination to raise the decibel and speed your reactions in order to deal with your frustration and anger about not being heard by your partner.

By slowing down, words become your force and your focus. Since the rhythm of most arguments is one of escalation, using the Imago technique will enable you to de-escalate before emotional reactions (along with shouts, threats, ultimatums) overwhelm you and hearing becomes impossible.

Margo Anand's work with Tantric Ecstacy is important in understanding the relationship of sex and an expanded moment. Since modern sex is too often a rushed event, even after marriage, she advises and teaches couples to fully explore their sensuality together.

It is not just the sexual act itself that's important, she teaches, but rather fully allowing ourselves to explore our own rhythms and the combining of those rhythms with another's in the midst of sensuality. Opening ourselves to pleasure for ourselves and our partner, a dance of giving and receiving, when we are present for each other, can lead us into realms of sexuality that we really long for, yet actually avoid in our haste to reach a climax. The joy is in the moment, yet we so often miss it in our rush to move on.

For optimum sex, the courting process is vital. You should pay real homage to your partner with words and small actions, first by admiring their clothes (through feel as well as description) as you remove them from your partner, then in paying loving attention to every part of your partner's body. The point is not to invest in the act but *in the process,* in being present through all the glorious elements of sex before orgasm—indeed, Anand stipulates that orgasm need not happen at all.

Scent, music, oils, food, flowers, feathers—all can add to the ecstacy by enhancing every sense, and the sexual moment can last, in linear time, for hours.

The use of ritual can be a tremendous help in overcoming trouble, sexual or otherwise.

For example, since most arguments most frequently occur when one spouse or the other arrives home, many people I know simply sit in their car for a few minutes before entering the house in order to allow them to adapt—or at least be more open to adapting—to the different rhythm they're likely to find inside. They are able to slow down; the cares of the day are allowed to recede; they're able to get more quickly into the present.

A friend told me that he had been in important meetings all day long, and had come home without pausing, to find his wife anxiously awaiting his decision on renovations for the kitchen.

"I exploded at her," he admitted sheepishly. "I simply couldn't handle another decision, so I took it out on her. She had every right to be mad at me."

His wife had a different outlook on the incident. "I shouldn't have hit him with it right when he came home," she told me when I asked her about their quarrel. "But I was excited and needed his help. When he didn't respond, I got furious. It was stupid. I should have waited till he cooled down. We should both have had a drink—then talked."

Simpler rituals—like a good morning or good night kiss, the sharing of dishwashing, the drink before dinner, mutual meditation (for meditation can be powerful when it is entrained with another's rhythm), the taking of an hour each evening for quiet conversation—can bring harmony to a relationship—as long as these simple acts are recognized as important, with both partners experiencing them, and are not just performed by rote or habit.

It's essential, too, to know that inevitable differences between you exist. Honor those differences—in many cases they're what attracted you to your partner in the first place. It's not enough to recognize them ("He's so much in the moment, he doesn't pick up his socks!"); you must accept them as fundamental aspects of your partner and thus allow your partner space for them without anger, sarcasm, condescension, or complaint.

Acceptance, which can only be achieved in a slowed rhythm, is just as important for outside, concrete realities as for personality differences. The person who works in crisis situations shouldn't be required to socialize. Dinner out and a movie can bring peace to a person housebound all day.

Of course you should discuss aspects of your partner that irritate you, but realize that some traits can't be changed, that there are some traits your partner doesn't *want* to change, and if they are part of someone you love, then honor them as you honor their bearer. And allow your partner individual time without upset. All of us have different time lines, and inevitably they will not always be in sync.

A man in a recent workshop told me he had been married for fifty-two years to the same woman and "had not spent a boring moment."

I didn't believe him.

But boredom, though it occurs in all relationships (indeed, is *necessary* in all relationships; imagine a relationship with nothing but stimulation!), need not be fatal.

Many people I know tell me they've grown accustomed to each other, though they're no longer excited by each other, and in this fashion their relationship goes on. But inertia is an unsatisfactory basis for a continuing relationship.

My friends Robert and Judith, who have been married over twenty years and have a relationship that seems (like wine) to get better with age, have a deep and active commitment to keeping the relationship alive. They've been through the difficult times, fought their battles, experienced the boredom—yet they stay present with each other through talk and adventure, and the relationship stays new.

As we've seen in the chapter on Self, the way to combat boredom is to sit through it until it dissipates, and this applies to couples as well. In relationships, a discussion of why the relationship has grown flat, a *feeling* of it until the flatness vanishes, is a good technique, but there's a lot more you can do to turn it into the creative force it can be.

Boredom in relationships stems from a monotony of rhythm, a sameness that permeates every day of the relationship. So the first thing to do is vary the rhythm, speed it up or slow it down, do something *different*.

Make a date with your wife and treat her as though you were courting her for the first time. Take your husband to a place he has never been. Plan special occasions, second honeymoons, treats, silly and serious presents. Dress in new clothes, wear your hair differently, make love in a different room, and in a different position.

A man I know met his wife returning from work on a bus. He had prepared a picnic basket, and they dined together at twilight on a blanket in a nearby field. When they got home, he asked her to wait outside—and he went in to light preplaced candles on all the steps leading upstairs to the bedroom.

In another kind of surprise meeting, a husband greeted his wife as she stepped off an early morning train from Westport to New York City. She had called him from their Connecticut summer house the night before, depressed by the recent death of her sister. He, already in the city, had recognized her distress, showed up at the train (she was coming into the city for a business meeting), and simply gave her a huge hug in the middle of Grand Central Station. "It's the nicest present I've ever gotten," she told him.

A couple who are close friends of mine play a game called "Swept Away, Whisked Away" as an antidote to the boredom of the refrain, "What do you want to do?" "I don't know. What do *you* want to do?" Whenever they got into that rhythm, they ended up doing something mediocre.

"Swept Away" makes one person the leader for a weekend; "Whisked Away" makes one of you the leader for a few hours. In both cases, the leader gets to pick what he or she wants to do, and the other must follow. In the "Whisked Away" times, it might be a trip to the ballet, which she loves and he doesn't; or to a ballgame— vice versa. But if the game is played fairly, the words "I don't like it" are forbidden, and it's the *act* of partnership, of shared experience, of *pure* experience, that is the governing factor. Nothing has to be repeated, nothing done regularly. The fun comes in the action, not the result.

Once, for "Swept Away," the wife told her husband to pack some light clothing. "We're going south," she told him on the way to the airport, "but I'm not telling you where."

The first leg of the journey was to Orlando, where they had to change planes. "I'll know as soon as we board the plane and the pilot makes his announcement," her husband said.

"Maybe," she answered.

In the airport, she blindfolded him, then left him momentarily while she spoke to the pilot.

When the plane took off, the pilot heeded her request. "Destination unknown," he announced.

This is not necessarily a good formula for all of life, but from time to time it can be thrilling.

Most relationships, of course, do not have the intensity or intimacy of spouses or lovers. But in all kinds of relationships, slowing down will enhance our own pleasure by allowing us to be more fully in the moment.

Most of us, for example, use the handshake as a perfunctory gesture, something forced on us by convention and speeded up by society. Yet if we take time with the handshake, looking into the other person's eyes, feeling the warmth of his grasp, *connecting,* then a bond is established and the relationship is taken immediately to a deeper level.

Other countries don't rely on handshakes for greetings or farewells. The French and Italians kiss both cheeks; Indians and Japanese bow; Egyptians embrace. All these are used, probably unwittingly, as a means of slowing down; too often, Americans rush through the greeting so they can "get down to business."

Since we are entrained with our society's rhythm, where "time is of the essence," we grow impatient with unpunctuality, and lateness is a sin. This is particularly true in business, but applies to social situations as well.

Yet Americans Indians, living in circular time, come to meetings virtually when they please. Chieftains attending meetings held at the Bureau of Indian Affairs often arrive two or three days "late." In Argentina, a friend related, they make social appointments and then ask whether the event will take place on "American time" (punctually) or "Argentinean time," when they can show up an hour or so behind schedule.

We think such people are rude; they are wasting our time. But a trip to the Caribbean will, I assure you, change your perspective when you shift from American time to island time.

When I go to the Caribbean, I drive an open van, covered by a surrey, which looks much like the local taxis. On many occasions, tourists approach me and imperiously demand that I take their bags or tell them the charges for a trip into town.

I don't care that they take me for a taxi driver (on the Islands, it is a compliment), but their rudeness appalls me. No greeting, no contact—just a demand. I feel the way I suppose highway toll-takers must feel: indistinguishable from an automatic machine.

When I complained of this to my good friend Zedie, who *is* a taxi driver (a truly courteous man pleased to allow people to cut in front of him in traffic), and asked him how he could stand it on a daily basis, he laughed.

"Steph, you know, them people from the north," he explained. "It's cold up there. We from the south where it's warm. You have to move fast where it's cold, otherwise you freeze. So they don't bother with words like 'hello' or 'how are you?' But they good people all the same."

When people are "different" from us, or speak "a funny language," the problem becomes more acute. Dr. William S. Condon of the Boston School of Medicine has found that, among tribes speaking different dialects of the same language, when the dialects are in rhythm, there is peace; if not, wars ensue.

So it is in our lives. I sometimes think the Gulf War could have been prevented if Saddam Hussein had understood that, to a Westerner, twenty-four hours meant precisely twenty-four hours, and if we had realized that to him such an ultimatum meant approximately a day, but one with a flexible limit, since time is experienced differently in Middle Eastern cultures.

Being present means noticing not only tasks but also people we normally take for granted. I don't mean you should walk down the street greeting everyone you see. But we can contact the people we deal with in our community in a human way, a way that reminds us that we're all in this life together. Again, it's a small thing, but it helps us remember that we're all related.

When we were talking about this in a recent seminar, Bruce acknowledged his chagrin about the way he'd been treating the casual acquaintances in his life.

> I've been going to the same dry cleaners for years. Every time I go, there are these two lovely people—I think they're from Taiwan—and they couldn't be friendlier. They'll greet me with a really genuine smile and warmth: "Mr. Simmons, how are you?" And me—I'm usually saying, "Here's my laundry and ten bucks and good-bye." Never hello, or asking how they are.

What does it take—thirty seconds? two minutes?—to make contact with another human being? Not to "network," exchange life stories, or tell them all about your work—but to simply make contact. That amount of time won't stop anything in our life. But it will make our days a little richer. We feel better about ourselves when someone makes contact with us, greets us in a friendly way, or says with sincerity, "You're looking good today."

These types of greetings get ignored when we have no time, but they give us an opportunity to make each other feel good, to interact in a way that says we care for another individual.

As Christ says, "Do unto others as you would have them do unto you." We have the opportunity to create friendliness in our world by taking the time to greet each other as human beings, rather than as machines performing tasks. In India, when two people meet, they bow and say the word *Namaste,* which translated means, "I greet the divinity that resides in each of us." Or as Ram Dass says of this, "I greet the place that when you're in yours and I'm in mine, then we're both here together."

After all, we have all found ourselves living together on this planet, having no idea how we got here, each of us pursuing our dreams and enduring the hardships of life. Taking a moment to recognize and greet another human being can be beautiful and deeply meaningful to all of us. Certainly this type of interaction can help in healing much of the turmoil and alienation that is taking place in our society today.

Pir Vilayat Khan told me of a time he was at a mass gathering in India. On leaving, half the crowd went one way, half the other. He caught the eye of a sadhu, a wandering spiritual seeker, in the other group, and for a moment, as he describes it, their souls interlocked before they passed on. It was interaction on a fundamental human level, an acknowledgment of the simple truth that all men are brothers, and he has never forgotten it.

Someone in class described a meeting with an African whom he considered stupid because the African spoke so slowly. It was only when he got bested in a business deal that he realized that *all* Africans of that tribe spoke slowly. It was the African's rhythm that had made the Westerner misjudge his intelligence. If the Westerner had bothered to make contact, he would have recognized their difference in rhythm. Rushed, he lost out in business and in human contact.

In all relationships, casual or intimate, take the time to slow down and make contact. Being in the moment with another person is the richest reward for the human soul.

CHAPTER TEN

CHILDREN

Lamentably, there is too short an interval
between the time when one is too young and
the time when one is too old.
—Montesquieu

I AM PLAYING a Nintendo game with my teenage son. Though he is a good athlete, I can still best him in one-on-one basketball, but at this game I don't stand a chance. Actually, I haven't won a single game from him in over two years.

It's not that I don't try. I'm in the moment playing the game, concentrating; no distractions deter my purpose. Yet Dan wins as easily as ever, and I refuse his offer of a second game with the feeling that one frustration from a child per day is enough.

He has out-thought me, out-strategied me, *out-rhythmed* me. Yes. Out-rhythmed me. And with that epiphany, my resentment vanishes, replaced by a sense of regret.

In this area, I realize, I am not up to speed. But I wonder if speed is what I should be looking for. We create games and programs that develop skills in speed, believing that being able to perform ever faster will best prepare our children for their future. Will Dan's skill at Nintendo in some ways presage success in society? Will he become addicted to the speed? I worry. What if the rhythm of Nintendo, so much society's rhythm, becomes his main operating speed?

Fortunately, the two of us have devoted time to other rhythms. He also feels comfortable coming to a meditation session—not for long, but he's willing to give it a try. We play a lot of chess together so that we can interact at slower rhythms as well.

It's vital to teach our children to function well at different speeds and rhythms.

Eli, my youngest son, is three and a half. Recently, I had a different rhythmic experience with him.

Lying together on a bed early one morning, we heard a bird. Its call was four beats, then a twenty-second pause, then another four beats, and so on: a steady, curiously cheerful rhythm that captivated Eli. We began to play a game, trying with a motion of a hand to note when the first beat would begin again. For five to ten minutes we entrained with the bird, lost in its rhythm. I could sense the expanding of the moment, a slowing down that resulted from our mindful attention. I was thrilled to see how my young child could stay so concentrated and present.

It reminded me of a top I had bought him the year before, which, when spinning, emitted a steady drone. Eli was mesmerized by it. He would sit and stare at it for long periods of time, watching and listening, and when it lost speed he demanded that I wind it again. Here again, the moment was expanded. Here again, time, for Eli, had shifted into a slower, mindful rhythm that held him in thrall.

Both events showed me what is possible in teaching and training our children. It's so important that they learn, from the earliest age, to be mindful, to be present not only for the speed of Nintendo moments, but also for the slower rhythms of life.

Too often we prescribe entertainment with a rapid rhythm for our children: If a young child seems restless or bored, we rush to fill the time vacuum with a new game or diversion. Jazzy videotapes teach spelling and numbers; we sit our children in front of a television set to divert them, then buy the toys and games that are off-shoots of the show. Even when they're alone they're not alone. They have television to keep them company.

Is it any wonder that when they begin school, they listen to raucous CDs or watch TV while they do their homework? It's as though they *must* multi-tract, and we somehow feel it might be good training for the workplace in their future.

As soon as they come home from school, we ask our children not how they are, or what they're feeling, but how they've done on their test or what they've accomplished. Their teachers test not only the extent of their knowledge, but also how *fast* they can get what they know down on paper.

Yet why do tests have time limits? For the children's sake, to see how quickly they can come up with the answers (rather than, given time, how many answers they know)? Or is it for the teachers' convenience? Two or three hours, and the monitoring chore will be over.

What if we gave five hours for a test that the fastest student could easily answer in three? Wouldn't that more fairly reflect how much each student had learned? Wouldn't it prevent the kid with poor handwriting or slower brain function (to say nothing of the more reflective kid, who wants to *think through* her essay answer) from coming home dejected instead of inspired, as my son Rahm once did, because he "just didn't have time" to complete his examination?

I asked him how he had done on a test we had studied for together the previous evening. His upset was clear, yet I was surprised, since he had known the material so well the night before. He told me he had known the answers to all the questions; in fact, of the ones he completed, he answered every question correctly. But he tends to read slowly, so questions (even though he knew the answers) were left unanswered, and he did poorly.

This reminded me of my high school and college years when I remember having occasional dreams (or nightmares, at the time) when I would awake with a start to the fear that I had overslept and missed the test I had been studying for. Why is there a time pressure in all of this?

A friend told me about her son, who is learning disabled and attends special classes. I could sense the stigma she, and I'm sure her son, felt was associated with this. As we discussed the situation, it was obvious that her son was extremely intelligent, yet simply operated at a different speed from what his teachers demanded. Her child was not stupid or a malcontent. Rather, he learned and expressed himself at a different rhythm. Perhaps he was an Einstein or a Picasso, for brilliance is about creativity and depth of understanding, not about the speed of performance.

Time-restricted tests measure information—how much has the child mastered, how quickly can he bring it to mind. What they don't measure is *knowledge* (a far different thing), since knowledge demands reflection, and reflection demands a slowing down in time. Indeed, adults today talk of an Information Highway, not a Knowledge Highway.

What if we taught mindfulness as well as arithmetic, scheduled rest time in grade school and high school, and encouraged children to listen to music, not necessarily play it? We don't because there "isn't enough time."

From an early age, we entrain our children into society's pace. "My Suzy's not a year old and already she knows thirty-seven words," a mother told me. "My kid could roll over by four months," another countered.

But what's the race? As parents, we are elated to see our children perform better than average. We use time as a measure for ourselves and push them faster.

We mold our kids into our rhythm and, as Alice Miller has so trenchantly pointed out in *Prisoners of Childhood,* we push them, too, to be replicas of us, to like what we like, to strive for our goals, to live up to our standards.

Such parents are future-oriented ("You did okay, but can you do better next time?"). Ram Dass calls the practice "somebody training," because the parents want to sculpt their child into a person who will delight the parents, who will satisfy the demands of the adult parents' ego with high performance. But actually we are denying the child access to his own core, his own self.

You'll have read enough by now to know that what we are doing is keeping the child from the present moment. We are forcing him to live in the future, and in essence we are preventing him from living in the now.

Yet young children have no sense of time. They, like animals (which never learn time), can locate themselves in space from infancy, but the words "later," or "soon," or concepts like "tomorrow" or "next year" are meaningless even to a four-year-old. Past, present, and future are unknown to small children. They live in the moment—and we try to yank them out of it as soon as we can.

My own life has been heavily influenced by the fact that there was always a high level of expectation in my family. It seemed to me I would never satisfy my parents' desire for my accomplishing more. High achievers themselves, they congratulated me on my accomplishments (for my accomplishments in a deep sense were theirs), but I always felt I could do more, and, when I failed, I had failed not only myself but them as well. In life, we experience both successes and failures; they come with living. Yet, to this day, when I fail either in business or in personal relationships, it seems that failure is all that exists, obscuring anything positive I've done.

A seven-year-old girl asked what time it was. "Twenty minutes to ten," her mother replied. "No," said her daughter. "I want to know what time it is now, not in twenty minutes."

No doubt you've had the experience of driving in a car with your children as they incessantly demand, "When are we going to get there?" Doesn't it seem contradictory to my observation that children are always in the present?

The cause of this is interesting. We are the ones who have announced the destination, put it into our children's heads that we are going somewhere. The problem is that they can't wait, they expect the destination "now." They are present. It's that the destination isn't present yet.

Instead of always imposing our rhythms on our children, we should let ourselves be drawn into theirs from time to time. Obviously, they'll eventually have to learn to entrain to society's rhythm—

school and work are essential parts of their lives—but we shouldn't fall into the trap of believing that a child's slow rhythm is worthless. Quite the opposite. It can be invaluable, for him and for us.

Our creativity is intimately associated with our natural internal rhythm. (During childhood, this rhythm must be strengthened and nurtured, rather than merely serve as a way to train a child to march at a faster pace.)

Teach your child to meditate. Designate a certain hour on weekends as nap time—for you as well as for your child. Read to her before bedtime. Sit and rock with your infant. Take walks and stop to smell the flowers or study an acorn or a leaf. Teach your child slow songs, play slow games. All of these will not only slow you two down, but also will bring you into a closeness with your child that no Nintendo game can equal.

I remember a morning when Eli and I were putting together a jigsaw puzzle. It was a sunlit fall day, the windows were open, and a gentle breeze caressed us, but Eli was concentrating only on the puzzle.

It was so simple—probably no more than twelve large pieces—that even a three-year-old could do it, which was precisely the point. Eli put it together with great glee, then broke it up and ordered me to "help" him again. I did, and did it yet a third time, when I realized that the activity was not boring, and that I was in a state of such blissfulness that I wanted the puzzle-making never to end.

The combination of the sun and breeze, the lovely fall light, and Eli's own powerful intensity created in me a deep sense of kinship with my child. At first I had resisted, because I had "more important" things to do. Yet once I allowed myself to be just with him and had entrained to his rhythm, we shared a wonderfully expanded moment.

In such moments we share a deep love that creates the true basis for our relationships with our children. After all, what else is there? Perhaps our sense of self-importance or guilt suggests we get busy or productive. But can busyness or productivity really be more important?

* * *

To experience such moments, as meaningful for the child as they are for the parent, we must be *with* our children, both physically and emotionally.

Physically comes first.

President Clinton's Secretary of Education, Richard Riley, reported that the fact that families don't have enough time to help their children learn was the major problem with American education. Not the lack of adequate schooling. The lack of adequate parenting.

The more time we spend with our children, the better off our children will be. I don't mean time spent in the same room doing our own work, paying no attention to our kids. Nor do I mean sitting with them by the television set watching *Sesame Street*. I mean being with them in the moment, *listening* to them, *hearing* them, taking their views, their questions, their needs seriously, and responding with seriousness, even if the questions seem funny and their opinions "childish."

When an infant has trouble sleeping, let it cry, advises Dr. Richard Ferber in *Solve Your Child's Sleep Problems*. But I believe that a child's sleeplessness is our problem, not hers, and too often we are asking an infant to adapt to our rhythm rather than her own. Sometimes some adaptation is necessary, of course, but for the most part why not let the child set her own sleep patterns rather than try to impose ours?

When a four-year-old cries, our usual response is to try to get her to stop. Why? Mostly because it makes us uncomfortable, both to see and hear our child crying and because we sense we are failing her in some way. If we can slow down, listen, sense what the problem is, then we can act appropriately instead of reacting to the tears.

Begin by just being with her and asking what's wrong. She probably won't be able to tell you directly, so you'll have to get to the reason through questions ("Did Daddy forget to read to you even though he promised?" "Is Mommy talking too long on the phone?"). The point is not to belittle, or scoff, or be sarcastic. The point is to listen, and to *hear*.

We tend to minimize our kids, to not really pay attention. We try to merely "handle" them, instead of really being with them.

A dramatic difference occurs when we truly come into rhythm with our children. I can watch Eli act like a brat or a tyrant, resisting my entreaties to do what I say. Yet the moment I slow down and switch to his rhythm, invariably he becomes the most adorable and wonderful child on the planet. It's this way with all children: Open our hearts and time to them, and they will become fully present with us and show us the beautiful side of their being.

When you're with a child in the moment, treating her like a human being, with dignity and respect, you're building her confidence and self-esteem.

I know a single mother who gave her daughter everything except herself. The perfect nanny, the "right" school, any toy or game she wanted—all were Rosie's.

The mother was a lawyer, who, as much out of guilt over the divorce, as well as a sense of "I'll show him!," worked long hours to make sure her child had only "the best." She usually arrived home exhausted, and when she played with her daughter, she did so perfunctorily, anxious to be doing something else—such as going to bed with a good book.

"I *hate* Rosie," she told me one day. "She's a spoiled brat. She doesn't appreciate what I've done for her. All she wants are more toys and more attention."

"Do you spend enough time with her?" I asked.

"Absolutely. Every weekend we do something together. I take her to the ballet or the circus. Even go with her and her friends for a picnic."

"Why not plan to spend a weekend doing nothing? Just the two of you together?"

"Doing nothing?" Her expression was one of horror. "I wouldn't know what to *do with her!*"

I explained my theory of spontaneous time. She listened reluctantly, even suspiciously, but in the end she agreed to try it.

Mother and child made no plans for the next weekend, just hung out together—and the result, the mother reported, was the best time they had ever spent. With no distractions, the mother simply focused on her child, listened to her for perhaps the first time, and realized that Rosie was a smart, caring, lonely little girl who needed attention and was bitterly resentful when her mother wasn't there.

They took a walk in the park, wandered over to the zoo, then the carousel. They had fun and laughed and just let the time pass.

Rosie's mother put timeshifting principles into practice, cut down on night work, and spent more spontaneous time with her daughter. However, the damage that had already been done ran deep, and it did take time for her to gain her daughter's trust. But eventually, she noticed a dramatic change. Her daughter *wanted* to be with her. The mother's guilt vanished, to be replaced by joy.

When parents are absent, there is inevitably a lack of rhythm between parent and child. If we don't timeshift for ourselves, making more time for our children and less for our work, then our children will be disrhythmic themselves, unaware of their limits, unsure of right and wrong, likely to act out their frustrations as Rosie did.

Two years ago my wife and I took Eli to Bali. I don't wish to romanticize that complex society, but one thing I found admirable was their delight in children—there, Eli was the star of our family. The Balinese carry their children, always, for the first six months. Their energy goes into them—*pours* into them—and the children are extraordinarily loving and friendly, for they grow up secure in being loved.

I have traveled to many places, and met different peoples, but I was especially struck by the loving nature of the Balinese. This love is a direct result of the love and attention given to their children, which they also received as children. There is a one-to-one correlation. It is a lesson for all of us.

Compare this to our society. If we want less violence and more human caring, it begins with giving more love and attention to our children, not simply teaching them how to "behave."

By now, we all know children with attention deficit disorder (previously called "hyperactivity"). The child will begin focusing on a particular project, but quickly loses interest. He can't sit still, is always active, and often talks and interrupts inappropriately. He has trouble making eye contact and seems uncomfortable with himself and others.

A therapist who specializes in working with such children tells me that they have marked rhythm disturbances. They can't keep a beat or dance in sync.

I believe this rhythmic disturbance underlies the marked increase in cases of ADD. The problem is that the pace and rhythm of society are increasing so dramatically that some children simply can't keep up, are unable to come in sync with the right rhythm. They are trying to shift their rhythms to meet those of their world's, yet they can't seem to get into gear. Like a racing car set in neutral, they expend an enormous amount of energy (and use up a lot of "gas") getting nowhere.

We treat these children with Ritalin, a drug that acts to *speed up* the body's system—yet the children seem to slow down. This apparent contradiction results from a speedup that enables the children, like the racing engine, to shift up, get into gear, and thus be in sync.

These kids are better treated if we teach them to slow down. Enormous patience is required, but they can be taught mindfulness practices, accept nap times, sit still for readings, dance to slow music, adapt to care and quiet. Certainly, it's worth trying this non-drug method.

To me, ADD children represent a paradigm for American children in general—an exaggeration, certainly, yet I see to a lesser degree frenetic children everywhere, out of control, knowing only the rhythm of speed and sensation.

ADD is a relatively new disorder; out-of-control "normal" children, in the numbers they have reached today, are also a novel phenomenon, yet we are, I believe, going to see more and more of them as the Nintendo and Sega generation reach adolescence.

Today's pace for children is ten times faster than it was for me, not only because there's so much more information (if no more, and perhaps less, knowledge), but because the toys of childhood—computer games, instructional tapes, television—entrain children into a rapid rhythm almost from birth. I used to watch my favorite old movies with my sons Rahm and Dan. But they hated the old "Three Musketeers" and liked the (to me) vastly inferior later version.

Our kids see too much violence on television, at a pace so rapid that they are numbed to notions of human pain and moral dilemmas. And parents, whether rich or poor, are often absent, and therefore unable, to counter these messages.

No wonder our children steal, fight, even kill, without remorse, for too often there is nobody around to teach them right from wrong, and the messages they get from characters like Arnold Schwarzenegger and Hulk Hogan is that violence is glorifyingly appropriate if the "good guy" wins.

Timeshifting is the only way to get the children to change gears, and we cannot teach them how if we do not know ourselves. And how do we teach our children to timeshift? There are many ways:

- From an early age, practice concentration exercises with your child. Have him listen to the reverberations of a bell, for example, or stay with a tone until it disappears.
- Severely limit television time.
- Read to your children, particularly at bedtime. This is a simple practice that creates entrainment, becomes a timeshifting ritual, and is a great way for parent and child to connect.
- Initiate spontaneous time with your child.
- Teach your child boundaried time, for himself and for you.
- Begin each family meal with a moment of silence.
- Remember to honor and share your child's rhythm as well as your own.
- Meditate with your child. (Thich Nhat Hanh always includes children in meditation. This does not mean they have to sit still; he simply wants to encourage them to experience the true nature of the moment.)
- At Christmas, give your child the best present of all: your time. Instead of shopping for another toy, give him a treat— take him to a movie or the zoo. Be with him rather than look for something to please him.

Remember that the biggest complaint of children is that they do not get enough time with their parents; and without a sense of family, a child is soon lost.

And I do not know of a single mother or father who, having shifted to a child's rhythm from his or her own, does not feel a sense of joy at being a parent.

CHAPTER ELEVEN

WORK

———

*Unlike other resources, time cannot be bought
or sold, borrowed or stolen, stocked up or
saved, manufactured, reproduced, or modified.
All we can do is make use of it. And whether
we use it or not, it nevertheless slips away.*
—JEAN-LOUIS SERVAN-SCHREIBER

BILL GATES ROCKS.

I'm not being metaphorical. The third-richest man in the world, founder of Microsoft, literally sits in a rocking chair during business meetings and rocks back and forth as the meeting goes on, obviously a means of creating his own slow rhythm and entraining others into it.

Tom Jackson, the president of Equinox, a consulting firm, starts each of his meetings with a "pause," a minute or so of silence. He uses this technique to break set, to shift from the rhythm engendered by urgency, in which there's always a crisis to resolve. The moment of silence allows each person to become more present, more peaceful, and to come into sync with everyone in the room. The investment of this time creates an atmosphere in which better communication takes place and fewer nonproductive arguments occur. Better strategies and decisions are the result.

I use the pause myself at all group meetings I run, and find it extraordinarily effective. Harried people come into my office with some crisis or other on their minds. The pause allows a shifting of gears, and it's amazing how much more calmly, *and how much more effectively,* we can discuss the crisis and come to grips with it.

Recently I went to a meeting at which there had been a heated discussion. Omega was in a growth spurt, and we had to hire new people for two departments without increasing the amount of office space. Not surprisingly, there was a turf war, with each person representing a view that was clearly affected by the impact the decision would have on him personally. This is quite natural, and it's often the first "gut" reaction, yet it limits the view of what really serves everyone, collectively, and is in the best interests of the organization.

I asked everyone to pause, and only after we had been silent for a while did we continue. We discussed how to approach the issues together, instead of from entrenched individual perspectives. Remarkably, a new solution suddenly emerged, a suggestion from one of the people most directly affected: We had a large office being used by several part-time workers. Why not partition it into two offices to accommodate the newcomers, and ask the part-timers to reschedule?

It was not a perfect solution, but it seemed to come from our group effort, nobody's nose was too out of joint, and there were no winners or losers. In fact, we felt that we all had won.

The principles of timeshifting are more important in the workplace than anywhere else. Mastery of these principles will, I assure you, lead to a more productive, less stressed, more rewarding work experience.

Before the Industrial Age, productivity had less to do with time than with the vagaries of the seasons. In an agrarian society, sun and rain, not man-hours, dictated a crop's bounty, and once the crop was planted or reaped, a worker could relax. The rest was up to nature.

Today, time is a measure both of productivity and efficiency. The more we work, we believe, the more we produce; the more we "use our time well," the better our work will be.

We are paid by the hour according to how much we can produce. Our recognition in money or fame is based on our productivity measured against time.

There are experts in "time management" who teach us to be even more effective by prioritizing our tasks and using every minute to its fullest. Other experts design our offices, workrooms, and kitchens so that "timesaving" devices (the fax, the phone, the dishwasher, the PC, the microwave) are within easier reach, leaving us free not to have more leisure time, but to be more productive. If we use E-mail, we don't have to "waste time" picking up the phone, dialing, and possibly getting stuck in a lengthy conversation. My computer can talk to your computer while you and I are talking in person to different people—carrying on two productive conversations at once.

Yet despite the fact that it is "easier" now to work more productively than ever before, the average full-time employee in the early 1990s worked 138 hours more in a year than his counterpart did twenty years earlier.

In the 1980s, perhaps because of Tom Peters's book, *In Search of Excellence,* "excellence" itself became a buzzword. In the 1990s, the buzzword is "faster"—if we can do each job faster, we will be able *to do more.*

We have not necessarily chosen wisely in our quest for more. We have clearly gained more goods, but at the expense of most of our time. Juliet Schor, writing in 1991 in *The Overworked American,* illustrated it this way:

> We could *now* reproduce our 1948 standard of living (measured in terms of marketed goods and services) in less than half the time it took in 1948. We actually could have chosen the four-hour day. Or a working year of six months. Or imagine this: Every worker in the United States could now be taking every other year off from work, with pay.

Obviously, we as a society have decided to trade our time for more goods and services.

Earlier in this book, we mentioned the Japanese word *kashori,* referring to the syndrome of sudden death in the workplace. This has now become widely acknowledged in Japan. However, when the issue first arose and widows complained to management and even the government about how hard their husbands had worked, they were told that it was an *honor* to die at work—just as widows in World War II were told what an honor it was that their husbands had died in suicide attacks on the enemy.

To qualify as a victim of *kashori* one has to have worked for at least sixteen hours a day for seven straight days, or twenty-four hours straight just before dying. Otherwise, it does not qualify as *kashori*. Computers turn off all office lights automatically at 10:00 P.M. in Japan. But if you look at the same buildings at 10:01, you'll see most lights back on, the switches manned by the still-present employees.

In America recently, a law firm was sued because a young lawyer committed suicide from the pressure of overwork. And a friend of mine once came to his office at a book publishing company to find a coworker, assigned to a rush project, dead at his designing table, a half-eaten sandwich in his mouth.

Workaholism has become rampant throughout our society. Stories abound of people like Neil Rudenstine, president of Harvard University, being hospitalized for severe exhaustion and stress from overwork. Fatigue syndromes and heart attacks are linked to excessive stress in the workplace.

In class, Marty commented that his wife is a workaholic, but given how much work they have to do in her business, he doesn't see any way around it. She used to love making pottery, he told us, but now doesn't seem to have time for it.

I turned to her and asked her if she could make the time.

"I don't know," she responded. "I'm afraid if I don't keep working, I'll be like them."

"Like who?" I asked.

"You know. People who never get anything done."

Her low self-esteem and fear of failure kept her trapped working. Until she faced this, the pottery wheel would remain idle.

We, like the Japanese, pride ourselves on being the last one to leave the office at night, or make sure we tell our coworkers how late we stayed up finishing the report, or worked through the weekend to nail a big new account.

I frequently hear from the same people, when questioned more deeply, that they don't really know what to do with their time off. They feel uncomfortable, guilty, and worried about whether someone else will misinterpret or destroy the work they've done—so they can't relax away from the job; they can't create a boundary and make the shift. Indeed, they come back to the office on a day off, just to check up on things.

The real issue lies with the emotional discomfort we feel, and as noted in Chapter Four, overcoming these work anxieties requires learning to sit with the bad feelings until we can shift gears and relax. We have become so entrained and habituated to our speedy rhythm of work that it seems almost easier to keep doing it, rather than to feel the initial discomfort that happens when we slow down. But if we don't learn to shift and relax, we become like the frog in the pan of water, and the stress eventually gets us in one way or another.

I have seen many people create or take on piles of work for themselves as a way of showing how needed they are. It becomes a measure of self-worth. They will insist that there is so much work, they are only responding to the external circumstances that are beyond their control. But there are plenty of other people I know who are not running from discomfort, who understand how to prioritize their time, plan their time, and create time boundaries. They seem to get all their work done without the same kind of stress and without a workaholic's temperament.

One cost of the drive for speed is lower quality. We are told to produce more, though the devices designed to make us move along faster can actually lead to a lowering of standards—or a neglect of thought.

"Please fax your response by this afternoon," urges a fax I received this morning, asking for the go-ahead on a project the sender and I had discussed. But wait a minute. The question is a complex one, requiring not a "yes" or "no" but a "maybe"; I really should spend some time, maybe days, to think it through. I should consider consequences and possible alternatives. But today there are a dozen more pressing matters requiring my attention, so without thinking much at all, I simply say "yes," uneasily aware that I'm not precisely sure what I've agreed to. It's the demand for a rapid answer, from one machine to another, to which I've entrained, and with some relief I do as bidden: I fax the go-ahead by the afternoon.

Years ago, when I was attempting to start the wellness spa, millions of dollars were at stake, and investors were breathing down our necks. There were decisions to be made and dates to be met in construction, in the hiring of staff, in the formulation of a publicity campaign, etc. I'm afraid we based those decisions on speed and productivity rather than quality of what we were doing, and eventually the spa failed. The more money involved, the more pressure to do it quickly. I've resolved never be caught in this sort of trap again, when time and quality become hostage to the Almighty Dollar.

Last winter, I had lunch with a famous novelist who was under a strict deadline to finish his book. "The company needs the income this year," he explained, "so they're pushing me hard."

"But what about the *book?*" I asked. "Don't you think it might be better if you gave it more time?"

"Sure," he said. "But if I'm late, I'll have let them down. They've given me a huge advance, and I feel under a tremendous obligation to—"

He broke off and shook his head.

One of my closest friends, Rob, is a lawyer who made a clear commitment many years ago to prioritize his time. At first, he was worried that if he took too much vacation time, or left his office early, he would lose clients or not make enough money. We all share that fear. But he discovered that while he could make more money if he spent more time working, the work itself would not be as good.

So he works shorter hours, with more time off for family and vacations, but he works at peak efficiency, knowing that the "down time" will be his self-given reward. He has not experienced a proportionate drop off in income. In his office, he is as intense and focused as anyone I know; he goes at it full speed. He could have more clients if he wanted them, but he doesn't. And when he goes home to garden or to build a stone wall, the office is totally gone from his mind. He has created clear boundaries in his life and successfully shifts between them. In his office, his clients get a lawyer at his best, fully there for them, rather then someone who wishes he were somewhere else.

Creating boundaries between work and other aspects of our lives is as essential as learning how to shift between them. Even in the workplace, choose certain areas where you can erect boundaries. Take no phone calls between nine and ten A.M., for example. Take a fifteen-minute solitary walk after going out on a business lunch—and have as few business lunches as possible. Schedule meetings without interruptions. Make at least one "personal" call to a friend every day.

Americans define themselves by work. The opening conversational gambit between strangers is "What do you do?" and the answer is always in terms of profession: "I'm a doctor, a lawyer, an accountant, a farmer, a truck driver."

I've often wondered what would happen if we changed the question to "Who are you?" or "What kind of a person are you?" or even, "What do you do for fun?" but I visualize the respondent stunned into silence, unable to answer. Recently I asked a pregnant woman, "When are you due?" She responded by telling me she was a financial consultant.

We value ourselves by what we produce or what we "do," and thus we value time accordingly. Often, we're considered to be doing a "good" job depending on how much time we devote to it. Workers coming in early or staying late at the office are praised, while a colleague, working short hours, *but producing as much or more,* is not.

Employees at large corporations now use the term "face time," which means putting in extra time at work, even if there's nothing to be done, just to look good to the boss.

When we work like this, our personal lives suffer. Judith H. Dobrzynski, writing in the *New York Times,* quoted Bob Israel, co-owner of a motion picture ad agency in Los Angeles, on the conflict between work and family.

"At some point during the day, I look at my watch, and I'm faced with, "Do I go home now and spend a little more time with my kids before they go to bed, or do I complete the work I'm staring at?" It really is a daily struggle. It sometimes causes conflict, and certainly presents conflict in my heart."

Mr. Israel generally solves his dilemma by staying at work, as I used to. Since you're reading this book, I'll bet you do, too.

For many of us, work is more important than anything else in our lives (particularly when we're young). Besides, we tell ourselves, there'll always be time to catch up on our personal relationships or our sleep, spend time with the kids when they're older, and have our fun when we can *afford* the time. We'll have enough time later to spend on introspective thought, to figure out who we are and what we feel. But we should remember, as Servan-Schreiber has urged, to view our *time* like a bank account:

> We think much more about the use of our money, which is renewable, than we do about the use of our time, which is irreplaceable.
> Unlike other resources, time cannot be bought or sold, borrowed or stolen, stocked up or saved, manufactured, reproduced, or modified. All we can do is make use of it.

Okay, we think, but we'd better get rich first, and then we can have it all. For as we all know, time is money.

Time is money.

To me, it is the most insidious belief in Western society, yet it is commonly, if not universally, held, and most of us live by it. It's a new belief, stemming from the Industrial Revolution. In agricultural societies, even today, it is mocked. In Indonesia, a friend loves to tease me by chanting, when I show up, "Time is money. Time is money." Not long ago, nearly everybody charged by the job; now we charge by the hour.

Actually, it's worse than that. Many lawyers now charge *by the minute.* Not long ago, when I needed a lawyer, I found myself writing down notes before I called him, so that I wouldn't waste a second trying to think of questions to ask when we spoke, so the necessary information could be communicated in as short a time as possible.

"How are you?" he asked when I called, and I could feel my resistance rising. I thought, *"Small talk! It'll cost a fortune!* Let's get on with the information transfer."

Where was the personal aspect to all this? Where was human communication? I didn't care. Time is money.

Such an attitude is destructive to our human nature at work. Actively engage in personal contact in the office. Give flowers on a birthday. Throw a small party for the coworker who gets promoted. Write a note of thanks when a coworker does you a favor.

This shifts the whole work environment from a place of anxiety to a place of friendliness and support. I'm not suggesting you "waste" time—just spend a few minutes being personally present.

The worker who bills by the minute (or the hour) often thinks like this: "I make one hundred dollars an hour. Our baby-sitter costs ten dollars an hour. If I work six more minutes, I can have the sitter stay for another hour. If I work another hour, I can hire the sitter, a cleaning lady, and a cook. If I work another *week,* I can add a chauffeur and buy a limousine. That way I'll be able to get to work faster, so I can work longer and earn more. After all, I'm worth one hundred dollars an hour, so it's not a good use of my time to be doing mundane chores!"

What such workers are doing, of course, is paying someone (or a lot of someones) to live their lives for them. They can't imagine doing the dishes, diapering the baby, mowing the lawn, or driving the car. They hate the lowly chores, sneer at anyone not attending solely to the megadeal, and can't imagine sitting in the balcony at a concert or traveling tourist class on a plane. The rest of us look at them as exemplars of "the good life," and we try to model their behavior as well.

Our continual quest to be freed of the mundane means we are saying that most of life is not worth being present for. We regain our time by reversing this process. Honor the mundane. Choose a chore you don't mind or that you actually like to do when you get home. Participating in ordinary life can be as enriching as spending extra time at work. Learn to live your own life!

We assume rich people are happy. We assume that if we were rich, we'd have more time to do the things we *really* wanted to do. If we could earn just so much, we persuade ourselves, we'd stop working so hard, and the rest of our lives would be a perpetual vacation, an eternal honeymoon.

Let me give you some examples from real life:

A fabulously successful arbitrager came up to me at a dinner party. "How I envy you," he said. "You seem to have so much time for relaxation. You don't seem stressed. You have the ideal lifestyle."

"You could *buy* that lifestyle," I told him—and he easily could. "Maybe you should consider taking a few months off."

"No," he said. "I'm stuck. I have to make enough money to maintain my duplex in New York, my house in the Hamptons, and our vacation home in Florida. Plus the nanny and private school for the kids." He sighed. "I'm supporting a pretty large nut. I have to keep going."

I realized that, with all his wealth, he had only increased his material responsibilities. His money had created more concerns and worries, and with them came more stress, rather than the relief we believe money can buy for us.

A builder responsible for the construction of over a million square feet of housing per year moaned to me that his business "was killing" him. When he was young he had loved his work, but over the years it had become drudgery.

"Then get out," I told him. "You have enough money to last a dozen lifetimes. What other things interest you?"

He paused a long time, thinking. Despite many suggestions from me, it appeared nothing seemed to interest him. "You don't understand," he said. "I don't like to do anything else."

It was true. This man had neglected to build himself, in any other way besides in business expertise. In business he was seen as an expert, at the pinnacle of his profession. Yet in most other ways, he was at a second-grade level. He was unwilling to be seen that way by himself or anyone else, so he kept working. He was rich only in money.

A couple I know, both of them brilliant management consultants, did so well as a team that they were able to launch their own firm, and soon had thirty employees. But a strange thing happened. As success built on success, they found that the work they once loved they now loathed; they became their own company's slaves, trapped on its treadmill. They had loved consulting directly with their clients, yet now they were more involved with the administration of others. They felt stressed, empty, and unhappy in their lives, despite their wealth. *But they wouldn't consider making the necessary changes!*

Complex factors come into play when people make lots of money. Instead of having more time, there seems to be less. Just managing and watching the money and investments becomes very time-consuming. The fact that they are rich becomes their identity; a vacation looms as a waste of money-producing time, and so it is not taken. How can it be worth one hundred dollars to lie for an hour on the beach? Money *demands* time, and rather than freeing us, it ensnares us. Material things become all-important, because they show the world how successful we are.

Paraphrasing Joseph Campbell, it can be said, "Follow your bliss; the money will follow." "Sounds good," many people say, "But I don't believe it'll work. I sure don't want to take the chance. I'll stick to my job, thank you."

This is a reasonable response, yet one that can often keep us imprisoned in a situation that isn't really satisfying for us anyway. Some of the most successful people I know are those who followed what they passionately believed in, doing what they wanted to do. I'm not defining success here as making the most money; rather, I'm describing those who have achieved satisfaction, joy, pride, and contentment from their endeavors.

Success is really about believing in yourself and trusting that if you are true to your inner voice, as well as listening to your mind, you will choose most wisely for yourself. The people I know who have been courageous in this way have invariably ended up the happiest. As if they were having an important meeting with themselves, they paused first to listen.

A friend recently quit his job as an account executive at an advertising agency to go into business for himself as a copywriter and consultant. Here's what he told me:

At first, I'd wake up at four o'clock in the morning with night sweats, convinced I wouldn't make another penny and couldn't take care of my family. Then I remember what you said about the connection between emotion and money—how much emotion is tied up in money, and I used the night hours to breathe and think.

Even though I had made all sorts of plans before I left the corporation, now I devised strategies I couldn't have seen when I was under such stress, and in the mornings I'd implement them.

It's been two years now, and I haven't reached the income level I earned at the corporation. But I'm my own boss, I don't have to sit through useless meetings, and it's a hell of a lot more pleasant to put pressure on yourself rather than have a boss apply it to you.

Sure I'm working fast, probably faster and harder than I did at the agency. But the fear is gone—fear of my ex-boss and fear that I'd fail when I worked for myself. And when I want to take time off, what's to stop me?

I've spent a good deal of time in "poor" countries, particularly in Asia and the Caribbean. There, pleasure, laughter, and humanness seem more authentic. People stop to admire the sun on the sea, rather than just take a picture of it to bring back as proof to their friends of how worthwhile their vacation was. Everyday life seems richer and fuller.

We have much to learn from them. I want to shout *"slow down"* at those who believe that only money can buy them a "better life." With all your money, you're still entrained in the ever-more-rapid tempo of Western life, without much chance for the emergence of the soul.

I believe there is a growing realization, both individually and corporately, that unless we slow down, productivity (at least the production of quality goods and services) will actually suffer. We must include play with work, nurture the self as well as the corporate animal, care for the inner as well as the outer human being—or we will become a nation of robots. Money will be our only goal; material possessions the only sign of achievement.

No doubt you are familiar with the Peter Principle, which states that you will rise to your level of incompetence. It suggests that you will be promoted as long as you do a good job, until you finally reach the level where you fail to perform and then will be stuck there.

I believe the Peter Principle is really about reaching our level of burnout, that level where we feel too much stress and dissatisfaction with our job to be performing at our best.

Nearly a hundred years ago, Henry Ford recognized how important slowing down was to his workers, and he cut their workweek from six to five days. He was shrewd enough, also, to understand that people would use their longer stretch of leisure time to drive—what was good for the public was in fact good for Ford. (By the way, Ford began his career as a watchmaker, no doubt gaining insight then about shifting time.)

Today, for individuals as well as for members of the workforce, shifting rhythm is essential not only to physical and mental well-being, but also to improved productivity. A good many management consultants believe this as much as I do.

If you're a manager, reward the producer of a rush report with a day off that is not counted against her vacation time. And make sure you don't use the same employee, good as she is, for one "urgent" assignment after another.

If you're the employee, see to it you take some boundaried time off, even if it's only an afternoon, using the methods described in Chapter Eight. If you can't do it any other way, take a sick day—for your mental health.

A businessman I know waits twenty-four hours before responding to any letter or fax. "It gives me time to think," he says. But he makes every unpleasant or difficult phone call the first priority in the morning. "Gets them out of the way," he explains. "I feel much calmer. Besides, if I waited, they'd be making me anxious all day."

CEOs who require intense, fast-paced responses will see their businesses function more smoothly if they reduce their employees'

pace in nonurgent times instead of continually urging them to go
faster. They could even teach their workers to pause, to change
their rhythms, to use the techniques described in this book for
speeding up and slowing down.

Ultimately, service and productivity would increase if telephone
operators, airline stewardesses, and fast-food handlers were actually
encouraged to work in slower rhythms, but with politeness, contact,
respect.

I remember a time at Heathrow Airport when an America-
bound flight was delayed and a crush of people surrounded the
purser, demanding alternative flights, even though none were available. The purser treated them like individuals, talking with them
calmly, refusing to entrain with their collective anxiety. Calm replaced chaos, tranquility prevailed, and an unavoidable situation became a time to savor. The passengers, I'm sure, chose the same
airline for their next flight. If all companies trained people to do
that, if they could teach amicability instead of rudeness, they would
get more business, lose fewer employees, and add to the civilization
of the world, rather than its discontent.

For individuals, we've already talked about the importance of
rituals to help us slow down. These are especially critical during the
working day. Use a picture or a prism on your desk to shift your
mind from work to the contemplation of something beautiful. Do
this regularly as a break that brings you into an awareness or "remembrance" of what's going on, rather than being reactive and "on
automatic" all day. Take three deep breaths every time your phone
rings before answering it. Use it as a break rather than feel more
pressure. Close your eyes and give full and mindful attention to the
caller. The communication will be deeper and clearer—and don't
worry: The other tasks will also get done.

Companies have long honored a timeshifting ritual by encouraging a cigarette break. Though clearly unhealthy in most ways, and
now no longer allowed in most office environments, it was nevertheless a positive means of slowing down. A worker could go into a
lounge or hallway, sit back, breathe air into his lungs, and relax. He
became connected with his breathing, thus changing his rhythm.
The problem was that ultimately cigarette smoking robbed him of
the capacity to breathe.

Now that we know how dangerous cigarettes are, I still urge you to take a break—a noncigarette break. If you feel foolish standing in a corridor simply taking in deep breaths, do it in the bathroom or go outside, but recognize its power as a ritual that shifts time for us.

The need for the coffee break is the one thing labor and management have always agreed upon since the advent of the Industrial Age: labor because of the break's timeshifting properties, management because coffee contains caffeine and its jolt gives workers added energy and speed. Unfortunately, we pay a price for this over the long haul. Caffeine adds artificial impetus to speed. Why rev your heartbeat when the pressure of the day keeps it pulsing rapidly enough already?

Read the paper at your desk before your workday starts. Drop into a colleague's office from time to time to chat about issues other than work. *Never* eat lunch at your desk, but use the hour to go outside for a walk and a sandwich, or at least for a change in environment. Exercise before work or during lunchhour. Get a shoeshine. Do your nails. Eat some raisins, really savoring them.

The point is to be conscious of the rhythm of the workplace *and to be conscious about shifting it*. You need to create for yourself boundaried time that is yours alone.

As we've already seen, this means you have to learn to say no, to keep those relatively brief boundaried minutes sacrosanct. And you must say no to too many simultaneous orders from the boss. Multitasking generally means multimistakes. A gentle "I'm sorry, but I'm already in the middle of a project. I'll get to the next one as soon as I can, but if it has to be done immediately, perhaps you could ask someone else" will be acceptable to your boss and save you stress.

Upon hearing this at my seminar, John insisted that, although he holds a high-level position in a corporation, part of the unwritten deal is that if there's a meeting at seven A.M. or six P.M., he is expected to drop everything and be available for it. And he doubts he can say no to his boss.

We discussed what would happen if he were to set boundaries and limits on his availability. "I probably wouldn't get a raise," he said. "Maybe I'd even be fired. But I'm not sure because I've never said no, and I don't want to risk it now."

I suggested he try it and get back to me. Needless to say, he found less resistance than he had expected. By being clear about his boundaries, he felt more empowered and even more respected by his peers.

There is always so much work that if you're willing to do it all, it will be gladly handed over. But if you respect your own boundaries and do your work well, other people will likely respect those boundaries as well, including your boss.

If boundaries *aren't* acceptable, if you find your boss's rhythm so out of sync with yours that you're in a perpetual state of anxiety, then you had best think of shifting not time but jobs. If you are constantly being pulled out of the moment, then you are being pulled out of life, and no job is worth that.

"What about this?" a workshop participant asked. "My boss seems perpetually mad at me. He seems to think everything I do is wrong."

I asked him if this was his boss's attitude toward everyone, for the problem was obviously less threatening if his boss was simply a louse.

"I'm not sure," he admitted. "But what if it's only me?"

I advised him to sit quietly with his feelings, try to understand whether they were rational or whether he was imposing his own inner doubts on his boss. If he could see where his boss "was coming from," I told him, he would be better able to understand the anger. And by finding the rhythm that connected them, creating a dialogue of understanding with his boss—by entraining with his boss rather than resisting him—his own anger would fade. If he could understand the pressures on his boss, he would be better able to get in sync.

The reverse is also true. A manager who understands the pressures on his employees is better able to create harmony in the workplace than the manager who imposes his own pressures (and fears) on his employees. In both cases, quiet contemplation of one's own feelings and about the causes for strife is essential. In both cases, timeshifting is the means.

A friend of mine, a psychologist, is often sent to areas of crisis or disaster to help organize the rescue workers. He tells me that the first and by far the most important thing he does is to gather the workers on his arrival, stand before them, pause, *and then talk slowly and calmly to them*. A man of enormous presence, he is simply getting them to entrain with his rhythm; he is entraining a team.

I think the antidote to the ruinous rhythm of today's workplace lies in such team entrainment.

You can do this in your work setting, too, without others even knowing what you're doing. At a heated meeting, change the rhythm by speaking slowly, calmly. This will slow things down, and it will get the others to listen to you. You might look at it as a kind guerrilla tactic—subversive to speed, and highly effective.

When commands come from the top, when plans are made by management without including the employees in the process, when reliance is placed on machines and computers rather than on people, when the CEO inspires fear rather than cooperation, the result is disharmony among the workers and a loss of productivity for the company. The best product is not being manufactured, or lesser service is given.

But when workers have a say in current and future planning, when there is true communication among all levels of a company, then the company will operate at maximum capacity, not because it is able to produce faster, but because it has been able to slow down.

For a long time, companies have tacitly recognized the need for networking among employees—hence the company picnic and the Christmas party. But these are often sterile affairs, full of artificial camaraderie removed from the hierarchical structure of everyday reality.

What I'm urging now is an approach already incorporated by many successful companies, where the sharing of ideas through talk and respect is the real entrainment. Ideas demand creative thinking, and creative thinking is impossible if the pace is rushed.

Management retreats, a practice becoming more and more common in American businesses, validate this idea. Sharing ideas with, and encouraging ideas from, all levels of the workplace will lead to the greatest efficiency and the best results.

Intracompany communication itself is getting simpler, which is one of the positive effects of computers. Consultants talk about the "alignment of vision" among workers and management, another way of describing entrainment. If workers can learn what the boss knows, if they can be allowed to understand the long-term goals of the company, if they can be encouraged to network the way that huge businesses are themselves networking with each other, then quality will be the result.

It's not easy. Getting workers to agree on a project, direction, or vision—really getting them "onboard"—takes time. Initially workers are suspicious. Disagreements are time-consuming, and management will often move so fast that workers simply go along without really feeling committed to the process. But this means the capacity for maximum success is not really there.

In a recent talk, the author Hedrick Smith described how General Motors and Ford each tackled the problem of a recent severe sales slump. Both cut costs as best they could. GM then introduced a number of technical innovations designed to speed productivity. Ford, on the other hand, adapted its policy of "Quality Is Job One," and went to its workers for ideas on how to implement it.

The workers recommended and helped design the new, more efficient tools with which they worked, and even recommended changes in their health plans and work conditions to give them greater security. Ford's turnaround was accomplished well before GM's. Coincidence? Smith didn't think so.

Japanese businesses have been described as being "holocentric"—a characteristic that significantly contributes to their dramatic success in the international sphere. Unlike systems that are more strictly hierarchical or pyramidal, a holocentric process fosters agreement among the entire working group on what we might call the "gut" level. (The corresponding Japanese word is *hara*: the body's "center," below the navel, that is described in many of the martial arts and in Zen practice.) The group entrains to the rhythm of this "gut feeling," and once everyone reaches agreement, this becomes the basis for a much more powerful way of proceeding. Members of the group have not only signed on in their minds; their feelings are aligned as well.

This process takes more time initially, yet it is a much more effective—and, in the end, time-efficient—way of working.

Communication among workers *requires* slowing down. Time becomes a friend, patience an ally.

As the founder of the Omega Institute, I have been leading programs on developing holistic businesses. I've been amazed at the overwhelming response to these programs. More and more people are deciding they are looking for work situations consistent with their ideals, rather than working for money only. There is a large movement of people dedicated to "right livelihood," those who desire a merging of social, lifestyle, and financial values.

I regularly meet people who are choosing to have more leisure time over higher pay. They usually report a higher degree of satisfaction and fulfillment. These workers are choosing to use their time not in the pursuit of consumerism, but in seeking experiences—the search, in other words, not for the material, but for the spiritual.

We have seen a rise in the number of enterprises devoted to wellness and spiritual advancement. Retreat centers, ecological resorts and journeys, and learning centers are rapidly expanding. Massage therapy is not considered New Age or unusual. Health food stores and bookstores, featuring as much philosophy and lifestyle as product are commonplace. Large companies like ClubMed or the Disney Institute have begun to focus in the areas of wellness, leisure, and continuing education combined.

We are coming into an age when industries that are service oriented, socially and community focused, yet financially successful, will proliferate; they are a major development waiting to happen.

If these businesses are to reach their greatest potential, all it will require is the commitment to a vision that honors a healthy lifestyle and social responsibility.

* * *

In Chapter Eight, we described different methods of timeshifting, and in this chapter have noted some of them as they apply to the workplace. Here are some others. Use them whenever and wherever, even if you have to slip away or make up excuses for doing something out of the ordinary.

In the Moment:
1. Take a few minibreaks during the day when you concentrate on breathing.
2. Get to meetings early so you can compose yourself before the others arrive.
3. Pause after you finish one task before beginning another. If possible, make the pause last several minutes.
4. Practice mindfulness by doing only one thing at a time, giving it your full attention.
5. Learn how to timeshift in the midst of busyness. While waiting for a fax transmission, or for the photocopying to finish, or for the elevator to arrive, timeshift into the present instead of feeling the rush and anxiety of tasks still waiting.

Boundaried Time:
1. Come to work ten minutes early and claim this time for yourself. Eat breakfast, read the newspaper, or make a personal call.
2. Set aside a regular time for planning—no interruptions, no crisis management, no attention to current issues allowed.
3. Don't work during lunch. If you *must* have a business discussion, finish it quickly and spend the rest of the time in casual conversation, enjoying the food.
4. Take a nap at your desk. (Actually, among top executives, the "power nap" is coming into vogue.)
5. In your calendar, make appointments with yourself. Use this time for planning, napping, or simple breathing and thought.

Spontaneous Time:

1. Leave the office next Wednesday afternoon without any plans. (Okay, so you're tied up next Wednesday. Make it a week from Wednesday.) Call it a doctor's visit, or simply play hookey. I know it's against company policy, and I'm sure you've been brought up to think it's wrong—but it's life-affirming.

2. Spend time at work with someone you barely know. Do not talk about business.

Honoring the Mundane:

1. Notice the simple things you do that you actually get satisfaction from, whether that is going over spreadsheets, using the computer, or tallying the sales for the day. When you have such a task, don't rush it, but just let yourself be present with it.

2. Practice "senseless acts of beauty" in your environment. Change the lighting, bring in flowers, rearrange the pictures on the walls, or the things on your desk.

3. Be in the present when you clean your desk, realizing how getting rid of the clutter helps clear the moment.

Time Retreats:

1. Make sure that on your vacation you leave work totally behind. Don't take work along, or a cellular phone. Don't leave your number with your office.

2. Plan a day of transition at home before you go back to work.

3. In between vacations, take a wellness day off once in a while, rather than a sick day.

CHAPTER TWELVE

SPORTS AND PLAY

———

*The mystical moment occurs as often as it does
in sport in part because you don't have to
have one. You are simply there to have a good
time or to pursue a particularly delicious
passion, when suddenly—it happens.*

—MICHAEL MURPHY

A CHILD AT play is a beautiful sight. There is no more moving example of someone being in the moment. Whether it is active play as part of a team, or quiet play (putting together a puzzle, facing an opponent across a board game, chasing a butterfly), the child is totally concentrated; the child is present.

As we've seen, being in the moment fosters creativity, and who is more creative than a child? No inhibition stops the rocket trip, the parenting of a doll, the heated colloquy with an imaginary friend. All these are certain ways for experiencing the feelings in the moment. What is going on is emphatically, energetically, totally *now*.

As adults, our play shifts. We forget what it's like to play for the sheer joy of it, but now play to win, or to avoid losing. We play with an eye toward the future. In quiet sports and games, we play with our heads rather than with our hearts, and we're often distracted—business or relationship worries break our concentration. It is sometimes impossible even to remember the score.

For a child, play is a natural impulse, a priority second only to sleeping and eating. For adults, play is a conscious act and usually a low priority—work, family, friends, "obligations" often come first.

Yet play is as important to an adult as it is to a child. It is a means of timeshifting, essential for living a balanced life—and it's fun.

Most of us don't know how to play. It's not that we haven't learned; we've forgotten! When we have time for ourselves, we watch television. We exercise, not for pleasure, but for the good of our health. When we feel guilty about "wasting time," we get back to work.

I've asked my classes to tell me what they like to do. Many have a long list of things—so numerous, they really can't get down to doing any of them. Others "don't know." I've seen their sheepish-ness when they admit that work is their only activity, and that they're uncomfortable doing anything else.

But lack of play for the sheer joy of it, for the connectedness of it, is a fundamental problem, says O. Fred Donaldson, author of *Playing by Heart,* who has studied play in wolves, dolphins, and children. Through play, he says, we can discern the difference between play-mate and contestant, learn how to touch and to connect, realize what fun it is to become beginners again, recognize the difference between power plays and power struggles, and learn how to take pleasure from change, not resist it.

In a forty-year study of Harvard sophomores, George Valliant concluded that lack of recreation time contributed significantly to a relative degree of illness over the years.

Imagine. One of the fundamental things we can do to maintain health is to play. And we don't do it nearly enough!

Sports, more than any other activity save war and sex (which many consider a sport; good sex surely involves play), can bring us, like children, clearly and completely into the present moment.

Even watching sports on television puts us *right there*—rooting for the athletes, concentrating on the skills they display. Except for news, sports (including sessions of congress, which a friend described to me, accurately, as "bull fights") are almost the only "live" events we see on the tube; virtually everything else is canned. But *participating* in a sport, either individually or as part of a team, holds a capacity for entrainment common to few other activities.

Sports have been likened to war. Teams have coaches (generals), captains, and players (foot soldiers). Victory is the desired result, and strategy, intimidation, "hitting," and superior "fire power"—all are used to win. All sports broadcasters use war metaphors—it's no coincidence.

Soldiers returning from the field have described the battle as "the best, most alive" time of their lives. Nowhere else have they been more fully entrained, more fully engaged.

We use sports as a means to sublimate the issue of survival. Without undue risk (except in a few sports, which I'll discuss later), this is a place where we can legitimately "go all out," thinking of nothing else, expending body and brain to their maximum—being one with ourselves and, in team sports, with others. Being one with the present.

Sports bring out the same emotions that are connected with survival; they provide an outlet for our anger and an entrainment with our primal body sense—all without the fear of battle. We are "safe" as our most basic selves.

What a healthy outlet all sports are! Beyond the obvious benefits to physical well-being, we also take a more positive approach to time through sports. In this aspect, at least, it makes no difference whether the sport is slow-moving (golf, jogging) or fast (tennis, basketball, handball, sprinting). All of them take us from our minds to our bodies—and, by concentrating on what we're doing, we lose the sense of time and therefore expand it. We expand the moment.

The professional athlete is a master of the expanded moment. In baseball, for example, a hitter speaks of the pitched ball as looking "large as a grapefruit"—even when the ball is coming at him at ninety-five miles an hour. He is able to hit it, often hundreds of feet, whereas most of us would run screaming in terror from the batter's box.

I remember a basketball game in which the Chicago Bulls, one point behind, had eight seconds left in which to score.

Eight seconds! As a spectator, that seemed too little time. *Hurry,* I thought. *Don't you realize how desperate it is?*

But to Michael Jordan, eight seconds was enough time, plenty of time, an eternity of time. Without haste—and surely without desperation—he dribbled the ball upcourt, complete master of the eight seconds remaining, about to expand them into precisely the amount of time he needed to win.

Yes, he made the shot. Yes, the Bulls won the game. And the magical effect for me—and for everybody else in the stands—was that his great mastery of time became ours. If he wanted those eight seconds to last until he had won the game, who were we to deny him? Somewhere in those eight seconds, we entrained with him, and his expanded moment became ours. Eight seconds? He seemed completely at ease. No sweat. It was remarkable.

To a lesser degree, many of us amateurs have had moments when "everything comes together"; when rhythm, adrenaline, our senses, concentration, passion, and our rudimentary skills have coalesced to put us "in the zone," a place where there is no linear time and we are the complete masters of our bodies and of the sport itself.

Recently, I played a basketball game in which I, literally, "couldn't miss." Difficult shots were easy; shots I never would have even attempted on an ordinary day I now took, *sure* of their success. For the time it lasted—and I have no idea how long that was—I felt an exhilaration no drug could produce.

As Phil Jackson, coach of the Chicago Bulls, notes, "Basketball is a complex dance that requires shifting from one objective to another at lightning speed. To excel, you need to act with a clear mind and be totally focused on what *everyone* on the floor is doing. Some athletes describe this quality of mind as a 'cocoon of concentration.' But that implies shutting out the world, when what you really need to do is become more acutely aware of what's happening right now, *this very moment."*

A friend of mine told me of a time ten years ago, playing tennis against an opponent precisely her equal, when both were at the top of their game; neither could "miss." The final score of their set was, under the old scoring, 24–22. And even today, ten years later, they still both talk of the set as one of the transcendent moments of their lives.

It is well known now that the mind as well as the body plays a vital part in sports, not through thinking but from a *cessation* of thinking, the ability to suspend the speed of the brain and enter into a sort of timeless trance.

An August 3, 1992, article in *U.S. News & World Report* discussed the whole subject of the mind/body connection in sports, emphasizing the work of Brad Hatfield of the University of Maryland. Hatfield had fitted expert marksmen with electrodes that measure the brain's electrical activity. He found that just before a marksman pulls the trigger, "the left side of the brain erupts in a burst of so-called alpha waves, indicative of a relaxed, trancelike state." In other words, during peak performance (and it need not be in sports—a painter, doctor, or businessman can experience the same phenomenon), the mind relaxes and the body is able to go into the "flow" that Bill Russell and others have described.

The article also noted the work of psychologist Dan Landers of Arizona State University, who monitored the brain-wave patterns of neophyte archers taking a fifteen-week course in the sport. As the archers improved, Landers found that their brain-wave patterns changed, and by the time they were expert, they showed the same burst of alpha waves shown by the marksmen in Hatfield's study. In time, Landers was able to train expert archers to control targeted areas in their brains. Those who could relax the brain waves in their left hemispheres did demonstrably better than those who could control the right hemisphere. The same phenomenon is common in golf, basketball, tennis, etc.—all sports that require a slowing down before the vital action occurs.

What athletes do in their "down time" is as important as the time spent at "peak" moments, the article continued. James Loehr, a sports psychologist who has worked with tennis stars Gabriela Sabatini and Jim Courier, teaches players to spend the twenty-five seconds between points visualizing a previous good shot, forgetting a bad one, relaxing, and then building up to the next serve.

Visualization, relaxation, and a sense of calm in the moment are all typical of the great athlete—and, as noted, not only of the athlete. Think how much better your own performance has been when you were relaxed, when you were so in command of your material that you considered yourself an expert. You were able to slow down, exist in the present—and triumph.

Although participation in any sport may draw you into the now, different sports have different effects.

Last year, ESPN televised a series of "Dangerous Games." These featured activities that some men and women do to achieve an adrenaline rush, a "high," which may last only a few seconds, but is unbelievably intense. To them, it's worth the arduous training—and the risk. Skateboarding, skydiving, white-water rafting, endurance cross-country hiking and biking, cliff-climbing: These and more made up the games, and all held the potential of serious injury.

On a recent airplane trip, I sat next to a businessman who was traveling west to climb El Capitan Mountain in Yosemite. "I like the challenge of death sports," he told me. "Nothing else—not even success—creates enough risk, enough drama, to get me going."

We've seen how addictive the effects produced by the adrenaline rush of risk can be. To me, there are better (and safer!) ways of attaining far more lasting highs, of experiencing expanded moments rather than shortened ones. The risk-focus equation described in Chapter Four is the theoretical answer. Sports can provide concrete illustrations, as in the Michael Jordan example.

Yet some people *crave* risk; they must have it. I know someone who goes to an airport, waits his turn for a plane, straps on his parachute—and jumps. He claims that all the hours he expends on this activity are worth the thrill of a few seconds' free fall. The risk that the parachute won't open heightens the excitement.

Another acquaintance, who races sports cars, tells me he has experienced thirty seconds of a "perfect" moment in ten years of racing. Those few seconds don't seem worth the effort of ten years, to me, yet he was exhilarated when he described them. I got the impression that he would have raced twice as many years for the same result.

We are all looking for "perfect moments," but to me such high-risk methods are too fast, too frenetic. How much better to be "in the zone" for extended periods rather than to risk one's life for a quick thrill. I understand my daredevil friends, but I want something with a different rhythm, a different effect.

So I play basketball, granted a sport with a fast pace, but without danger, in which I am a member of a *team*. This is a terrific advantage for me, because in team sports the whole notion of entrainment, of rhythms in sync, becomes vital, whether it is on an amateur or professional level.

My favorite basketball announcer was Bill Russell, who was able to predict that a particular team would "go on a run." Sure enough, the team would score ten or twelve points in a row—and then, just before the spree ended, Russell would tell us the run was about to end—and end it did.

I was never quite sure how he knew. Having been a great professional himself, he could *feel* a team's rhythm the way viewers like me cannot. The phenomenon of entrainment explains, I think, why teams go on winning and losing streaks, why all of a sudden all the members of a baseball team "get hot," or their bats simultaneously "grow cold."

My mother told of playing in a bridge tournament with her regular partner when everything suddenly "clicked," and their communication, in the carefully proscribed language of bridge, seemed as easy and as natural as conversation. For hand after hand they did not make a wrong bid or play a wrong card, and they won the tournament easily, though there were many higher-ranked players in the competition.

What except rhythm explains why one sculling team, of exactly equal strength to its competitor, will nevertheless pull ahead and win by a comfortable margin? Why else can the fiftieth-best tennis doubles team knock off number one?

Many people, of course, prefer and derive equal pleasure from the slower sports, and going back to the extensity graph we can see that a game of golf or a hike in the woods can produce as great a "high" as mountain climbing.

In golf, the beauty of the surroundings and the pleasure of the walk are more than adequate compensation for a sliced drive or missed putt—indeed, I have friends who don't keep score, but just play for the beauty of it.

Jogging, walking, swimming, aerobics, tai chi, yoga, and cycling—for exercise *and* for relaxation—depend on becoming one with one's body, and in taking in the peacefulness of one's surroundings, so much so that people often say they "forgot" what they were doing, and were aware only of their inner selves and their surroundings.

In this way, sport is similar to meditation. It is a time without thought. Martina Navratilova said, when asked why she lost a match, "I started thinking." Sadaharu Oh, Japan's greatest home-run hitter, speaks of the "Zen" of baseball. My friend's grown-up son asked him to go to Shea Stadium to watch the Mets with him. "But the Mets are a terrible team," his father said. "I don't care," his son replied. "I want to go to a *game.*" And, he could have added, "I want to bond with you through the shared experience of a sport we've both loved since my childhood."

At Omega, Jena Marcovicci, a professional tennis player and former instructor at Williams College, once hit back and forth with me *with no net,* all the while playing a recording of drums. "I teach people to get into a rhythm," he explains, "and then to match their tennis to that rhythm." He was teaching "the inner game of tennis," timing into one's own natural rhythm and getting into the flow of the game. Even in competition, controlling one's own flow is the most effective way to win.

In horseback riding, riders speak of their oneness with the animal, in a sense with all nature, just as sailors speak of their oneness with the waves. The power of the rhythm from the movement of the horse or the waves creates an entrainment field that resonates with our inner nature.

My wife loves to dance and knows how important it is to concentrate on movement in the moment. When she is at her best, she loses inhibition and becomes at one with her own body and with the music with which she has entrained. In Africa, different neighboring tribes beat drums in different rhythms, reflecting their different cultures. Finding the right rhythms, for us as well as the tribes, is essential to sports and to life. When we find it, we develop mastery of ourselves.

Sports, of course, is only one kind of play—and only one way to fill leisure time.

At Omega, Joe Killian gives a course called "Playing for the Fun of It" in which he teaches people to have a good time. He shows them how to get silly, to drop inhibition and insecurity—and to laugh.

Laughter is often the result of play, or it can be play itself. There's a wonderful game where everybody puts their head on someone else's belly and they all start to laugh. Artificial at first, the room soon erupts in genuine laughter, and a great feeling of joy takes over. Laughter is indeed, as Norman Cousins showed, the "best medicine."

I think we must bring play and laughter into the workplace and into personal relationships. A publishing acquaintance tells me how, during a particularly traumatic time at his company, he and two others decided to play a game of no-stakes poker as a means of breaking the tension. Soon they were laughing, loudly and open-heartedly. The door to the office burst open. "How *dare* you laugh at a time like this?" their boss bellowed. The door slammed shut. Their laughter redoubled. And no, they were not fired or even reprimanded. Passing their boss's office a few minutes later, they heard him laughing, too.

Don't run from play, from "joking around," or from spontaneous fun. Play and laughter are wonderful ways of coming into the present (you may be anxious when you work, but never when you play). All other animals gambol, frolic, and cavort. We are supposedly the most intelligent animals of all, yet we don't seem to learn from the natural behavior of the creatures around us. Play is endemic to children, too. Our productivity-oriented society has made us forget what fun it is to be a child.

★ ★ ★

Exercise is vital.

"I'm too busy to exercise today. I'll do it tomorrow."

How many times have you heard it? How many times have you said it?

If you feel that you don't have the time, then shift your priorities. We all need to create time for exercise. Walk briskly for an hour every day, play tennis three nights a week, go dancing twice weekly, do yoga daily, or play golf regularly. The essential thing is to plan a regular schedule of exercise, and to stick with it!

The only rule is to do something you like. Exercise can be dull or exciting, a chore or a pleasure—it depends on what suits you. If you get tired of what you initially liked, change it. And if you grow too old to keep up with the most strenuous sports (one day, I know, I will have to give up basketball), find a more age-suitable way to exercise. But no matter what, don't stop.

A doctor I know was an avid tennis player—the game was his favorite method of timeshifting. But a complication arose during an operation he was undergoing, which resulted in the need to have his right leg amputated—making it impossible for him to play anymore, and leading to a depression so overwhelming that it affected everything in his life. Then he discovered sailing, and fell in love with the deep rhythm of the sea: a different exercise, a similar result. His depression lifted. His life resumed.

Entrain with exercise. Make it an essential part of your life. And—soon!—watch your vitality grow, feel your whole body open to a thousand new stimuli, and know the joy and pleasures that live in a healthy body.

HEALTH

―――

*We have forgotten that our only goal is to live
and that we live each day and that at every
hour of the day we are reaching our true goal
if we are living. . . . The days are fruits
and our role is to eat them.*

—JEAN GIONO

THE MIND AND the body are connected, and the health of one affects the other. This is an old concept. In the Middle Ages, the "humors"—anger, for instance—were directly related to body organs; a "bilious" man suffered from disorders of the liver and gallbladder. But by the start of this century, with the coming of psychoanalysis, mind and body were looked at as separate entities in the West; we began to believe that diseases of the body were unrelated to the mind, and vice versa. "It's nothing. It's all in your head," doctors told their patients, and the patients went away believing they weren't sick, just a little crazy. No connection was made between illnesses like an ulcer or a back problem with psychological states like stress or depression.

In the East, energy, body, and mind were and are always looked at as one—"holistic" medicine means exactly that: treatment of the body and the mind as a whole. But the idea of body-mind medicine—a direct connection between the central nervous system and the immune system—is just now resurfacing in the West.

The scientific terminology for body-mind medicine is

psychoneuroimmunology. This has become a major area of interest in medical research, which explores the relationship and pathway that goes from the mind through the nervous system and the endocrine (hormonal) system finally to the immune system. Dr. Steven Locke's book, *The Foundations of Psychoneuroimmunology* (1985) has pointed the way in this field. He has followed this with *The Healer Within,* which gives clear explanations for the lay reader, as does Dr. Joan Borysenko's book, *Minding the Body, Minding the Mind.*

When it comes to practical applications, Jon Kabat-Zinn and Saki Santorelli at the University of Massachusetts Medical School have developed the Stress Reduction Clinic, offering relaxation programs to patients referred from every specialty within the hospital. The emphasis is on using mindfulness practices along with yoga to teach patients how to come into the present, experience their particular problems, and thus learn how to effect change. The results have been extremely successful. Kabat-Zinn has published numerous studies, among them one that shows a marked reduction in chronic pain from various causes that remains reduced even four years after patients participated in the mindfulness program.

The Omega Institute has been offering a mindfulness training program with Kabat-Zinn and Santorelli, and it is remarkable to note how many health professionals attend, with plans to bring the techniques back to their own hospital or medical practice.

Writers like Norman Cousins, who in *Anatomy of an Illness* showed that laughter is an effective curative method, have been joined in their beliefs by the medical community. We know now that depression can go hand-in-hand with cancer, that anxiety causes ulcers or exacerbates asthma, that "tension headaches" exist—and conversely, that joy produces health, calm prevents the onset of many diseases, and that a "sound mind in a sound body" is not just a maxim of the ancient Romans.

This is not to say that by eliminating strong emotions we will eliminate disease, or that by eliminating disease we will eliminate strong emotions. I am talking here about a *connection,* about the vital role the mind plays in the functions of the body, and vice versa.

If you're frightened, your pulse quickens. If you're anxious, it's hard to breathe. Depression, anger, stress, fear, love, happiness, and serenity all have physiological components.

I believe that the development of body-mind medicine—which has responded to the unnatural separation between the physical and the psychological—came about as the direct result of the speeding up of the moment. In Chapter Three we saw the differences between mental and emotional time—the first is fast, the latter much slower. If we do not slow down to be in the moment, we live only in mental time, and it's easy in that realm to separate mind and emotion, mind and body. By living in mental time—in a speeded-up world—with the resultant repression of emotional issues, we increase the chance of disease. The faster we go, the more likely we are to separate mind from body, and thus the more susceptible we become to a variety of diseases that have the lack of communication between mind and body as their root cause.

In *Emotional Intelligence,* Daniel Goleman quotes the results of a series of studies involving several thousand men and women. People who suffered from chronic anxiety, depression, pessimism, hostility—even cynicism or suspiciousness—were found to have twice the risk of disease (asthma, arthritis, ulcers, heart attacks, etc.) as those without chronic troubling emotions. "This order of magnitude," Goleman points out, "makes distressing emotions as toxic a risk factor as, say, smoking or high cholesterol are for heart disease." No wonder there is such a growing interest among doctors in body-mind medicine!

We all must be interested. Good health lies in the slowing of the moment. Work through the emotions, and the diseases caused by repressing them will be less likely to surface. Learn to slow down, to experience the emotion and then let it recede, and the body becomes less vulnerable.

Learn to timeshift, and your chances for good health dramatically increase.

At the end of my medical school education, I spent four months at a hospital in a small Himalayan village—this was where I met Shri Bhagwan.

The contrast between the Western medical model that had been consuming my life for the previous four years and my experience in rural India was staggering. There I was witness to all manner of parasitic disease and a variety of diseases stemming from malnutrition. Tuberculosis, which I had never seen in real-life patients, was almost epidemic here. Surgical operations were performed, but often without some of the most basic laboratory techniques and essential diagnostic information.

From the window in the room where I lived, I could see women carrying huge cans of milk up and down the paths along the hills; men carried even heavier loads of wood. Conditions were less than sanitary; even the rudiments of hygiene were difficult to maintain. But the air was clear, and there was never a lack of exercise for the inhabitants.

In that village, out of the hundreds of patients I saw, with every imaginable disease, there was only one instance of a heart attack. The victim was a visiting American professor.

Heart disease is a direct outgrowth of Western culture, found in societies in a hurry, in which life is rushed. It is the most dramatic disease of the shortened moment, though by no means the only one. It is the disease of the workaholic.

Researchers Ray Rosenman and Meyer Friedman label people most prone to heart attacks as type A. These are the people who bolt their food, talk fast, lean over the tracks to see whether the train is coming, and get impatient in traffic jams and supermarket lines. They'll help others who aren't getting a job done "fast enough," multitask themselves, never have "enough" time—indeed, are in competition with time itself.

In a twenty-year study of 3,500 men in the San Francisco area, Rosenman and Friedman found that type A's were four times as prone to incidences of heart attack than were type B's. Type B people feel no sense of time urgency, take life more slowly, play for fun rather than to compete, and do not work as hard or as frantically.

More recent studies have implicated the role of certain emotional states, most specifically hostility and anger, in increasing the likelihood of suffering cardiovascular disease. A study group of heart-attack patients at Stanford University Medical School was taught methods to control and lessen their angry reactions. There was a dramatic reduction in the rates of second heart attacks for those who had been trained versus the group with no training. Fundamental to the training was learning to shift rhythms, to slow down into a mindfulness that allows one to better deal with the anger, rather than allow the quickened intensity of hostility.

Dr. Dean Ornish has demonstrated dramatic success in reversing coronary plaque buildup in patients with severe cardiovascular disease. His program includes a stringent low-fat diet, as well as an emphasis on relaxation training and yoga. Most of us are aware of the role of diet in heart disease, yet the Ornish program is not as effective without the timeshift that results from the yoga and relaxation.

Even though we know the destructive effects of rapid emotions, indeed of speed itself, we still drive ourselves faster and faster. Time is money. Time is productivity. Life's a sprint, not a marathon. As the hero of Willard Motley's *Knock on Any Door* says, "Live fast, die young, and have a good-looking corpse." There is enormous denial in us if we live this way; if we stopped to feel what was going on in our bodies, we would timeshift.

Early on in my practice, I heard many stories of patients who had sudden heart attacks "without previous symptoms." I used to believe those stories, but now I'm convinced that the symptoms were there, only the patient *didn't listen to them,* didn't *feel* them. Remember the story of the politician, which starts this book.

They didn't give themselves time.

Just after my medical training, I took a job at an HMO. There I was given a quota of patients per hour: To meet it, I was required to see a new patient every ten minutes. That was some twenty years ago. In today's modern medicine, physicians often make diagnoses in seventeen seconds. They size up the symptoms of the patient as soon as he walks in, analyze them, and send the patient on his way—to bed at home, to a hospital, with a prescription; anything that'll satisfy the symptom—content that they've done their job. Indeed, if the symptoms persist, somehow they blame the patient.

The patient is content, too. He "knows" what's wrong (an expert has told him) and what to do about it. He can get on with his business in the least possible time.

Of course, what both doctor and patient are treating is the symptom, not the underlying cause. What's left out entirely is the *whole person*.

An eighty-year-old woman told me the story of a time when she had trouble lifting her right arm. She couldn't raise it above her shoulder without enormous pain; she found it difficult to dress or to eat.

She went to see an orthopedist whom she had not previously met.

"It's aging," he said, barely looking up at her. "There's nothing you can do about it."

"I don't think it's aging," she said. "I think it's something else."

"I tell you it's aging. I've been a specialist in joint diseases for forty years. I've seen plenty of such cases."

"I don't think so."

"Trust me. It's aging."

She waved her left arm frantically in front of his face. "See this arm?" she cried. "How come I can lift it? It's eighty years old, too!"

Her doctor, like so many others, didn't take the time to *be* with her. To him, she had no core, no history, no soul. The doctor, as so many doctors do, made an immediate diagnosis on the basis of the symptom only, and would not be shaken from his belief. He was completely "tuned out" to his patient's words and feelings.

In my own practice, I consciously force myself to slow down. Early in my career, for example, a man with a condition related to hypothyroidism handed me a book written by a physician that described new approaches to thyroid disease. "No other doctor was even willing to *read* it," he complained. "But it would tell them much better than I can exactly what's wrong." I borrowed it from him, read it, and was able to help him, and I learned a new approach to a health problem I frequently saw. Too often doctors are experts who dispense their knowledge without realizing that people can be so intimately involved in their own illnesses that their input is vital to finding the cure. We doctors have a great deal to learn in this regard.

I try to listen not only to the patient's words, but also to his feelings. I've found that my consultations generally start with discussion of a specific illness, yet soon seem to be about stress and coming into the present. The likelihood is that when you're sick, you will be stressed. To get beyond the stress—*behind* it—takes the time of both doctor and patient.

Doctor and patient are operating on different rhythms. The patient is anxious, afraid that his symptoms are serious, and worried that the diagnosis will mean bad news. The doctor, on the other hand, is hurrying. Her waiting room is full, this patient doesn't seem too sick, and she has to get to the hospital to begin her rounds. Both are unable to get into the present. They are almost speaking different languages, and neither is "here" for the other.

I consciously slow down with a patient because a patient will often be confused, even contradictory, in his description of what troubles him, and his confusion in turn confuses me. But if I spend the time to listen, I can better determine the root cause of the ailment—and treat that rather than just the symptom.

The cause I often discover is stress or anxiety. Patients with sleep disorders (or chronic fatigue, panic attacks, or even asthma), for example, are so worried about getting enough rest or enduring the next anxiety attack that their problem is exacerbated. I try to teach them to go into the present, *not* to will themselves to sleep or to fend off the next attack, but—since stress comes from resistance—to simply go with their present feelings, to flow into a nonresistant state where there is only the now. It isn't difficult; it's *easy*. But it takes the practitioner's time to help the patient attain that state—it takes the ability to shift time.

I also ask patients to write out a list of questions before they come to see me. Most people suffer from "white-coat syndrome." It's well known, for instance, that patients' blood pressure rises when they see a physician, and in their anxiety, they forget much of what they've come to ask. I have a friend whose father, a man of ninety, complains continually to his daughter and wife about ailments ranging from deafness to spinal stenosis. But he tells his doctor only that he is "fine," or "the same"—and after the doctor has left, he complains that the man "doesn't know medicine—any idiot can see how sick I am."

Evidence continues to mount that clearly indicates stress may be the most significant factor in the widest array of illnesses that afflict us. As reported in numerous journal articles, with more being published monthly, the link between stress and disease is widespread. Stress has been shown to affect immune system functions, causing an increased susceptibility to viral infections and the common cold. It has caused an increased incidence of colorectal cancer, and it impacts the rate of metastases in advanced breast cancer. Stress directly increases risk of cardiovascular disease, and in children increases the risk of diabetes. Graves Disease (a thyroid condition) and inflammatory bowel disease are more prevalent with increased stress.

The role of stress can be further illustrated by a study that was conducted of LeMans race car drivers who had their blood-fat levels checked before and after the race. Their levels rose an average of one hundred points afterward, far more significant than the impact expected even from a fatty diet. The negative health effects of stress appear in all aspects of physiological function. Stress is a modern disease; a disease of speed.

Recently, a woman with a thyroid condition came to see me. The condition had cleared, but was now replaced by severe anxiety attacks, which no medicine seemed to help. It took me awhile to get her to face what it was that made her fundamentally anxious.

"I'm not getting enough air," she said.

"Anything else?"

"I'll never find a medicine that works."

"Anything else?"

"I'm afraid I'm going to die!"

Right. The thyroid condition had been threatening. It had been cured, but the threat remained, at least in the woman's subconscious. Once she was able to face her fear of death squarely, the anxiety attacks disappeared in a week.

Most doctors don't have the time to truly listen; and most patients would rather not pay attention to what is really happening in their own bodies. When seeing a patient for the first time, doctors take medical histories, inquire about emotional condition ("Depressed?" "Trouble at home?" "Working too hard?") in a perfunctory way, and then prescribe. If the medicine doesn't work, they try another medicine. The patient goes back to work, or back home, with the feeling that both he and the doctor have done their best.

The doctor has listened to the (often confusing) "facts"; the patient has "described" his symptoms. Both are satisfied. Yet both have failed.

Neither has taken the time to be in the present. Neither has slowed down enough to be able to see the whole person. Both are caught in the pace of work and money, of speed and stress, and have been unable to shift time. So the doctor goes home with the nagging feeling that perhaps "I could have done more," while the patient may be heading for a more serious illness.

As Daniel Goleman states in *Emotional Intelligence:*

Historically, medicine in modern society has defined its mission in terms of nursing *disease*—the medical disorder—while overlooking *illness*—the patient's experience of disease. Patients, by going along with this view of their problem, join a quiet conspiracy to ignore how they are reacting emotionally to their medical problems—or to dismiss those reactions as irrelevant to the course of the problem itself. That attitude is reinforced by a medical model that dismisses entirely the idea that mind influences body in any substantial way.

Four years ago, a woman came to me for treatment of breast cancer. I sent her to a surgeon who removed the tumor and later monitored her progress. Two years later, he picked up a questionable shadow in an X ray and recommended invasive tests to determine if the cancer had reappeared.

The woman had been coming to me steadily. Though I was no longer directly responsible for her care, I was "the only one she could talk to"; the doctor who would understand her "human" side.

She was terrified of the test, of any operation, and could only express that terror to me, she said. Her surgeon was battling her disease; she was battling her *illness,* which comprised both the possible tumor and her terror. We needed to weigh the degree of her terror against the need for exploratory surgery.

I spoke to the doctor, then to the patient. It seemed to me that the surgery was necessary, but I was able to tell her the news gently, calmly, and persuade her that *this* surgery was not frightening, and it was worth it. The only true risk was in ignoring the shadow.

I was treating the *whole* woman, mind and emotion as well as body. She submitted to the procedure. The cancer had not reappeared.

As a physician, I've focused on wellness and health. In the practice of holistic medicine, one attempts to treat the whole patient, to look at her entire psychological and physiological way of life, and to work with preventive medicine.

Western medicine concentrates on sickness and disease. I and other doctors learned to recognize pathology, the abnormalities of the cellular and metabolic functions of the body. We were never taught what health is. Health was defined as not having the disease, and so we learned to cure the illness but not how to prevent it. Prevention, other than a few general precepts from doctors, is up to us.

One of our foremost health and nutrition experts, Dr. Jeffrey Bland, categorizes our physical condition into three states: optimal health, vertical disease, and horizontal disease.

The first is self-explanatory; the third refers to those pathological diseases which, literally, lie us low. The second, vertical disease, refers to those ailments that afflict so many of us, yet we put off dealing with them. These are not ailments that are life threatening or incapacitating. They are the nagging backaches, headaches, fatigue, indigestion, skin rashes, or chronic pain syndromes to which we have become accustomed. We promise ourselves that we'll deal with them as soon as we finish our next project at work, or when the kids graduate from school, or when we get our next vacation, or *when we get the time*—which we already know never comes unless we become self-responsible for its creation.

Western medicine is accustomed to treating horizontal diseases— and for spotting incipient disease in an outwardly healthy body, which is why you should get regular checkups, even as you learn to become the master of your own health.

Have a heart attack, and your chances of survival in the West are far greater than anywhere else in the world. Our machines can detect minute cancers, and our instruments can remove them with the least possible damage to surrounding tissue. We fight bacterial infections with the most sophisticated and effective drugs; we can remake limbs, reconstruct damaged faces, transplant organs, prolong the life of the dying, and rescue the two-pound premature baby from what, in other societies, would be certain death.

Our medical system is unparalleled when it comes to crisis care and technological intervention for the late stages of disease. In fact, thirty percent of the money spent on health care is for the last six months of life.

We call it health care, but a more accurate name would be disease care.

Where our doctors—we ourselves—fail is in the treatment of the far more common, and initially far less serious, vertical diseases. (I say "initially" since vertical disease, if not treated correctly, will lead to horizontal disease.)

In other words, we are experts in dealing with pathology, but amateurs in treating the whole person, and procrastinators when it comes to treating ourselves.

What we want is instant gratification. We are always hungry to get it "now," but are unwilling to take the time to be here for what's actually going on.

"I know a guy who fell from a ten-story building," Steve McQueen says in one of his movies. "As he passed each floor on the way down, he said, 'So far, so good.' "

With our vertical diseases, we are like the falling man.

- Headaches? Probably eyestrain. We'll have them checked out just as soon as we've finished the week's work (only we don't).
- Neck pain? Comes from sitting too long at a desk staring at the computer. Next week—we swear it—we'll start going to the gym (only we don't).
- Anxiety attacks? With *that* boss, who wouldn't have them? What we need is to take a good three-week vacation (only we don't).

- Shortness of breath? Bet it comes from not getting enough exercise. Tomorrow, we'll walk to work (only we wake up late, so we don't).
- Getting a little paunchy around the middle? Right after New Year's, we swear it's only fruits and vegetables for us (only it isn't).

Basically, we and only we are responsible for our own health, yet we take care of our cars better than we take care of ourselves—at least we take our cars in for five-thousand-mile checkups.

I think that what we'd all like to do is drop our body off (like a car) at a doctor's, take our brain to the job, and pick our body up again after work, bloodstream changed, joints lubricated, rattles eliminated. Let the doctor do it, we feel. *We* don't want to be involved.

We don't want to think of diets, exercise, or the elimination of stress factors. We look for the quick fix, the instant remedy, and we *love* the doctor who tells us, "Take two aspirin and call me in the morning."

The contrast between a quick fix and taking time is illustrated by the story of Nancy, a woman in her mid-thirties, who developed multiple sclerosis. She came to me, as she had gone to many other doctors, looking for "answers"—and I, like the many others, told her there was no definitive cure. I did, however, put her on a program of a special diet, vitamins, and exercise, which, while not curative, radically alleviated her symptoms by improving her health. Despite occasional flare-ups, she was at last able to face her condition squarely and realistically, and regain enough vitality to go on to become a yoga teacher.

She invited me to address a meeting of the local MS Society, and I was struck at once that only two of the forty-some members looked healthy. They were the two following my regimen; fighting their disease and not giving in to it. They were the only ones who did not make a beeline for the soda and doughnuts available at the breaks.

The others, I realized, were looking for news of a cure. Once that was denied them, they went on to a different gratification, the doughnuts and soda which had been rather thoughtlessly provided for them. Doughnuts and soda are by no means part of a healthy diet, and probably my listeners went back to more appropriate food at home. But here they seemed to be saying, "Why me? And *if* me, then life is lousy and I'll enjoy myself now, no matter the consequences."

Nancy's success was that she faced the fact that MS was her lot, and she didn't give up. She threw her energy into making her life as successful as she could, investing her time in being healthy. She had expanded the moment of health by not running from her fear of the disease, but facing it as fully as her life.

With many patients, there is often shame or guilt or the sense of victimization. Nancy did not choose to have MS, but her ability to accept it has opened her to the possibility of living well within the confines of this diagnosis.

Everyone else wanted an instant cure, and without a "magic bullet" they wanted any type of "feel good" that was available. This is the model of denial and avoidance, wherein there is no possibility of slowing down to experience the disease, to accept it, and even to befriend it. By doing just that, Nancy was able to create a life of health beyond what most in her condition are able to achieve. Slowing down to be present, to accept conditions as they are, gives us the opportunity to ultimately effect the most positive changes. Nancy and others I have worked with are living examples of this.

Most people with any kind of serious illness look for the miracle cure. The less aggressive take the aspirin, the diet meals-in-a-can ("all the natural ingredients your body needs"), the pep pills, and the antidepressants—and when the headaches go away, when they begin to lose weight, when their vitality improves, and their depression recedes, they think they're cured. (Only they're not.)

Consider that slight pain, if left unattended, will eventually worsen. Vertical disease, if allowed to linger, will become horizontal disease.

It *takes time* to be healthy, and it's an investment more important than the time you put into work. We can't simply "drop into" good health, as much as we'd like to. Health takes effort; it doesn't "just happen." But most people are only concerned with their health when they're feeling bad.

Optimal health only occurs when the body is in rhythm with itself (a regular heartbeat, regular breath, regular eliminations, etc.) and this is only possible when we've slowed down and are in the present moment. As we'll see, disease slows us down, and the prospect of death brings us squarely into the present.

But then it's too late. How much does it have to hurt before we are willing to stop and listen? How much pain do we have to feel? How many headaches, anxiety attacks? How much obesity or shortness of breath?

I believe that sometimes we *create* diseases in ourselves (unconsciously, of course; my statement implies no blame and should generate no guilt) simply to force ourselves to stop to feel. When we're sick—particularly when grievously ill—we reshape our priorities and rethink our lives. There is nothing like pain or the fear of death to bring us into the moment.

How nice if we could entrain with wellness instead! How nice if we could recognize how vital rhythm is in creating a healthy life.

It's well known that the body has circadian rhythms. If viewed in terms of health, we see that hormonal levels fluctuate throughout the day and month, as do levels of blood sugar, minerals, and enzymes. We are likely to be upbeat in the light (think how good it feels to go outdoors on a sunny day!), depressed in the darkness. The great director Jose Quintero told me that he became nearly suicidal directing a performance of Eugene O'Neill's *Long Day's Journey into Night* during a Norwegian winter. "It wasn't the play so much as the lack of light," he said. "No matter what time I went out, it was always dark."

Until recently, the theory that the body's organs are in different rhythms with each other has been ignored in the West, but it lies behind all Chinese and other oriental medicines. Today, we know how dramatically important body rhythm is, and we've learned to change treatments according to the time of day and the season. Certain types of chemotherapy, for example, are more or less effective depending on the body's rhythm. All human cells work in sync with each other—cancer is fundamentally a case of cells running amok, out of rhythm with the other cells of the body.

Just as cancer develops further through disrhythm, we can look at the healing effects of entrained rhythm. Dr. David Spiegel of Stanford University Medical School studied a group of women with advanced breast cancer. He created support groups for women to express their experiences with the disease. There were no differences in treatment methods, yet when they were compared to women who faced their cancers alone, those in the support group lived *twice* as long. There are other possible explanations, but I have no doubt that the ability to come into the moment with a group of people, to be able to slow down and share feelings, creates an entrained rhythm that truly affects the healing process.

Deepak Chopra, M.D., who is both Western trained and steeped in Ayurvedic medicine from India, is an expert in both conventional and alternative medicine. I recently had the opportunity to ask his thoughts about the role of rhythm in health and disease. He believes that "the universe is a cosmic dance, our biological rhythms are part of this dance, and when our body is in harmony with inherent rhythmicities of nature, we experience wholeness. Health is the return of the memory of wholeness. The first manifestation of disease is a disruption of biological rhythms, which means we are no longer in step with the cosmic symphony." He has begun to further explore the role of music and rhythm in health.

Robert Becker, M.D., and Andrew Bassett, M.D., have pioneered the field of electromagnetic energy as it relates to human health and disease. Their work showed how bone fractures that were mending poorly could be fully healed with the use of electromagnetic coils. The Japanese have begun using magnets to cure headaches and many other conditions. In fact, some have postulated that the needles used in acupuncture act like antennas, passing along electromagnetic currents that help the body return to its normal rhythm.

There is great potential in the field of electromagnetics. I believe that medicine will be transformed by the knowledge that develops in this area. It is fascinating to note that the curative effects directly result from rhythmic wave impulses, which interact with the body's subtle rhythms—tuning the inner rhythms of the body to the delicate balance of health.

As we've seen, stress underlies most disease, and stress is arrhythmic. But rather than acknowledge the dangers of arrhythmia, we virtually foster it with caffeine to help the day "get started" (it's like racing a car motor before it has had a chance to warm up), creating a pace that starts fast and gets faster as the day progresses, and a workload so vast, "there aren't enough hours in the day" to complete it.

To counteract the rush, we take "downers," usually in the form of alcohol, then "veg out" in front of a television set from which images fling themselves at us in rhythms as fast or faster than the pace we've endured all day.

Jon Kabat-Zinn has shown that mindfulness and meditation are vital in the treatment of illness. Recently, the National Institutes of Health have acknowledged that biofeedback and meditation are an effective therapy for certain conditions, and have recommended that insurance companies reimburse patients for following these approaches.

Wellness (a good word, I think, for *positive health)* lies in our control and no one else's. My goal as a doctor, and as the writer of this book, is to show you how much more beneficial it is to go *by yourself* into positive health, and how this simple act of self-empowerment will let you live longer, minimize stress, fill you with the air of wellness (indeed, good breathing is a keystone to good health), cut down on depression, and improve your work life and your personal life. It can fill you with a spirit *in the moment* more pleasurable than any risky sport or drug-produced high.

Wellness is in *our* control. When we attain it and if we keep it up, all the other pleasures the world has to offer become more alive—and so do we.

The other day, a ninety-year-old patient came to see me and immediately took off his shirt. "Hit me in the stomach," he said. "Hard as you want."

I didn't, but I laughed and asked how he had gotten such strong stomach muscles.

"Sit-ups," he explained. "Added them to the jogging and the shadowboxing."

I examined him. He had the body of a man twenty years his junior.

"Why did you come to see me?" I inquired.

"Just showing off."

In his case, and in yours, the old adage of "use it or lose it" applies. Like the backup systems in spacecraft, our body's organs have reserve capacity—it's why we have two lungs instead of one, why if one kidney fails, the other can take over.

But reserve capacity can take you only so far, and if you misuse the organs (by smoking, or by allowing fat to accumulate around the muscles), you'll soon find yourself in trouble from which exercise may not be enough to extract you.

To achieve wellness, we need not only a good diet and exercise, but also to adopt a slower, steadier rhythm, and an ability to feel firm and confident about our well-being. If we incorporate the exercises for timeshifting described in Chapter Seven—if we specifically focus on healthful measures—we'll feel better and *be* better.

My own prescription for health includes:

- Regular exercise—sports or dance or play—on which we focus and for which we make ample time.
- Daily meditation and relaxed breathing.
- Fun and laughter (it's better than an apple a day).
- Time spent on the enjoyment of meals—avoid "power lunches."
- Time spent on preparing meals with fresh and wholesome foods. (Avoid fast foods; generally they are a melange of the worst chemicals, preservatives, oils, and sweeteners.)
- Treating your body with love and affection by scheduling regular massages and body work.
- Making health a priority by taking health retreats; vacations that nourish body and soul.
- Honoring and acknowledging your health.

Time spent on health will prolong life. This investment pays the best dividends.

CHAPTER FOURTEEN

AGING

At the age of eighty-five, Pa Kin, the greatest
poet of modern China, had just been
decorated by President Mitterrand and was
invited to visit France. "To meet whom? To
find what of interest? You realize," he added,
as though to apologize for these questions,
"my feeling is that I only have seven dollars
left to my name—and I don't want to fritter
them away on peanuts."
—JEAN-LOUIS SERVAN-SCHREIBER

AMERICAN SOCIETY IS most afraid of the very stage of
life that has the potential to be most happy and most fulfilling. To
us, aging is anathema. It's as though every new wrinkle requires a
smoothing cream, every gray hair a dye, every aching joint a lini-
ment. We run from aging, we deny it, and we are embarrassed by it.

Aging depresses us. It reminds us that we are mortal, and dying,
and so we look on each of its manifestations with horror.

We all live in linear time, a straight arrow that goes from birth to
death. Aging reminds us that our end is near. The fact that we are
wiser than before, that we can have the time to think and to meditate, that our pace has at last slowed so we can appreciate our
surroundings and our relationships, seem to offer little solace. We
are older. Soon we will die.

In societies dwelling in circular time, however, all this is different.
The elderly are honored, not ignored; listened to, not shunned. An
aging person, having experienced more of life, has many things to
teach his younger friends—not about facts, necessarily, but about
emotions, feelings, instinct, and experience. In autumn, she can feel

the approach of winter, knowing as no young person can that inexorably after winter comes—once again—spring.

Elders are the wisdom-keepers in circular time cultures. When a crisis arises, it is the elders to whom people turn for advice. If there is a flood or other natural disaster, Grandfather will know what to do. If there is sickness, Grandmother will have the remedies. For they are the wise ones.

In the West, though, technology supplies the answers, and technology is the province of the young. Our children are taught about nuclear science, computers, aerospace design, etc. Their elders are considered behind the times. Because we value information over wisdom, elders are considered useless by the young, even as a burden to society. And the elders begin to believe it themselves.

Paradoxically, the one aspect of aging we look forward to, the one we "can't wait" for, the one we "put in our time" to achieve, is retirement. But once we get there, we hit a wall.

I think it is the wall of time. Suddenly, we have time without knowing how to spend it, as though someone had given us a million dollars when we were stranded on a desert island. Our work, which has defined us, and given us our self-esteem, is no longer available to us (we've told ourselves we don't *want* it anymore), and thus we think of ourselves as useless, as a "burden" to our children. For some people, the experience makes them feel like prisoners; it makes them feel like they are "doing time."

If we've planned for retirement well, we have adequate money. We can be lazy, we can go fishing, we can watch television all day long, we can go to the movies in the afternoon, we can travel, we can garden, and we can stay up all night and sleep till noon. Many of us—most of us!—get busy again, and go back to work, in some form or another.

Since nothing in our work life has prepared us for a life of leisure, and because we have been taught all our lives that idleness is "unworthy" and that to "do nothing" is a sin, we volunteer at the local hospital, we work on political campaigns, we stuff envelopes for charities, or we take part-time employment. No one has taught us how to *enjoy* retirement. What we're really doing with all this activity is trying to escape our upset about being seen as useless, our fears of infirmity and death. If we face our feelings squarely, we need to face the certainty of death. Anything, we think, is better than that. So we announce with pride that we "don't have the time" to do nothing—meaning we don't have the time to be in the moment. We continue to fill our days with activities long after we really have to. And the happiness and relaxation we long for continue to elude us.

Sylvia is a woman in her mid-seventies who retired from a professional career a few years ago. Her retirement first led her to winters in Florida and summers up north with friends and relatives; she had been widowed some years back.

This routine left her dissatisfied and unfulfilled. She came to a program at Omega on health and wellness, and was so taken with it that she decided to spend the summer living at Omega as a staff member, immersed in the learning community. After participating in activities ranging from Brazilian dance to African drumming, from sessions on wellness to seminars on timeshifting, her spirit soared. She became more alive and vital.

Those who age most successfully, like Sylvia, are the "learners." I know of many people who have gone back to college simply for the joy of learning, to keep their minds active. "I feel like a child again," an eighty-three-year-old woman told me. These people are quite literally entering a new life. "What are you doing *that* for?" an acquaintance asked his mother, seventy-six, who had begun a course in philosophy at Skidmore. "For spirit," she replied. "For growth."

Still, it is perfectly permissible—even gratifying—to do "nothing." I know a retiree who used to cringe with guilt when he told friends he wasn't doing anything. Soon, though, he gave the same answer with a grin, with pride, even with arrogance. He found that doing "nothing" suited him, and by relaxing into it, by letting himself into each day's "nothingness," he found a contentment he had never felt before. "I really enjoy my life," he said, when I asked him to be more specific about the experience. "I walk, read, listen to music, watch television. No schedule, no pressure. I sleep well. I really get a kick out of telling people I'm doing nothing! They're so stressed out, it seems they want me and everybody else to be working as hard as they are."

One complaint of the elderly is that time passes more quickly than when they were young. One reason is familiarity.

Do you remember the summer when you were five, or perhaps seven, when you were aware of the sunshine, the languor, and the games, and the friendships, and it seemed as if summer would never end, would go from one golden day to another into infinity? Do you remember the summer you first fell in love?

When you're elderly, summers don't have that feel any longer. You've been through seventy of them, and now there is sadness associated with the pleasure. You may remember unhappy events that occurred in the summertime. One summer becomes much like another—hurtling us toward the end. "Just another summer," we think. "Nothing special."

But they *can* be special. At one of my workshops, a woman announced that the past summer was the best of her life.

"What did you do?" I asked.

"I watched butterflies."

At dusk each day, a swarm of butterflies had entered her garden, and played there until sundown. The woman would hurry home from her errands or from visiting her grandchildren to make sure she was there in time to watch them. To her, they brought beauty and peace. They brought her into a moment that lasted all summer.

We need to timeshift, to expand the moments so that we are *present* in every summer—and fall, winter, and spring. The woman who rushed home to her butterflies was doing just that: she used a ritual, entrained with nature, made each day "longer" by participating in the newness of life. When we timeshift, each season can be full, lasting, infinite.

Sociologists at Duke University recently completed a study on longevity in which they discovered that people who were flexible in facing loss—who could confront their initial grief, work through it, and go on with their lives *in the present*—had a greater chance for long life than those who dwelled in their grief. This latter group was living in the past, very much masking their own fear of death by mourning the loss of another person, and by doing so they were unable to savor the moment or exist in the now.

Much of our fear comes from watching the deaths of our parents;

we use them subconsciously as role models. If they died with fear, we are likely to be fearful also. But if they accepted death calmly, even with relief, then our own fears are probably mitigated—and our chances for a long and happy old age become vastly enhanced.

In my workshops, I ask students how long they think they'll live. Almost all of them relate their answer to their parents: "My mother lived to seventy, my father to seventy three. I hope I can make it to seventy-five, since I take better care of myself than they did."

This sets up a self-fulfilling expectation. The chances are that these responders *will* die around age seventy-five. But there are people who routinely live longer lives, such as Russian Georgians, or Afghanistani Huzans, or the Peruvian Vallacanbabans. For them, seventy is middle age, and if you can picture yourself living past one hundred as a physically and mentally vital person, then I'm convinced your life-expectancy will expand.

In fact, when Alexander Lief of the Harvard Medical School first studied the potential causes of longevity, he found that the most significant attribute of these people was individual and social expectation of living more than one hundred years.

Positive expectations affect health as well as aging. For example, cataract patients who have confidence in their surgeons do better than those who are mistrustful of their treatment. Cancer patients are taught to visualize healthy cells attacking diseased ones in order to overcome their illness. Bernie Siegel, M.D., has worked extensively with the effects of a positive attitude in cancer patients. The Simontons have done similar work.

Yet as we age, most of us live in fear, positive that the next illness will "get" us, sure that our infirmities will worsen and our memory will fade. Even so, we are surprised and disappointed when our fears are realized.

We need to face aging optimistically, recognizing that we can maintain our present state of wellness.

Think back over the past few years. What do you remember? Can you recall what you were doing on October 5, 1995, at ten A.M.? Can you remember what you did at work last Thursday? With whom did you have lunch two days ago?

And your first kiss. Do you remember where you were, what the kiss felt like, the expression in your partner's eyes? What costume did you wear at Halloween when you were five? What did you wear to the last dinner party you attended? What about the last time you took a plane versus the first?

What lingers in the memory are only the moments when we're truly present, whether those moments were momentous or ordinary. The rest of the time, when we're doing things just to get them finished, simply going through the motions of life—all of those days, months, years recede into a gray blur.

My workshop participants are often stunned to realize how much they don't remember of their own lives. When I ask questions about what they recall, everyone's answer has to do with a deeply felt event. It might be joyous or painful, embarrassing or fearful, but it's something that fully captured their attention—mental, physical, emotional.

Clearly, something that arouses great emotion or passion pulls us into the now. A car crash, a fire, an intense night of lovemaking. Novelty will bring us into the present, too, partly because doing something for the first time tends to arouse emotions, and partly because new situations inherently demand more attention than situations with which we're familiar.

In Sufi practice, a key word is "remembrance." That is the way you get in touch with God. When we get lost in the flow of life, if we are too busy to feel, too rushed to truly see and hear, then remembrance is lost, and we are lost from ourselves, from our center, from our world.

If you miss the event when it happens, it's gone forever, because we only recall what we were present for the first time around. What happens, then, when our memories begin to fade as part of the aging process?

Our memory is made up of *past* present moments. Senility is uncomfortable when we want to extrapolate from those past presents directly into the now. If you've lost your past and are afraid of the future, you will be disoriented in the present.

Our loss of memory has the potential to make us more alive in the present. That's why some people do so well with senility, while others—uncomfortable and fearful in the present—do not. Those who have spent their lives avoiding the present moment continue to resist, and accordingly feel unhappy.

I've seen old people rail against their failing memory, but if they could accept it, if they could shift from regret at a lost past to the consciousness of a vital present, they would find peace and joy in their lives and in their spirit. My grandmother was happily senile; she was okay with it. She is my role model, and was one of the first to teach me how important the present really is. Senility has, after all, been called a "second childhood." And how many of us would not wish for another childhood if it were offered?

All this requires is timeshifting. Too many of us have no idea of how to come into the present—we have simply not experienced it—so we don't know what to do with ourselves when confronted with the prospect of aging. As we approach death, we feel increasingly fearful, since we haven't yet learned to sit comfortably in the present. As our memory wanes, we will feel more comfortable with ourselves if we have already had experience with the now. The more we practice being in the present today, the better we will be able to cope with aging tomorrow.

In *The Fountain of Age,* Betty Friedan points out that there are practically no old people in television commercials, and those that we do see—like the ninety-year-old man waterskiing barefoot, or the wrinkle-free, silver-haired couple delighted that they had taken out adequate insurance when they were young—are really youths in disguise, cartoon figures having nothing to do with the vast majority of the elderly.

Let's not even *think* of the elderly, television commands. Stay younger longer—indeed, for as long as you can—and then disappear!

Of course this goes counter to the fact that with the aging of the baby boom generation, more and more people are growing old, and it seems strange that our society does nothing to encourage them, would rather not have the "burden" of taking care of them, and altogether wishes they would simply go away.

Why can't we change our attitude and look at aging as a positive force? If we could, it would transform our society, but to do so requires accepting the present moment as it is. Aging is a natural biological process in all living organisms. As each of us ages, our body changes. We develop wrinkles, our muscles begin to atrophy, our reflexes get slower. To resist this only denies the reality of the moment. Learning to timeshift is about recognizing the rhythm and reality of the changing moments of our life process. We do get slower, which is only negative if we expect to be operating at the faster speed of a youngster. When we consider how much better able to appreciate life we are when we slow our rhythm, then the grace of aging and its slower pace can be seen as something positive, another stage in the beauty of life.

There is also a significant role that elders can play that will give a great benefit to society. To receive material benefits, they should impart spiritual ones: a knowledge of history; a sense of hope; love. Rabbi Zalman Schachter-Shalomi, for example, in his book *Spirit and Eldering,* points out that contiguous generations are always at odds. He advocates a "rent a 'bubba' " program whereby grandparents can team up with their grandchildren to teach them from their own experience and wisdom. The problem, he believes, is in getting the middle generation to agree.

You don't even need to teach only your own grandchild. One woman, Jean, told our class she had never had children of her own and now, in her seventies, felt a longing for an extended family. One of her neighbors was a single mother with three children who seemed to be struggling with her life. She lived at a distance from any close relatives and worked all day to make ends meet.

Jean offered to become a foster grandmother, unusual and virtually unheard of in our society, yet vitally needed. The result has been an overwhelming success for everyone involved. Jean has a loving and supportive family in her life because she is able to generously offer her own support and love. The family has adopted her, and she has adopted them.

When Jean told this story, there were many teary eyes of elders in the class. They no doubt longed for similar connections. If they are moved to look, they will find them.

Ram Dass tells of the time he first realized, at age sixty-two, that he was elderly. Buying a ticket on the train between Westport, Connecticut, and New York City, he was asked what kind of ticket he wanted.

"You mean I have a choice?"

"Yes. Regular and Senior Citizen's. Senior Citizen's is three dollars cheaper."

Of course he bought the cheaper ticket, but then realized with a shock that he had donned a new coat, a coat of age, a coat made by our society, which fits *all* people over sixty, no matter their health, no matter the age of their spirit. He realized that in American terms, he was no longer necessary, just one of the aged who, to the young, was taking from society more than he had put in, at least in terms of Medicare and Social Security. But he still has plenty left to offer! His thoughts have matured along with his body. He knows things he can teach us all.

What a contrast to the society of India, where Ram Dass' Indian friends greeted him with, "You look older!"

His American nature rebelled. It sounded so much like an insult to him! But he soon realized the greeting was a compliment. He realized that saying "You look older!" means you are wiser. His friends were honoring him as they honored all the elderly: as people who had much to teach, for they had experienced a great deal more.

We can import such an attitude. But first the elderly must choose to embrace it.

When we're young, we think of the future as vast and exciting. As we get older, we think of it as transient and filled with pain.

But it doesn't have to be.

Aging is only another stage of the present, and as such can bring us as much pleasure as any other time of life. Ram Dass describes a meeting with a ninety-year-old psychiatrist who, hale and hearty, was still seeing patients on a daily basis.

At first, Ram Dass was envious, but then he realized he would choose another path for himself. Life is composed of stages, he says, of which aging is one, and he believes in different modes of speed for the different stages.

Aging is a stage when we slow down, and when our physical condition deteriorates to some degree, even with the best medical care and attention. The mind can stay sharp and alert, but it also slows somewhat. We experience a natural reversal of the fast pace we live at during our highly productive years.

This is a contemplative time, an introspective period of life. There is less energy for physical exertion, although many elderly people describe needing less sleep as they age. There is much to experience in life from this different vantage point. Those who prosper in this time are those willing to be present for the experience, rather than deny it through fear, or by pretending they are still "young."

Let's *graduate* to aging, and not resist it, for as we know, resistance means stress, and stress makes us suffer. We speak of the "quality of life" factor in old age, but we can only achieve this if we slow down to be in the now, if we look neither with longing to the past, nor with fear to the future.

Success in aging seems most directly related to an attitude of acceptance instead of resistance or denial. Rather than focusing on a model of perpetual youth, it is recognizing the natural cycle of life that includes the aging process and the preparation for it. In this regard, consider the following:

- Visualize your retirement before it comes. Look to the future without fear, seeing yourself as you want to be.
- Before retirement, take extra vacation time or reduce your working hours. Begin to feel what having more free time is like so you can learn to pace yourself.
- Involve yourself in learning. Look for the joy and wonder of it. Don't pursue knowledge for any material benefit, but for the process itself.
- Exercise both your mind and your body. Reading and jogging are equally important.
- Regain spontaneity. Try new things. Don't let yourself become "sclerosed" or set in your ways. Experiment with life.
- Listen to the young without necessarily agreeing with them or following their example. You are wiser, but they can be wise, too.
- Spend time with children. Take the opportunity to play with them.
- Give of yourself to the young as a friend and a mentor.
- Allow yourself contemplative time. Settle into the present moment.

CHAPTER FIFTEEN

DEATH AND DYING

*We shall not cease from exploration and the
end of all our exploring will be to arrive
where we started and know the place for the
first time.*

—T. S. ELIOT

"ALL THIS TIME, I thought I was learning to live, when all along I was learning to die."

So said Leonardo da Vinci, and we are likely to read his words, smile knowingly, think to ourselves "how wise"—and be glad that they don't really apply to us.

We're right: They don't.

Most Westerners run from even *talk* of death. True, we cry at movies like *Terms of Endearment* when dying is unrealistically romanticized; we weep at funerals, cheer when the "bad guys" die on television, and shudder at newspaper accounts of catastrophes, though we soon get over it. But as for the thought of our own death, while we know in our mind that death is inevitable, we expend untold energy denying it, sensing somewhere in our untrustworthy heart that we are immortal.

We deny death because we are afraid of it. This fear is so deeply ingrained that it, above all other factors, keeps us from being fully in the present.

When we are alive, our death exists in the future. If we spend our days worrying about death, we essentially live in the future. In that sense, death robs us of life before we die.

It takes attention to hold off death. We plan. We become anxious. We busy ourselves so we do not have to think about it. And we lose contact with present time and present place where wonder and joy—and not death—exist.

"But I'm not afraid of death," people have told me, "only of some terrible disease like cancer, or some awful injury."

Yes. But probably they are afraid of death as well. Actually, fear heightens our experience of disease or pain or death, whether it be our own or a loved one's. If we can face calamity directly, then we will experience it as a part of life. When it comes to death, we must recognize that its mystery is unfathomable.

Ram Dass tells of a student who went to a Zen master.

"What can you tell me about death?" the student asked.

"Nothing," the other replied. "I'm a Zen master. Not a *dead* Zen master."

One way to come to the feelings of death is through meditation. Indeed, Philip Kapleau, author of the brilliant *The Wheel of Death*, points out that meditation itself is a "dance" of death, for ultimately death is both the end and the beginning.

I remember with awe an elderly man in my class doing his first meditation. He seemed shaken when it was over, and I asked him why.

"I'm afraid of death," he said.

He had immediately come to a place where he was alone, by himself, facing universal issues. It was remarkable to me that in such a short time he could reach this place that most of us hide from, avoiding any consideration of our true fears. He was overwhelmed, and I empathized with him, having undergone an equivalent experience.

My own fear of dying stems from childhood. When I was eight or nine, my grandfather died, and the words "really" and "forever" buzzed in my head. He was *really* dead; he would be dead *forever*, never to return to spend time with me. I couldn't sleep for months. If death had happened to him, it would happen to me. I would really be dead. I would be gone forever.

Until children understand the concept of time, they cannot conceive of death. Knowledge of death is the prime cause of a child's loss of innocence. Until faced with an understanding of death, children are intrepid daredevils. That is one of the reasons we must watch them so carefully.

It is in the realm of death that the Western concept of linear time is most destructive. In cultures in which people live in circular time, they do not fear death; they look upon it as a blessing. In Bali, for example, funerals are celebrated like births, with equivalent joy and ceremony. For the Balinese, death is simply part of the continuum of birth, life, death, and rebirth. As Voltaire said, "After all, it is no more surprising to be born twice than it is to be born once."

The Sufi mystic Jalal ud-Din Rumi, perhaps the greatest of the Persian poets, wrote:

> I died as a mineral and became a plant,
> I died as a plant and rose to animal,
> I died as animal and I was a man.
> Why should I fear?
> Was I less by dying?

Death is in our lives, and we must recognize that as an unalterable fact. Recently, the six-year-old daughter of a friend was killed on a camping trip in the Adirondack State Park. My friend and his son and daughter had spent an idyllic few days there, close to nature and close to one another.

As they were leaving, they crossed a highway that cut through the park and the girl was struck by a car traveling sixty miles per hour. She died instantly.

The tragedy was unspeakable; my friend and his son will have to struggle terribly to get through their grief and guilt. But taken objectively, one can see how difficult it is to make a timeshift in a world where the slow rhythm of nature clashes with the speed of modern society's most familiar totem, the car.

In the middle of nature, the pace of society intruded in a most horrendous way. (Which is not to say that nature itself can't be cruel, violent, full of death.) Death sometimes has no meaning except that it exists; it can be expected or unexpected, and to live life in fear of death denies life itself.

Death does not exist in the present moment. In the now, there is only life, with its range of emotions and myriad feelings, its universal bounty.

In my timeshifting workshops, I try an exercise. I ask the members to imagine the next six months. It is a time of perfect health and physical well-being; there is plenty of money and, if they choose, they do not have to do another day's work.

At the end of the six months they will die.

How would they spend those months? I ask. What would their priorities be? I put on a peaceful, beautiful piece of music and let them imagine those six months and their feelings about them.

For most workshop participants, it's an extraordinarily disturbing exercise, and I've been touched by the seriousness and the sadness etched on their faces. Many of them have not come face-to-face with imagined death in so direct a fashion, and their initial reaction is one of shock. Almost always, they take a minute or so before they begin writing, and then they often quickly cross out what they had started to write, pause, think some more, and begin to write again, obviously with greater seriousness.

Some start without much depth: "I'd tell my boss off, get good and drunk, and *then* decide what I'd do"; "I'd have sex with a hundred women, without ever worrying about AIDS"—that sort of thing.

Then the answers get more thoughtful. The most common is, "I'd take a long trip with the person I love, visiting all the places in the world I want to see."

But that, too, gives way to deeper sentiments, and when I go around the group, asking for answers, then I hear about solving relationship problems with a loved one, spending time with the children, and not changing anything because life is good. But by far the most common is, "I'd spend all my time with the people I love."

Yes. Human relationships count most when the prospect of death looms before us, and the exercise clearly points that out. The most dramatic responses are from people who have an estranged relationship with a loved one.

Joe began speaking about his father and how upset he had been about their argument over money; they hadn't spoken for two years. The thought of his imminent death made Joe realize he wanted to heal the rift before dying. So during the exercise, he made amends with his dad. When he shared this with the group, all of a sudden he realized, "Why am I waiting? I need to resolve this now!"

We are all in the process of dying; we just don't know when it will happen. Why not resolve issues and express our love now, before it's too late?

Senator Paul Tsongas once said, "No one on his deathbed ever said, 'I wish I had spent more time at the office,'" and that attitude is reflected here.

It's wonderful that so many people are able to say that they wouldn't do anything differently. Isn't this something we all aspire to? What is more satisfying than contentment?

Long after the participants have gone home, I'll get letters telling me how the exercise forced them to look closely at their lives and, in many cases, made them alter their priorities. What they're doing is mapping out times for themselves, time in the present with the people they love.

Facing death squarely means being squarely in the moment. And the ultimate moments are spent with a loved one, not with a boss.

This, fundamentally, is what our life is about.

Elisabeth Kübler-Ross, in her book *On Death and Dying,* brought this country face-to-face with the *fact* of death. She told us we did not have to run, could not hide, and could approach death with equanimity, even calm.

Even though the book caused a tremendous stir, and several later works by different authors expanded on her themes, only some people listened then, and not enough people are listening now.

Americans see death as a kind of failing or disgrace, like bad breath or body odor. No *strong* person would die, we seem to say. And so the strong deny it or run in terror, pretending that death is *not* a fact, not a certainty. At the same time, of course, they do everything possible to prolong life, even when that life is submerged in pain or hopeless senility.

When we deal with the dying, we're adept only at dealing with the *business* of dying. We build more and more sophisticated instruments of "salvation," an end-care technology that costs billions of dollars to save—what? Lives?

Yes, lives, but surely not the kind of life any of us wishes for.

Partly, I believe, this lust for machines stems from doctors' own fear of death, a kind of subconscious belief that by prolonging life in others, it will prolong their own lives. Too, if they substitute a machine for human contact, then they won't get "infected" by their patients; death will pass them by.

Thus the use of machines obviates for the medical establishment the need for human contact.

This is the most tragic facet of our need to prolong life: the fact that we'll do anything to save the patient, rather than take into account the patient's human needs and desires. I've witnessed dehumanization in hospitals, doctors as callous as prison guards, and all because of their own fear of death.

We tend to praise the "impersonal" physician. If he got *involved* with all his patients, how could he maintain his objectivity, his sanity? What would his own life be like if he became "emotional" with each of the people under his care?

So we laugh at movies and books that show doctors joking about their patients and about death. But the impersonal physician is limiting his own life, not protecting it, and the laughter I've heard in emergency rooms is hollow.

Many of us have had direct experience of the loss of a loved one and know how difficult it is personally to face the death of someone close. Underlying this discomfort is the fear and pain surrounding our own death, for we know that it is inevitable. Our discomfort, like the physicians', comes from our uncertainty about what is in store. At the same time, the more we can directly face the experiences of loss that come into our lives, however unwanted, the better prepared we will be for our own death. If we can feel someone else's physical and/or emotional pain, we will be better able to deal with our own.

Attention to the psychological and emotional needs of the dying is a relatively new phenomenon in American society, particularly for its nonreligious members. The hospice movement, until recently bitterly criticized as "warehousing" the dying, or "despairing" in its attitude, is now seen as the humanitarian effort it has always been.

Many health-care professionals, doctors included, have come to realize that "taking care" of a patient goes well beyond looking to his physical comfort, or prolonging his life.

Joan Halifax, a dear friend and Buddhist shaman, has described the immense *mutual* benefits of simply being with a dying person, with no agenda and no time constraints—just two people coming into the moment. Her work with the dying is an outgrowth of her personal commitment to being mindful. Being with someone who is dying means being stripped of the social niceties that surround our usual interactions.

Ram Dass has described the same phenomenon. He has worked with the dying for many years, and has made society more aware of their concerns. Psychologist Marsha Greenleaf, who counsels the dying both in hospitals and in her office, writes of the vital importance of giving the dying their voice, letting them determine the manner and method of their death according to their psychological needs.

An old friend, Wavy Gravy, has made a career of dressing as a clown and visiting the terminally ill in children's hospitals. To me, this is an act of tremendous courage, but to him it offers enormous spiritual rewards.

In my early years as a doctor, I counseled people that having cancer was an *opportunity* for the patients, since it often forced them to resolve relationships, to bring their affairs in order, and to strive for spiritual peace.

In my heart, though, I didn't believe it. I knew it conceptually, but had no firsthand experience myself or with patients.

Then one day I met a woman with cancer, who described herself as "more alive than when I was supposedly healthy." She became closer to her husband than ever before, she told me, and had joyfully reconciled with the rest of her family. "I started living my life in the present," she explained, "in a way that I had never felt before. This disease has helped me fully appreciate what I have in my life." A devoutly religious woman, she accepted her disease as a "blessing," with all its positive implications.

It's true that facing death has the remarkable side effect of bringing one into the present. If we are allowed to keep our humanness, if we entrain with someone who is fully human, too, then dying is indeed an opportunity for fulfillment, perhaps the greatest opportunity of all.

With all the stories and differing perspectives we've learned about death, it still remains the greatest mystery. Death is elusive, inevitable, unfathomable. It is feared as a plunge into the unknown void, yet it is but a natural step in the progression and unfolding of life. My favorite Zen story, as translated by Roshi Philip Kapleau, on the death of Master Tenno, suggests both the simplicity and myriad levels involved in reaching an understanding of dying:

> When the Master was dying, he called to his room the monk in charge of food and clothing in the temple. When the monk sat down by the bed, Tenno asked, "Do you understand?"
>
> "No," the monk replied.
>
> Tenno, picking up his pillow, hurled it through the window, and fell back dead.

CHAPTER SIXTEEN

PLANNING AHEAD

---

*I arise in the morning torn between the desire
to improve the world and a desire to enjoy the
world. This makes it hard to plan the day.*

—E. B. WHITE

As LONG AS we keep hurtling forward, trying to do more
and more in less and less time, we will continue to feel anxious and
stressed. What we must do is slow down enough to *plan*. Initially,
people react negatively when I mention planning ahead in class,
because it seems contradictory to plan and to be present in the
moment. That's because most of the time we aren't really willing to
take the time to make plans. Plans govern the future, and most of us
look to the future with fear. What if our plans don't work out?
What if something unexpected comes along to stop us? What
if . . . ?

So we get anxious and flee from planning and the feelings it
evokes from the past and the present—instead of being mindfully
attentive to creating our plans and being willing to feel our doubts.

Many people I know have never succeeded because of their fears
and doubts, rather than because of a lack of talent or creativity. My
close friend Tom came to see me one day for advice about starting a
business venture related to his music. His idea was to create a series
of musical recordings that would affect people's moods in positive

ways. He had been working in this field for many years, and now had discovered a way to market his music to hospitals, health care centers, etc., so that people would be soothed by it. He would also be creating a profitable business for himself.

He had done a lot of thinking and research, he told me, and his idea seemed brilliant to me as he described it. However, as he spoke about it, he would say, "But you know me. I'm pretty lazy when it comes to this stuff. I just don't know if I can go ahead with it." Or, "I know I should speak with other people in the field, but what if they don't like the idea?" Or, "You know, it seems it will be a lot of effort, and I'm not sure anyway that it will work."

The project never got off the ground, despite its creative brilliance.

Many of us do the same thing in our relationships. It can take couples years to decide whether to get married ("What if the romance disappears when we live together?" "Will I have to give up my independence?" "In three years, will I still find him/her attractive?"). Often, the doubts are so paralyzing that the relationship atrophies and the couple drifts apart without ever really knowing what happened.

Our fears of the future, our self-doubts, and our unwillingness to sit with those feelings often keep us trapped in circumstances that we know we can change—yet we can't seem to find the path.

My point is not to avoid planning, but to plan for the future *in the present*. Now. Without fear. Without our plans being so carved in stone that the future seems preordained (the suburban house, the two-car garage, two children, a minimum fifty thousand dollars a year), yet without being so vast that the future will be disappointing if the goal is not met. We must make plans, knowing that the path will always be circuitous.

Here, in the present, look at the future as a beam of light coming from a distant light tower. It serves as your directional beacon; aim your step toward the light. You can be as specific or grandiose as you would like, as long as this vision doesn't become a weight around your being that keeps you from the present. Plan for and visualize the future, then let go of it.

Its power shows up in any moment that a choice presents itself to you. For instance, when you leave home in the morning, depending on your destination, you automatically know whether you're going left or right. You may be offered a promotion at work, which means more pay but perhaps less opportunity to be with your family. Or you might have to choose between two different jobs that will mean significant differences in lifestyle. If you allow yourself to be present with your feelings about your choices, and locate that beam of light in your future, you will know whether to go left or right; you will be aligned with the choice that is most consistent with your vision.

But suppose you decide you no longer want to follow in a particular direction? There is no commitment to consistency, only to the truth you feel within yourself this moment. Feel free to create new plans whenever it seems appropriate. Planning is not for the purpose of living in the future, but for realizing that our life, like a river, takes many turns. To follow an inflexible and unchanging straight line is unnatural and stressful. Our commitment is to the present. Our power is bringing our future into the present. Planning helps us to do this.

In my workshops, I ask participants to think of where they'd like to be in five years—where they want to live, how they want to work, with whom they wish to spend their days, what state of health they wish to feel, what kind of spiritual growth they want to be experiencing, where they want to be traveling, and how they want to spend their time. These are, of course, plans made in the present, but if they can visualize that light, and if their decisions about their life are made with the beacon of light in mind, then the decisions become clearer, and the path will unfold with less stress.

Susan, a professional photographer, wrote down a full range of plans and visions for her future. Most important was her desire to travel to distant areas to do her work. Being visually oriented, she began by creating a montage of five beautiful landscapes that she had seen in magazines, and decided she would visit them all within three years. Her travels took her to the Southwest deserts, the Canadian Rockies, archaeological ruins in Jordan, and the Maine coast. Then a friend invited her to a small village in Mexico for a vacation. Upon returning, she looked at her montage and realized the village was the site of the fifth picture, even though she had never consciously known where the picture had been taken. She had brought her future to the present.

I have spoken with many people who seem to have a knack for creating positive outcomes. Usually they are people who hold visions of the future, and they are willing to be present for success as well as for failure. We cannot be so arrogant as to believe we can control our fate, though as Spinoza said, "Chance favors the prepared mind."

"I don't know what I want to do," a nineteen-year-old tells me.

"At least," I ask, "do you know what you *don't* want to do?"

He nods.

"That's a start. As you begin to acknowledge to yourself what *isn't* the direction, you'll understand where you *are* going," I say, and indeed it is a start. As he grows older, the light will become clearer.

Many people, of course, don't plan at all—they just "go where life leads them." Such people are generally anxious and fearful; life, it seems, leads them too often toward unhappiness and chaos. If, alternatively, they could *lead* their own lives, much of the anxiety and fear would automatically disappear. It's the same principle as that of mastering time or having it master you.

In a 1953 Yale survey of undergraduates, only 3 percent had clear plans for where life would take them. Twenty years later, those 3 percent had accumulated total assets greater than those of the remaining 97%!

A set agenda, such as the twelve-step program for alcoholics or drug users, may work for addicts, but it is far too specific to be used as a model for life. Immerse yourself in the flow, and remember that the river bends.

At the end of my workshops, I ask the class to take ten to twenty minutes to write down a stream of thoughts about the issues of the future I had brought up at the beginning of the session: the future of their relationships, their health, their play, their environment, their lifestyle, and the time they set aside for inner growth.

It would be an excellent exercise for you, too. I don't grade the papers; I usually don't even see them, although some participants are so moved by the experience that they share their thoughts with me, often months after the workshop has ended. If you do the exercise seriously, you'll be astonished at how much more brightly the light of the future will shine.

And what happens if the plans go awry? If you suddenly discover that the road you've chosen is the wrong one, that you are headed toward a future you no longer want?

When that happens, let the future go; you'll get back to it. Return fully to the present, for that is the only place to know yourself, and it is there and only there that the future is to be found.

My friend Captain Dave lives on a sailboat in the Caribbean, making his living by painting local scenes and selling T-shirts. I see him every time I visit St. John. "I'll be back in five years," he told me at our last meeting.

"Really? What are your plans?"

"I'm going to sail around the world. No itinerary. I'll just stop when I feel like it, stay as long as I want, then push on, literally blown by the wind."

Off he went. He wrote from Fiji to say he liked it there and had decided to spend an extra month. I haven't heard from him since, but I think of him often because it seems to me that his five-year plan, aimless as it might appear, is actually more reliable than most.

There will be sudden crises in his life, causing change and re-evaluation—there are for all sailors—but it seems to me he has found his light and is following it. It wouldn't be *my* light; I'm far too wedded to Omega and my family life. But it seems to me that, more than anyone I know, he is open to the moment—living in the moment—and there are times I envy him.

He has discovered what is important to him, and will head into his future undeterred.

Finding what's important is a fundamental factor in all planning. Often, though, we're too distracted by crisis, by the desire *not* to think but to do, by the rush and tumble of our everyday lives, to figure out what "important" is.

Stephen Covey, in *The Seven Habits of Highly Effective People,* makes a vital distinction between "urgent" and "important." Urgency has to do with events that intrude upon us and demand our

immediate attention. These events can be important crises and dilemmas that have to be taken care of *now,* or they can be the daily
interruptions and nuisances that also grab our immediate attention,
like unimportant phone calls, unnecessary business meetings, or
family squabbles over whom to invite for Thanksgiving. Importance refers to those things that go beyond the immediate and are
aligned with the overall direction we have chosen in any aspect of
our life.

Sometimes it is essential to respond to the immediate situation,
yet spending time without urgency is vital as well. It is then that we
can plan, and prevent the crises and demands constantly pressuring
us.

Patently, planning ahead is important but not urgent, and it is in
this area, Covey says, that we should spend more of our time. He
suggests that we shift our time from the urgent and not important to
focus on the important role of planning. Yet if this were simple,
then everybody would do more of it; obviously, since we do not,
there is difficulty and resistance. "Important but not urgent" is a
difficult distinction to make.

Urgent and Important

Urgent and Not Important

Not Urgent and Important

Not Urgent and Not Important

If we view this from the vantage of frequency and amplitude,
frequency representing urgency, amplitude representing importance, then we can understand why we feel uncomfortable with
planning. Since we are continually responding to urgent situations
and interruptions all day long, we become entrained to the fast
frequency of urgency. Whether important or trivial, we are habitu-

ated to the fast pace. In fact, even when there is nothing urgent or important happening in our lives, we tend to continue the fast pace. Television or video games, for example, are hardly urgent, yet we play them since they keep us going at the quickened pace of society.

In order to plan, we need to slow down the frequency and up the amplitude—that which is most important. Essentially, we must give serious consideration to what we want in the future through unhurried, undistracted, concentrated thought. It is initially hard to change pace. At work, we know how difficult it is to set aside time to write the report or come up with a new plan; at home, the needs of a child intrude, as do business phone calls or calls from friends.

Timeshifting is required—recognizing the faster, urgent rhythms that have us entrained and then being able to shift into the slower rhythms necessary for planning. We've already seen how closing our office door, taking time off with our spouse, carefully setting up boundaried time, etc., can allow us to timeshift. Without such rituals, without slowing down, we are unable to plan, and thus we remain in demand, putting out brushfires all day and ultimately bemoaning the fact that we are always stressed and in a hurry. In slowing down and giving our attention to the important—giving our *time* to the important—we prevent many of the problems that arise, and thus we give ourselves the gift of ultimately having more time. Though seemingly paradoxical, it is in slowing down that we gain time in our lives.

The following stories illustrate what I mean.

A man in my class told me that his job as financial manager for his firm was always being interrupted by coworkers with questions about immediate problems. "I can never get my budgets done," he complained. "I have to work overtime, weekends. I never have time for my family. And what thanks do I get? At best, lip service. Everybody takes me for granted."

What's important is the budget; what's urgent are his colleagues' demands. Yet he is actually adding to the crisis mode by failing to erect boundaries, by being unable to say no, and by devoting too much of his time to the immediate rather than to the long-term.

"Slow down," I told him. "It's your only chance."

One of my Omega colleagues was so good at creating boundaries that she was able to devote most of her time to planning. At first, one of our managers complained to me that she wasn't working out well; her predecessors had done much more work, he said. They were always at their desks well after business hours.

In fact, my colleague was doing a remarkable job, and her department ran more smoothly than at any previous time. This wasn't because she was working longer or faster, but because she was working more efficiently and was better able to plan ahead. "Let others take care of the crises," was her attitude. She devoted her time to the long-term and thus reduced the number of crises.

A couple I know, both high achievers, fought for three years over the issue of phone messages. She had moved into his apartment, but when a call was for her and he answered the phone, he often failed to tell her about it, particularly when the message was personal rather than business. It drove her wild.

"But it's only your friends," he'd say. "They'll call you back."

Their fights were fierce and destructive—so critical, in fact, that they talked of breaking off the affair, even though they loved each other.

The relationship was important and the issue was critical. Finally they each took off a day from work and spent an afternoon in a "neutral" place (a coffee shop) to discuss what was really happening. Numerous psychological factors, they discovered, lay underneath the battle.

Although he loved her, he realized that her moving in felt like a sort of invasion, which he subconsciously resisted. And although she knew she loved him, she hated the control over her his "ownership" of the phone represented.

Once they had each slowed down and aired their differences, they both came to a solution so simple that they were amazed they had not thought of it years before.

They put in a second phone line.

In order to effectively plan, to devote our time to what is important rather than just urgent, we must slow down, shift our pace, keep out intrusions, create boundaries, be mindful, and focus on long-term issues. This is the effective way to prevent problems in the future, and thus reduce the time we need to spend dealing with crises.

It's why so many people take work home during the day to avoid the interruptions of the office. It's why so many people take the phone off the hook when they make love or simply want time to talk. It's why vacations are important, why time outdoors is vital, and why concentrated play with children is so good for us all.

It also explains why some authors have been able to overcome writer's block by setting up boundaried time. They give themselves three hours each morning, for example, during which they don't have to write, but are not allowed to do anything else. Usually, after a while, they get down to writing.

Sometimes I come into work on Sundays, when no one else is in the office. It's time I've carved out for myself; not to catch up on the week's unfinished chores, but to plan long-term for Omega and to consider its present problems and opportunities in quiet conditions.

But when I do, I give myself time off during the week to devote to things other than work. It's not overtime, it's *different* time. The more we balance time in this way, the fuller our lives will be.

In Chapter Thirteen, we saw how Dr. Dean Ornish has been able to reverse coronary plaque buildup in his patients who have cardiovascular disease with a program combining diet, yoga, and relaxation. That program is rooted in Q2; Ornish prefers planning ahead to treating the crisis of an attack with bypass surgery or last-minute heroics.

Interestingly, his approach was rejected at first because most other doctors felt that patients would be far more willing to have their chest cut open than to slow down to the constant hard work of changing their unhealthy lifestyle.

To plan ahead for one's health, one's relationships, and one's life, requires timeshifting. Native Americans have long accepted the practice of seeing life's future from a perspective free from the pressure of the everyday. There is the long tradition of the Vision Quest, where one leaves everyday life behind and journeys into the wilderness to get new ideas, new visions. In our planning, too, we must step back, enter Q2, and separate the important from the urgent. Otherwise we will be unprepared for a future in which the unexpected forces us not to act but to react. By being prepared, we are better able to exploit opportunities where we find them.

CHAPTER SEVENTEEN

SOCIETY

—

Everywhere, people are straining to set aside time for things that are felt to be humanly important: being with loved ones, enjoying nature, studying ideas, or engaging in some creative activity. And more and more it is becoming a losing battle. There is no issue, no aspect of human life, that exceeds this in importance. The destruction of time is literally the destruction of life.

—JACOB NEEDLEMAN

PRACTICE RANDOM KINDNESS AND SENSELESS ACTS OF BEAUTY

So reads a bumper sticker I've been seeing frequently of late. I believe its popularity comes from a deep social "knowing" that this is something needed, despite the fact that so few of us heed its commands. Yes, we are extraordinarily capable of *premeditated* kindness and acts of beauty, but we are too busy—don't have enough time—to include them in our daily routine. We have to think about them; they don't come naturally.

They are materially nonproductive. No benefit accrues from them, except for the soul.

I began following the bumper sticker's dictum. For one small example, learning from my Caribbean friend Zedie, who is courteous *by nature,* now when a driver tries to cut in front of me, I wave him ahead with a smile—if he's in such a rush, why not? Maybe his wife is about to have a baby and he has to get home as fast as possible.

It's so easy to switch our perspective and it makes us feel so much better. Much better than being angry at someone rudely cutting in line, and along with it feeling our inner tension mounting. It's remarkable to act kindly and then witness the effect that generosity of spirit has on another human being—and on oneself.

These opportunities surround us during our day. Whether it's giving directions to someone who is lost, or saying hello to toll collectors on the bridge (even giving them tips—letting them "keep the change"), or helping someone at work beyond your own responsibilities.

These opportunities are endless, so I'm not suggesting that you now become burdened by becoming a full-time Good Samaritan. Sometimes we truly don't have the time or inclination, though often we are governed by a mood of irritability related to the pace of the moment. If we allow the speed of our lives to imprison us in a routine of rushing that precludes this type of human caring, we all create a society that walls us off from each other.

My wife is remarkably present and generous with her time for others. It comes from a true sense of love for people. I often appreciate how her caring and concern creates such positive feelings. Caring and concern don't take much time. Simply dropping our preoccupation with busyness is all that's necessary; being present for life that is going on around us all the time.

I've learned a lot being around her, which has enabled me to notice more and give of myself in situations that aren't necessarily my job or role or responsibility. It's about being present as a human being. In many regards it's like the perfume of a flower; it's just there.

Do I think of myself as selfless, a "saint," a "paragon"?

Not at all.

Whom am I benefitting? The strangers, I suppose, though except for a momentary flicker of surprise, they're likely to think nothing of my actions, awash as they are in the impersonal sea of our society.

Myself? Absolutely. I'm truly *happier* when I perform my random kindnesses.

Random kindness and senseless acts of beauty take time. That time is there for all of us, only we don't seem to know it exists.

Jim Buglione—or Jimmy Bugs, as we fondly called him—volunteered for many years at Omega, doing whatever was necessary, helping out with mailings or kitchen work or answering phones.

He had been in the military and suffered disabilities that affected his health, primarily poorly controlled and recurrent epileptic seizures.

I had first met him as my patient, then he became a fixture within the Omega community. He wasn't really staff or a paid employee, yet he embodied all the principles of our organization. When he suddenly died last year, his death was met with deep sadness and shock by everyone at Omega. We gathered in our conference room to share our thoughts and feelings. For me, I was most struck by how much Jimmy had given of himself to all of us there, how deeply he had touched each person. Stories poured forth. About how he had brought flowers to a man he didn't know whose wife had died, even though he had to walk a few hours to get there (Jimmy couldn't drive because of the epilepsy). About how he brought treats to staff members, or mysteriously arrived in someone's office just when she needed help or a friend to speak with.

We often think that those with titles are the ones "making it all happen." I run Omega; Jimmy had no title, no official status. Yet he truly cared and gave deeply of himself, and he remains an inspiration to me. His legacy of kindness is one of the things that makes Omega special.

Time is like wool, Rabbi Zalman Schachter-Shalomi observes. It comes in long strands—yet we cut it into short pieces.

When the skeins were longer, they bound families, communities, societies, and nations together. Previously, as many as three generations lived harmoniously in one home, the members of a community were bound by religion and shared interests into a united whole, and different groups—religious, social, racial—worked together for the common good: one nation, indivisible.

We have spoken before about the role of music as an entrainer, a rhythm that bonds two people in a relationship, or in this case brings a group into sync. Often, music has been used by communities to hold them together—in African tribal meetings, in Balinese dance rituals, and in many South American cultural gatherings.

An extraordinary but little-shown movie, *Latcho Drom,* without dialogue, uses its musical soundtrack to depict how Gypsy tribes live from India to Turkey to Romania to France. Their often tragic lives, rent by the atrocious treatment from outsiders, are bound by the deeply emotional music shared by all in the community. They live a nomadic life without apparent roots. It is the music that has kept their culture intact, while other communities have perished. Their spirit is expressed by that music, communally shared. They are connected in a unified rhythm of the soul. Curiously, studies of Gypsies indicate that their language has no words for "future" and "past." Time is only the present.

Today, because we have cut the wool too short, most of us have no communal music. Rap music is the only example I can think of today; until Jerry Garcia died, a subculture found the music of the Grateful Dead a bugle call to the spirit.

Little binds us anymore. Relationships are transient, and people marry with the attitude that if it doesn't work out, they can always divorce. Our children leave home, communities fight each other, the term "special interest groups" is no longer pejorative, race is set against race, generation against generation. "Ethnic cleansing" has become a term we all understand. That the term even exists is a fact hideous in its nature.

Even the employer-employee relationship has changed. It used to be that a worker, if he were loyal and conscientious, could count on equal loyalty from his boss. Now, people are fired for "reasons of scale," because "economics demand it," because CEOs are beholden to faceless stockholders rather than to the people they command.

Time—and, principally, the concept that "time is money"—is at the root of our lack of societal caring. The need for instant gratification, the drive for more and more goods and more and more services, and the desire to "have it all" have produced an "I'm all right, Jack" attitude in us individually that by definition excludes others, even our spouses, parents, children—and certainly community.

Five hundred years ago in England, one of the Oxford colleges built a "great hall" using huge oak timbers for beams. The dining hall is still in use, but recently the beams needed to be replaced because of rot. The current college administrator, deliberating and researching for a solution to the problem, found in the records of his counterpart five hundred years ago that an oak grove had been planted near the college at the time of the erection of the dining hall—*specifically* so that the large timbers would be available when needed. The great old trees were harvested and used for the purpose foreseen five hundred years ago.

Imagine us doing that in America today. Instead of centuries or decades, we plan ahead by years or months or days—or often not at all.

All of our building, for example, is short-term. Our sidings might last fifteen years, our cars five. Reaganomics led to increased debt because people wanted a tax cut *now* to be able to buy more things *now*. Our highways have become overused because we gave up on railroads as a too-slow means of transporting goods. Our federal buildings have so rapidly deteriorated, they look like left-overs from communist states. Cities like New York and Los Angeles are being rebuilt on a continuous basis.

Ed Bacon, an architect, is a city planner, responsible in part for the rebirth of Philadelphia. He was derided because he thought thirty years ahead—not because it was too short a time, but because it was too long. He fought battles with the local politicians who wanted immediate solutions to urban problems, yet were unwilling to consider plans that went beyond five years.

Our infrastructure is crumbling because we built two-lane high-ways without thinking that soon there would be so many cars we would need three. Sports arenas erected thirty years ago are deemed too old because they have no domes, luxury boxes, or artificial grass. Our computers "improve" so rapidly that today's is literally obsolete tomorrow. "Change," "growth," "new"—these are the words by which we live and by which some of us prosper.

Yet we find ourselves with holes in the ozone layer, undisposable nuclear waste, endangered species, polluted streams and rivers. One hundred years ago (a very short time!), there was no need for a federal environmental agency—the environment had not been threatened.

We take virtually no preventive measures to spare our environ-ment, as we take virtually no preventive measures to spare our health.

I've written earlier about how the fast-and-growing-faster pace of American society mitigates against any long-term thought and inhibits us from reflection. When it comes to our land and our resources, the problem becomes particularly acute.

Americans look at land as an *investment*. We buy and sell it without setting foot on it, much less stopping to savor its beauty or smell its flowers. Developers build on it, paper manufacturers cut down its trees, miners dig into it and put nothing back. People who want to fill in a marsh for a housing development have never experienced the marsh.

Not long ago, we loved our land and experienced it through our senses—we were part of nature, not users of it. We listened to the waves, not the sound of boom boxes on the beach, and we responded internally to the prolonged rhythm. If we killed an animal, it was for food, just as other animals kill for food. It was a maintenance of the natural balance.

Yet the more we go into our minds, the more we lose the capacity to feel—the more, in other words, we get divorced from our emotions and our senses—the more we will bulldoze and blacktop. Nothing but speed and the lost capacity for entrainment with nature can explain the insanity of letting our environment deteriorate.

Some segments of this book were written in a tent at Maho on the island of St. John. When I moved from that tent to a modern house—four walls, a ceiling, windows shutting out the outside—I was struck by the difference in me that the "isolation" produced. In the tent, I could actively feel the rhythms of nature. Inside, I had to remember them.

All of us must entrain with the deep rhythm of the earth. We must find a balance between its rhythm and society's, return to and feel the deep pulsing that dominates mankind, not individual man.

Land—nature—is God's gift to us, the most precious asset in our lives. And today we treat it as a profit center!

We have seen that the best way to slow down is to experience natural rhythms. Past cultures knew that; those living in circular time know it today.

A culture so out of balance with its environment will not survive, yet most politicians will not even go with environmentalists to endangered areas before they vote to destroy them.

It is only by slowing down to appreciate our environment that we will be saved, yet the political response is to go full speed ahead, even faster, putting us more out of touch with our natural senses and feelings, and thus out of touch with our senses, our environment, our world.

Society's pace is eroding, too, a man-given gift: democracy.

The democratic process takes thought, discussion, argument, synthesis—time. In order to truly understand issues, we must hear both sides of a reasoned argument, have facts at our disposal, study, weigh, ruminate. In order to evaluate a candidate, we must listen to his ideas, ask probing questions, consider his truthfulness, understand the ramifications of what he has to say.

What a mockery speed makes of this!

"Tell me, Mr. Candidate," the moderator of a televised presidential debate asks. "How would you reform our national health-care system?" He looks at his watch. "You have three minutes."

Three minutes. As though an answer is *possible* in that time. As though anything but a series of surface slogans could serve as a response.

The other candidate gets one minute to reply—and on the late-night news, for those of us who watched *Taxi* reruns instead of the debate, both answer and reply are cut to ten or fifteen seconds each.

Sound bites are loathesome words, and a hideous concept. Politicians rely on them, pundits decry them, "spin doctors" compose them—and we all hear them and believe they represent a candidate's position, a candidate's *wisdom.* All we have to do to balance the budget is cut government spending. There are too many cheats on the welfare rolls. I can cut taxes without cutting services. Yeah? Well *I* can cut services without pain to their recipients.

These are nonsense syllables; advertising copy.

Our increasing reliance on sound bites is not the politicians' fault, it's society's—and our own, since we have entrained with society's rhythm. And so we vote on the basis of the emotion of the moment, and come up with short-term, shortsighted solutions.

We are a nation of consumers: fast food (what a phrase!), aspirin, Prozac, "wonder" drugs, "instant" weight-loss regimens, Nordic-Tracks, SSTs, computers. We want answers, and we want them *fast*.

It's no wonder, then, that the fast answer, the simple solution, is what politicians hand us. I'm talking here not only of presidents and congressmen, but of PTA participants, members of town councils—anyone responsible to a constituency—and it's no wonder we are satisfied with their response.

It's much easier to vote quickly and reflexively than to study the issues; to judge on a candidate's looks and eloquence rather than content. The political debate is "won" not by the man with the better ideas, but by the candidate with the quicker zinger. (And we find out who "won" by an opinion poll conducted *within seconds* after the debate concludes.) Even in that long-ago time of 1960, Richard Nixon "lost" a debate to John F. Kennedy because he sweated under the television lights. If he hadn't, most political analysts agree, he would have been elected.

Revolt! I am tempted to cry, but then I stop myself. For revolution does not bring peace either to the land or to the revolutionary; it, too, is part of the jagged, frenetic pace of our world. Yasir Arafat will never know peace, nor did Nathan Hale, nor Che Guevara, nor Eldridge Cleaver, nor Susan B. Anthony.

For an ounce of doing good, Ram Dass says, you need a pound of sitting still, and I would add that our desire to do good becomes a problem if we merely respond by doing.

In Hong Kong, members of parliament—all of whom wished to do good—actually got into a fistfight when their views collided. Martin Luther King and Mahatma Gandhi were perhaps the greatest revolutionaries of all precisely because they preached nonviolence, and the rhythm of their revolutions, while immensely powerful, was slow.

I think that revolutionary anger, like all anger, hides a deeper, slower sadness about the essential human condition, and it is through contemplation, not action, that we can come to terms with it.

Combat, territoriality, conflict; sickness, aging, dying: these are not foreign to human life, they are inescapable parts of it. We are capable of evil as well as good; greed is in our nature along with altruism.

We cannot run from the tragic aspects of ourselves; we can only conquer them by facing them squarely and incorporating them into our knowledge of ourselves as whole.

We *must* slow down. We must move from our heads to an examination of our hearts.

The true revolution is an honest respect for the differences of others; forgiveness of their sins because their sins are ours. We must, above all else, learn compassion.

How can we learn compassion from anger?

Only through time.

A study of the Athabascan Indians in Alaska revealed that when they are accused of a crime, they are more likely to be convicted of it than are Caucasians.

The reason is rhythm.

Athabascans pause before speaking. Bid them good morning, and their return greeting—no less sincere—will come not in seconds, but *eventually*. Ask them if they're guilty, and their denial will come after an equivalent delay.

Aha! we pounce. They had to think about their answer. Obviously, guilty as charged.

Yet all they did was respond in their rhythm, one that incorporated the pause, not the one common to American life.

Once we could pause, too. Jews and Christians paused with their Sabbaths, communities with their blue laws closed shops for the weekend—all these contributed not only to a slower pace, but also to a *change* of pace.

Advisors say that when you go to another country, you need to check on four things: gifts, greetings, formality, and *concepts of time*. Most people in France take off the month of August. In Germany, lunchhour is truly time off. In Spain, *siestas* are sacrosanct.

Even in Europe, though, pause is rare. Here, in America, it is virtually unheard of. Stock-trading never stops, for example; Store after store advertises itself as "Open 24 Hours"; through television, you can buy a new dress at three o'clock in the morning.

As Juliet Schor points out, we are praised for putting in "long hours"; and the statement, "I haven't had a vacation in three years" is applauded by bosses and envied by less obsessed coworkers. ("If I work as hard as Henry, I'll get that raise.")

Yet this is the atmosphere in which violence escalates, in which teenagers burn homeless men because they're bored, "like the action," and don't have time even to consider, let alone feel, what it is they have done.

Violence flourishes because it is a way to *feel*. Caught in the rhythm of television violence, consumed by the need for a quick fix, for gratification, needing the addictive high that comes with risk, more and more we turn to fists and bats and knives and guns. Instead of waving them ahead when other drivers cut us off, we shoot them.

When we live only in short moments, it's easy to understand why violence escalates, why movies can only elicit emotion by more and more graphic depictions of sex and mayhem, why boom boxes and ambulance sirens get louder. *Something* has to penetrate to get attention in a world without feeling. So we wail and fight and ingest images that are more and more horrific.

What we lose is compassion. As we have less time for our inner selves, we have less time for others. Unless we can shift time, unless we can entrain with slower rhythms and unburden ourselves of the frantic pace at which we exist, civility will be lost.

And as we lose civility, we are on the brink of losing civilization.

CHAPTER EIGHTEEN

THE FUTURE

Live in the present
Do all the things that need to be done
Do all the good you can each day
The future will unfold
—Peace Pilgrim

THE GERMAN JESUIT priest and Zen master Hugo Enomiya-Lassalle, in his book *Living in the New Consciousness*, describes the evolution of man's consciousness in its relationship to time.

First, he says, there was "archaic consciousness." It existed in man who experienced himself as totally one with the universe, and thus at one with time, essentially *without* time, since time and space and ego were submerged into the whole. Archaic man had no experience of past or future; he would not have understood the concepts. (This is similar to the animal experience of time. A cat or dog exists only in the present, with no thought of future or past.)

Next came "magical consciousness," when man was still without individuality, still (unconsciously) perceived of himself as one with nature, living in circular time, but was already on the "decadent" path—one in which the self began to extract itself from the whole—which led toward "mythical consciousness." In doing this, man had divorced himself from the universe and nature, and thought of his own ego and soul as different from others'. Here, time became important, since individual life and death existed in time, even though it was still circular time with cyclical rebirth.

With Plato came the start of conceptual, rational thinking, the emergence of "ideas." This ushered in the period of "mental consciousness," which meant that what was perceived by the mind was in fact what *was*, and man thought of himself as distinct from the universe, from the flow of time and the condition of nature. The same concept started earlier in the East, but man never divorced himself entirely from the concept of oneness with the universe. It is with mental consciousness that we in the West look at time today.

The process of evolution must continue, Enomiya-Lassalle believes, taking our consciousness into the fourth dimension, in which all previous states of consciousness exist and are integrated, so that past, present, and future, linear and circular time, the archaic, the magical, the mystical, and the mental are fused and raised to a new level.

This new state, this fourth dimension of time, is, in effect, undefinable further, but in it we would both retain our individuality and remain part of the whole, feel the past and future in the present moment, recognize time as an entity yet be an indivisible part of its flow, be both self and all humanity.

The fourth dimension remains in our future. I believe, along with Enomiya-Lassalle, that we must strive to attain it.

Creativity, says the sculptor Hans van de Bovenkamp, is bringing the future into the present.

Great art, wrote the naturalist Loren Eiseley, consists in so rendering a common thought or emotion that we cannot encounter that thought or emotion without thinking, if only subconsciously, of the work of art. Try, for example, after seeing a Van Gogh sunflower, to look at a real sunflower uninfluenced by his rendition of its essence.

Both men are taking us toward that fourth dimension, in which present and future can coexist, and a sunflower can be both ephemeral and eternal.

If we can experience time as both linear and circular, if we can be both one and One, then practical applications to all aspects of our lives ensue.

We have seen how anxiety-producing it is when we are locked

into linear time, one in which we can make natural rhythm speed up (we can, for an easy example, "artificially" time-ripen a tomato), when "time is of the essence," when we are surrounded by alarms, bells, and whistles that urge us toward speed, when even our internal clocks are set by society's rhythm and we wake up startled, without an alarm, to get to an appointment on time.

We have seen how restful it is when we fall into the rhythms of nature, when we entrain with the waves of the ocean, rather than the electronic waves from a computer or television screen. And we have seen how Western society values the electronic over the natural, how a worker's time is "valuable" to us all, while a vacationer's has little worth to anyone save himself.

But, argues Jeremy Rifkin in *Time Wars,* what if time itself is democratized, if we all shared equally in time, had equal access to the past, present, and most particularly the future? Our society would become less combative and less rushed, our politicians would look toward the long-term protection of the environment, and the future would be seen as something we all have in common—something valuable, something part of us *now.*

We are in a critical point in human evolution, he writes, for we must determine whether we can embrace ecological instead of man-made time, whether we can incorporate spiritual/sacred time, rather than techno-speed, into our everyday life. Rifkin says:

> Political tyranny in every culture begins by devaluing the time of others. Indeed, the exploitation of human beings is only possible in pyramidal time cultures, where rulership is always based on the proposition that some people's time is more valuable and other people's time more expendable. In a democratic time culture, everyone's time is valuable and no one's time is any more expendable than another's. In a culture where the sacredness of time comes first, there is no other way to view time.

The concept that everyone's time is equally valuable is truly revolutionary.

*   *   *

Just as a vast misuse of our ecology—the stripping of our timberlands, the rape of our hills in the search for coal, the dumping of toxic waste, the concretizing of our marshlands—led to the environmental movement, so, I believe, the misuse of time in today's society should lead to a "time movement."

Its philosophy would incorporate the following:

1. Rifkin's ideas on political change. He believes, for instance, in a resorting of political persuasions from left and right to "power rhythms"—the ones our politicians have now—versus "empathetic rhythms," aimed at matching society's tempos with those of the natural world.

2. Larry Dossey's analysis of the "hurry sickness." This is expressed as heart disease, high blood pressure, or depression of immune functions, leading to an increased susceptibility to infection and cancer.

3. Joanna Macy's writings. She believes in the essential need to consider time in long skeins, to counteract the "hectic fever" imposed by society on our brains, rendering us incapable of considering long-term solutions to such issues as toxic waste.

4. Juliet Schor's argument about work. She thinks that the reason we rush toward money, consumption, long hours, and stress in the workplace is simply because we don't know how to treat work as only a *part* of our lives and thus have no idea how to step into a new area where rest becomes as important as work, and contemplation as important as consumption. It's a place where we can live virtually stress-free, with only a portion of the *things* that imprison us.

A time movement—a marshaling of forces that would allow us to slow down, to relax, to think of over*work* as wasting time and play as valuable—is not so far-fetched an idea. If even a businessman like Henry Ford could realize that time off increased the value of time on, then this and future generations can surely make their need to be in the present known, and the rhythms of peace, of nature, of play, of solitude will become part of society's rhythms once again.

The movement must start now. It is not hyperbole to argue that without it, we become automatons, replaceable parts in a vast in-

dustrial machine, made merely to run the machine until we ourselves (not it; never it) run down.

All of us plan for the future. We take out life and health insurance, for example, write wills, set up college funds for our children
and retirement funds for ourselves.

These are relatively new practices, and even today many societies
would not understand them. The *community* will take care of the
aging in those societies, make sure they live comfortably when
they've stopped working, tend to them when they're sick, guarantee the correct passing on of their goods when they die. The community will educate the children, repair catastrophes that befall
house or farm, come together for all citizens' protection.

We desperately miss this form of community in a society that is
ever more alienated and fragmented. I believe that the false security
gained by the "paperwork for the future," our society-forced insurance hedging against future calamity, makes the warding off of
death a constant priority, and takes us from the present into a future
filled with darkness and little hope.

Indeed, if you ask most Americans about the future, they will tell
you they view it with pessimism, not only for themselves individually but for mankind as well. Sooner or later there will be an atomic
war and all species will be eradicated. We will return to the Ice Age.
Global warming will fry us in our beds. A plague will kill us off. We
will become subservient to computers and no longer masters of our
fate.

Every heat wave or cold snap leads to dire predictions. Our science fiction is mostly apocalyptic. Our movies depict savage wars,
fires, environmental devastation. We will have more sophisticated
weapons, they seem to say, not more sophisticated people.

One of the tragedies of future planning in America is that it is so
short-term. We protect ourselves against tomorrow, but give no
thought to the far future—indeed, in our anxiety about the near
future we seem to disregard the distant future and our descendants
in our haste to make sure *we're* okay.

Can we, like the Jews of the past, think seven generations ahead?
Do we know what to do with the nuclear waste accumulating in
our temporary storehouses? Do we care if tomorrow's increased
profits will lead to eventual catastrophe?

What is it we are leaving to our children? Politicians give them lip service ("building a better world"), but do they really believe it, when they turn over public land to private development, satisfied that they've repaid the largest investors in their previous campaigns? Can they really believe that if they allow the destruction of our natural resources, the pollution of our rivers, the destruction of our land?

Joanna Macy writes movingly about two visits, a year apart, to British Columbia to visit her son. The first time, the mountains were untouched; on the second visit, the cedar and Douglas fir were cut down to leave huge areas of stubble. And for what? For paper diapers.

Do politicians really believe that postponing decisions on the disposal of nuclear waste will build a better world for forthcoming generations?

Societies in circular time think about the generations ahead, for those future generations are one with the present. To them the human race is one being, so of course it must be revered and protected, now and forever.

In contrast, in linear time, we think of ourselves. Who cares if we disenfranchise our children or grandchildren? The world is coming to an end anyway. Let's get what we can while we're still around to enjoy it.

Individually, of course we care about our children, and most of us want them to have a better life than we did. But as a culture, this appears not to be true, and it looks like this feeling of despair for the future will only deepen as our government becomes more and more a tool of special interests.

As Dan Goleman points out in *Emotional Intelligence,* when he tells a story of a mother and father giving their lives to save their handicapped child during a train crash, our parental instincts are so strong that if it's a choice between our salvation or our child's, the child is invariably chosen. Yet we live in a society that seemingly has no similar instinct for its future generations.

As we've seen, when it comes to our health, we take too few preventive measures. When it comes to society's future, too, we
~ke little effort at prevention, but rather spend fortunes to shore
/:he environmental mistakes, the jerry-built communities, the

defective planes or dangerous cars we have produced through greed for today and lack of planning for the future. We deny the future until we're "there"; *then,* in horror at what we ourselves have wrought, we pay to correct the past.

Yet for us to survive as a society, we *must* invest in the future—invest money, thought, effort, present time. For any species, its future is in its progeny, and if we *want* a future—for ourselves, for our children, for humanity—we will have to shift time to be able to ensure it.

In *Ageless Body, Timeless Mind,* Deepak Chopra makes a superb distinction between time-bound awareness and timeless awareness.

> Time-bound awareness is defined by: external goals, deadlines and time pressure, self-image built from past experience, fear of change, fear of death, distraction by past regrets and future worries, and insecurity.
>
> Timeless awareness is defined by: internal goals, freedom from time pressure, action focused on present moment, reliance on intuition and leaps of imagination, detachment from change and turmoil, no fear of death, and positive experience of Being.

Indeed, I would say, it is precisely the ability to shift time that will take us back and forth between time-bound awareness and timeless awareness, and it is the ability to shift to timelessness that will govern the future: ours and society's.

I believe, with Jeremy Rifkin, that we are at a critical point. We must be able to embrace ecological and artificial time, and incorporate sacred time into our techno-speed environment, or we will lose our humanity.

It is critical because it is becoming more and more difficult to withstand the rhythm of modern America. Think of Juliet Schor's comparison of the workplace in 1948 and 1991—if we shifted back to the rhythm of 1948, we would have to work only half as much as we do today—and conditions in 1948 were hardly uncomfortable! If we cannot incorporate the ability to timeshift to a slower beat, if not everything needs to be "new," or "speeded up," then, as Alvin Toffler points out, the shattering stress and disorientation caused by too much change in too short a time will overwhelm us. Indeed, in many cases, it already has, as evidenced in the cacophony, the shattered relationships, the violence, and the greed that surround us.

As humanity plunges forth into the future, we stand at one of the most significant crossroads in our evolutionary history. As the great evolutionist Loren Huxley correctly observed, "Mankind is evolution conscious of itself for the first time." This means that to some degree, the future is in our hands. We can choose the path we will follow.

The apocalyptic worldview as represented in current science fiction, in almost all movies that attempt to peer into the future, from *Blade Runner* to *Road Warrior* to *Strange Days,* shows a rapid unraveling of the strands that hold together the human family. Environmental degradation; ethnic strife and battles; urban violence and decay; increasing on-line interactions favoring information communication over relationships: All these point to the fact that our society is imperiled. The sheer magnitude of the speed-up all around us will surely plunge us into a darkness that will become less habitable for future generations. For we will not be physiologically able to evolve to match the speed at which changes around us are occurring. This could leave us with little hope as a society.

Yet the alternative is possible if we are able to shift, to consciously choose our future. It's possible, if we as a society—the human race—are willing to consciously embrace our potential as creatures who feel and care for each other, and are willing to slow down enough to let this happen.

If we are willing, there is a future that we can pass on to our children and grandchildren. We can feel proud and responsible *now* for its creation. It is not out of our reach. It requires our conscious effort to live truly in the present with a compassion for others as well as for ourselves.

Therein is a society in which there is plenty, not measured by how many goods we have, but by a real quality of life. The creation of this future depends on our timeshifting, slowing down collectively into the present. We can use our technologies, be able to function at full speed, but know we can also exist in the full range of human rhythms.

The view of our positive future will look like this:

- I see shorter work hours and consequently fuller employment, based on the European movement that has already begun.
- As a result, I see the growth of a leisure-time industry, devoted not to consumerism but to service. More adult education classes, with time to immerse oneself with inner-directed study, artistic interests, sports and movement, and time spent in nature.
- I see computers programmed to entrain with our slower rhythm, and they become, not our masters, but servants in *our* time.
- I see people using holidays *as* holidays, not as excuses for shopping sprees—imagine a Christmas season devoted to meditation (now, it's famous for being the most anxiety-filled time of the year), a President's Day actually devoted to the study of history.
- I see an education system teaching four Rs, not three—the fourth being Relaxation.
- I see our children being given time as well as space, so they can *be* children and know there is a slow track as well as a fast one within which they can find their own rhythms.
- I see more and more people working within their own environments to help slow their rhythms, particularly as working from home through the fax, modem, E-mail, etc. *(advantages* of the new technologies) becomes easier.
- I see a rededication to communities, such as retirement communities or the co-housing projects pioneered in Europe, where people dedicated to each other's support can share services, goals, and ideals. The trend will be toward developing interdependent living situations, resembling the villages of old.
- I see that there will be more parks, more marshland, more wilderness areas, in direct contravention of the trend today, as more and more of us entrain with the healing rhythms of nature and the earth.

- I see more and more people involved in contemplative practice and meditation.
- I see more courtesy, and more kindness toward strangers.
- I see the creation of more rituals for sacred time.
- I see the honoring of doing nothing, praise for inactivity, cheers for those whose goal is expanding time, not income.
- I see the evolution of humanity so we can navigate in the fourth dimension, where time is at once past, present, and future.
- I see most of us in the present moment, for the future is in the present.
- I see a present so deep, so profound, that we feel not only the rhythms of the earth, but can tune in to the rhythm of the cosmos itself, where there is no time, only awareness.
- I see the ability to shift time, and in so doing . . .
- . . . I see there is hope . . .
- . . . And I see love—for humanity, community, friends, family, self.

A Final Word

A<small>T THE END</small> of my workshop on time, I ask the participants to pick three ideas about timeshifting they can incorporate into their lives.

Here, at the end of this book, I ask the same of you.

Some of you might want to go deeper into this eternally fascinating subject, and study the great, profound, and difficult teachings that range from relativity physics to mysticism, from Plato to Shakespeare to the Dalai Lama.

Most of you, though, will return to your lives, your lovers, your work, and your play and remain much the same as always.

But what if you paused for five minutes of solitary thought before switching from workplace to home? Or if you looked at the future as a beacon of light? Or spent more time in the wilderness? Or began to listen to Mozart?

I do not suggest you can take in all aspects of time, only concepts that suit your own lives and selves. All I really ask, in fact, is that you realize that you have the ability to shift time, that it is not difficult, that its rewards are life-enhancing, even life-giving.

Timeshifting is, in fact, the door to the present, itself the way to the past and future, and thus to the fullness of existence through a deep knowing and entrainment with life.

Bibliography

Suggested Reading

Almaas, A. H. *Diamond Heart: Elements of the Real Man.* Berkeley: Diamond Books, 1989.

Chopra, Deepak. *Ageless Body, Timeless Mind.* New York: Harmony Books, 1993.

Covey, Stephen R. *The Seven Habits of Highly Effective People.* New York: Simon & Schuster, 1989.

Csikszentmihalyi, Mihaly. *Flow: The Psychology of Optimal Experience.* New York: Harper & Row, 1990.

Dass, Ram. *Be Here Now.* Boulder, Colo.: Hanuman Foundation, 1978.

Enomiya-LaSalle, Hugo. *Living in the New Consciousness.* Boston: Shambhala, 1988.

Goleman, Daniel. *Emotional Intelligence.* New York: Bantam Books, 1995.

Hendrix, Harville. *Getting the Love You Want.* New York: Henry Holt, 1988.

Jackson, Phil. *Sacred Hoops.* New York: Hyperion, 1995.

Kabat-Zinn, Jon. *Wherever You Go, There You Are.* New York: Hyperion, 1994.

Kapleau, Philip. *The Wheel of Death.* New York: Harper & Row, 1971.

Lara, Adair. *Slowing Down in a Speeded Up World.* Berkeley: Conari Press, 1995.

Leonard, George. *The Silent Pulse.* New York: E. P. Dutton, 1978.

Moore, Thomas. *Care of the Soul.* New York: HarperCollins, 1992.

Nhat Hanh, Thich. *The Miracle of Mindfulness.* Boston: Beacon Press, 1987.

———. *Peace Is Every Step: The Path of Mindfulness in Everyday Life.* New York: Bantam Books, 1991.

Rechtschaffen, Joseph, and Robert Carola. *Minding Your Body: 100 Ways to Live and Be Well.* New York: Kodansha International, 1995.

Rifkin, Jeremy. *Time Wars.* New York: Simon & Schuster, 1987.

Rinpoche, Sogyal. *The Tibetan Way of Living and Dying.* New York: HarperCollins, 1992.

Schor, Juliet B. *The Overworked American.* New York: Basic Books, 1991.

Servan-Schreiber, Jean-Louis. *The Art of Time.* New York: Addison-Wesley, 1988.

General Readings About Time

Burns, Leland Smith. *Busy Bodies: Why Our Time-Obsessed Society Keeps Us Running in Place.* New York: W. W. Norton, 1993.

Campbell, Don, ed. *Music: Physician for Times to Come.* Wheaton, Ill.: Theosophical Publishing House, 1991.

Campbell, Jeremy. *Winston Churchill's Afternoon Nap.* New York: Simon & Schuster, 1986.

Chusmir, Leonard. *Thank God It's Monday: The Guide to a Happier Job.* New York: New American Library, 1990.

Davies, Paul. *About Time: Einstein's Unfinished Revolution.* New York: Simon & Schuster, 1995.

Eiseley, Loren. *The Firmament of Time.* New York: Atheneum, 1975.

Fiore, Neil. *The Now Habit.* Los Angeles: Jeremy P. Tarcher, 1989.

Fraser, J. T. *Time, the Familiar Stranger.* Amherst: University of Massachusetts Press, 1987.

Grudin, Robert. *Time and the Art of Living.* New York: Ticknor & Fields, 1982.

Hall, Edward T. *The Dance of Life: The Other Dimension of Time.* New York: Doubleday, 1983.

Hope, Murry. *Time: The Ultimate Energy.* Rockport, Mass.: Element, 1991.

Housden, Roger. *Retreat: Time Apart for Silence and Solitude.* San Francisco: Harper San Francisco, 1995.

Langer, Ellen. *Mindfulness.* New York: Addison-Wesley, 1989.

Lightman, Alan. *Einstein's Dreams.* New York: Random House, 1994.

Morris, Richard. *Time's Arrows: Scientific Attitudes Toward Time.* New York: Simon & Schuster, 1985.

Russell, Peter. *The White Hole in Time.* New York: HarperCollins, 1992.

Rybczynski, Witold. *Waiting for the Weekend.* New York: Viking, 1991.

Sheldrake, Rupert. *The Presence of the Past.* New York: Random House, 1988.

Body/Mind and Health

Anderson, Robert A. *Wellness Medicine.* New Canaan, Conn.: Keats Publishing, 1990.

Bland, Jeffrey. *Nutraerobics.* Cambridge, Mass.: Harper & Row, 1983.

———. *Your Health Under Siege.* Brattleboro, Vt.: Steven Greene Press, 1981.

Borysenko, Joan. *Guilt Is the Teacher, Love Is the Lesson.* New York: Warner Books, 1990.

Chopra, Deepak. *Quantum Healing.* New York: Bantam Books, 1989.

Cousins, Norman. *Head First: The Biology of Hope.* New York: E. P. Dutton, 1989.

Dossey, Larry. *Space, Time and Medicine.* Boulder, Colo.: Shambhala, 1982.

Garfield, Charles A. *Peak Performance.* Los Angeles: Jeremy P. Tarcher, 1984.

Kabat-Zinn, Jon. *Full Catastrophe Living.* New York: Doubleday, 1990.

Kübler-Ross, Elisabeth. *On Death and Dying.* New York: Macmillan, 1969.

Locke, Steven E. *The Healer Within.* New York: E. P. Dutton, 1986.

Northrup, Christiane. *Women's Bodies, Women's Wisdom.* New York: Bantam Books, 1994.

Ornish, Dean. *Stress, Diet and Your Heart.* New York: Holt, Rinehart & Winston, 1983.

Pelletier, Kenneth R. *Sound Mind, Sound Body.* New York: Fireside, 1994.

Selye, Hans. *Stress Without Distress.* New York: Lippincott & Crowell, 1974.

Spiegel, David. *Living Beyond Limits.* New York: Ballantine, 1993.

Walford, Roy L. *Maximum Life Span.* New York: W. W. Norton, 1983.

Weil, Andrew. *Natural Health, Natural Medicine.* Boston: Houghton Mifflin, 1990.

Philosophy and Spirit

benShea, Noah. *Jacob the Baker.* New York: Random House, 1989.

Bergson, Henri. *Creative Evolution.* New York: Henry Holt, 1911.

Dalai Lama. *Awakening the Mind, Lightening the Heart.* New York: Harper San Francisco, 1995.

Dass, Ram. *How Can I Help? Stories and Reflections on Service.* New York: Knopf, 1985.

Daumal, Rene. *Mount Analogue.* Boston: Shambhala, 1992.

Eliade, Mircea. *The Sacred and the Profane: The Nature of Religion.* New York: Harcourt Brace Jovanovich, 1959.

Friedlander, Shems. *Submission: Sayings of the Prophet Muhammed.* New York: Harper & Row, 1977.

Goldstein, Joseph. *The Path of Insight Meditation.* Boulder, Colo.: Shambhala, 1993.

Goleman, Daniel. *The Meditative Mind.* Los Angeles: Jeremy P. Tarcher, 1987.

Khan, Pir Vilayat. *Toward the One.* New York: Harper & Row, 1974.

Kornfield, Jack. *A Path with Heart.* New York: Bantam Books, 1993.

Levine, Stephen. *A Gradual Awakening.* New York: Anchor Books, 1979.

Nhat Hanh, Thich. *Being Peace.* Berkeley: Parallax Press, 1987.

Rumi, Jalal al-Din. *Unseen Rain.* Putney, Vt.: Threshold Books, 1986.

Suzuki, Shunryu. Edited by Trudy Dixon. *Zen Mind, Beginner's Mind.* New York: Walker/Weatherhill, 1970.

Teilhard de Chardin, Pierre. *The Phenomenon of Man.* New York: Harper & Row, 1959.

Wilber, Ken. *Sex, Ecology, Spirituality.* Boston: Shambhala, 1995.

Work and Business

Autry, James A. *Life and Work*. New York: Avon Books, 1984.

Celente, Gerald, and Tom Milton. *Trend Tracking*. New York: Warner Books, 1993.

Covey, Stephen R. *First Things First*. New York: Simon & Schuster, 1994.

Durning, Alan. *How Much Is Enough? The Consumer Society and the Future of the Earth*. New York: W. W. Norton, 1992.

Hawken, Paul. *The Ecology of Commerce: A Declaration of Sustainability*. New York: HarperCollins, 1993.

Peters, Thomas J., and Robert H. Naterman, Jr. *In Search of Excellence*. New York: Warner Books, 1988.

Schumacher, E. F. *Small Is Beautiful*. New York: Harper & Row, 1973.

Whyte, David. *The Heart Aroused: Poetry and the Preservation of Soul in Corporate America*. New York: Doubleday Currency, 1994.

General Interest

Donaldson, O. Fred. *Playing by Heart*. Deerfield Beach, Fla.: Health Communications, 1993.

Friedan, Betty. *The Fountain of Age*. New York: Simon & Schuster, 1993.

Harner, Michael. *The Way of the Shaman*. New York: Harper & Row, 1980.

Hendrix, Harville. *Keeping the Love You Find*. New York: Pocket Books, 1992.

Chung-liang Huang, Al, and Jerry Lynch. *Thinking Body, Dancing Mind: Taosports for Extraordinary Performance in Athletics, Business, and Life*. New York: Bantam Books, 1992.

Levine, Stephen and Ondrea. *Embracing the Beloved*. New York: Doubleday, 1994.

Macy, Joanna. *World as Lover, World as Self*. Berkeley: Parallax Press, 1991.

Murphy, Michael. *In the Zone: Transcendent Experience in Sports*. New York: Penguin Books, 1995.

Norberg-Hodge, Helena. *Ancient Futures: Learning from Ladakh*. San Francisco: Sierra Club Books, 1991.

Rilke, Rainer Maria. *Selected Poems of Rainer Maria Rilke*. New York: Harper & Row, 1981.

Schachter-Shalomi, Zalman, and Ronald S. Miller. *From Age-ing to Sage-ing*. New York: Warner Books, 1995.

Weiss, Brian L. *Many Lives, Many Masters*. New York: Fireside Books, 1988.

Acknowledgments

In my life I have often dived headfirst into the future, believing, falsely, that I knew what to expect. My undaunted dive into the overwhelming realm of writing was cushioned by the support and encouragement of many friends and colleagues for whom I have much love and gratitude.

My deepest thanks are to my parents, Fran and Joe, who have always believed in and respected whatever path I have elected to follow, especially when it veered from one they might have chosen.

My heartfelt gratitude goes to Richard Marek, whose masterful support and expertise helped to raise the writing to a level beyond that which I could have accomplished alone. Carole Douglis's early collaborative efforts were instrumental in moving this project forward, and I cherish her continuing friendship and belief in this work. I feel fortunate to be working with such great literary agents, Ling Lucas, who has become such a trusted friend, and Ed Vesneske, Jr., whose last-minute editorial help was vital. I am grateful, too, to Lori Lipsky, my editor at Doubleday, who saw the possibility of timeshifting and applied her publishing expertise and editorial skills to the book's final form. Also at Doubleday, I thank Frances Jones, Jayne Schorn, and Ellen Archer for their much appreciated help in making this book a reality.

There are many friends whose wise counsel and encouragement have been both meaningful and important. I thank Amina Eagle for her assistance and continued encouragement; Dan and Tara Goleman for their wisdom and advice—their knowledge of this field and of the joy and struggle of the writing process has helped greatly; Harville Hendrix for his help, direction, and a friendship I much value; Owen Lipstein for suggesting I write an article on timeshifting for *Psychology Today;* Zedi Jennings and Hamilton Eugene for teaching me about "island time;" June and Phil Jackson, Saki Santorelli, Jeffrey Bland, Richard Perl, Ellen Wingard, Arnie Weiner and Nancy Lunney for their help; Robbie, Katarina, Hans, Mickey, and Steven for their continued encouragement and for being there for me as friends; Elizabeth for going through it with me all these years and still being supportive; Dan and Mia, who grow more beautiful and wise with time.

I feel fortunate to work with people at Omega Institute who have been so supportive and understanding during times of stress, especially during the birthing process of this book: Lois, Harry, Skip, Andrea, Allan, Lisa, Jean, Ila, Kathleen, Ian, Jamine, Jim, Kim, Kathi, Gumby, Paul, Leeta, Jamie Lee, Susan, Jo Anne, Mary Ann, Kacie, Elaine, John, D., and Jane. A special thanks to Dinabandhu and Tom for their commitment to Omega and our relationship. I feel privileged to work with the Omega board members whose support on many levels has meant a great deal to me: George Kaufman, Robert Gass, Mirabai Bush, Gail Straub, and Gary Krauthamer.

In my life there have been certain people who have been mentors, friends, or sages whose presence has so deeply influenced my journey that they have become part of my cellular structure. Chuck Meyer, who was there for me when it all started. Jan Holcman, who created sound. Pir Vilayat Khan, who had a dedication to a vision and asked me to join it. Shri Bhagwan, who opened the door to what is possible. Ram Dass, whose commitment to discovering truth and whose love and friendship have been a constant inspiration.

And finally, my thanks and love to my wife and dearest friend, Vasant, whose companionship has created many cherished moments, who has taught me about love and shown me the possibility of being real in the present.

OMEGA INSTITUTE FOR HOLISTIC STUDIES

Stephan Rechtschaffen is President and a founder of the Omega Institute for Holistic Studies. Omega Institute, the nation's largest and most progressive holistic learning center, is at the forefront of personal and professional development. Every year more than fifteen-thousand people attend workshops on our campus in Rhinebeck, New York, which is located in the Hudson River Valley on eighty acres of rolling woodlands and lawns.

THE COMMUNITY

Founded in 1977, Omega is recognized worldwide for its broad-based curriculum, world-famous faculty, and unique community spirit. In its nineteen years of providing a combination of education and vacation, Omega has become a model for a new kind of educational center: the learning community. As in a village, learning, socializing, and celebrating naturally intertwine as part of the fabric of community life. When people gather in a place of beauty for a common purpose, a certain kind of culture is born—one where learning is experiential and profound, where deep friendships are forged, and where both celebration and inner reflection occur spontaneously.

FACULTY AND COURSES

Programs at Omega explore new ideas in health, psychology, relationships, arts, sports, nature study, and spiritual understanding. The distinguished faculty and artists who teach and perform at Omega are leaders and innovators in their fields. Some of the faculty include: Maya Angelou, Deepak Chopra, M.D., Joycelyn Elders, M.D., Matthew Fox, Ram Dass, Thich Nhat Hanh, Christiane Northrup, M.D., Thomas Moore, Robert Bly, Bernie Siegel, M.D., Jon Kabat-Zinn, Marion Woodman, Olympia Dukakis, Paul Winter, Phil Jackson, Bill Walton, Babatunde Olatunji, Harville Hendrix, Pir Vilayat Khan, and the Drepung Loseling Monks.

OMEGA ON THE ROAD

Omega offers workshops and conferences throughout the United States, including St. John in the Virgin Islands. Our conferences bring together prominent thinkers, artists, mystics, and teachers who, together with the participants, create an experience where inspiration, healing, and transformation occur.

To receive a free catalogue please call: 1-800-944-1001.

About the Author

Stephan Rechtschaffen, M.D., brings more than twenty years' experience as a physician and leader of workshops on health and personal growth to *Timeshifting*. He is a pioneer of the wellness movement and a founder of the Omega Institute for Holistic Studies in New York's Hudson River Valley, a world-renowned center for holistic study of health, culture, spirit, and the arts.

Dr. Rechtschaffen offers presentations, workshops, and consultations on timeshifting based on the material in this book, and otherwise related to wellness and health. For further information about upcoming programs, please write or call:

Omega Institute
Attn.: Amina Eagle
260 Lake Drive
Rhinebeck, NY 12572

1-800-944-1001